STILLMEADOW
DAYBOOK

GLADYS TABER

Stillmeadow
Daybook

ILLUSTRATED BY EDWARD SHENTON

Parnassus Imprints
Orleans, MA 02653

Published by Arrangements with
Harper & Row, Publishers
All Rights Reserved

Parnassus Imprints Edition
Published May 1989
ISBN 0-940160-42-0

The quotations on page 26; on page 161, from "The Chilterns"; on page 180, from "Pine-Trees and the Sky: Evening," are from THE COLLECTED POEMS OF RUPERT BROOKE, Copyright, 1915, by Dodd, Mead and Co., Inc.

The quotation from "Quite Early One Morning," by Dylan Thomas, on page 90, is from QUITE EARLY ONE MORNING, by Dylan Thomas. Copyright, 1954, by New Directions.

The quotation from "The Lake Isle of Innisfree," by William Butler Yeats, on page 103, is from COLLECTED POEMS, by William Butler Yeats. Copyright, 1934, by The Macmillan Company. Reprinted by permission of the publishers.

The quotation from "Farewell," by Walter de la Mare, on page 251, is from COLLECTED POEMS, by Walter de la Mare. Copyright, 1920, by Henry Holt and Co., Inc. Copyright, 1948, by Walter de la Mare. Reprinted by permission of the publishers.

For Jill,
The mainstay of Stillmeadow

Contents

STILLMEADOW
DAYBOOK

Foreword

I SAT on the old stone steps this morning, paring potatoes. It was one of those mild sweet days in early spring, with a sense of beginnings in the damp sunny air. Whenever I lifted my eyes to look at the blue Connecticut sky, and the soft line of hills that roll away toward Litchfield, Hollyberry Red, the young Irish, thrust her velvet muzzle in the pan and neatly removed a potato. Then she flew around the yard, tossing it in the air, and catching it.

Especially Me followed after, his eager cocker ears flying, his golden paws twinkling over the young grass. Six other cockers were at the far edge of the yard, hunting the big plump bunny that lives under one of the storage houses.

There is something about the task of preparing vegetables that gives a woman a reflective mood. I wondered how many tons of potatoes I had pared since we put our roots down here in these forty acres of stony Connecticut soil. The woods and fields, old orchards and brooks seem to have always been the home place, the cliffs and swamps, and sweet hay meadows have a sense of timelessness about them.

And so does the little white farmhouse, as steadfast and secure as it was when it was built in 1690. How many lives has it sheltered down the long years before welcoming me and mine, I wondered. The very first moment I saw it, with its steeply pitched roof, little windows with bubbly glass, and worn lintel, I knew I belonged to it.

Twenty years later, I felt it even more true. Old houses, I thought, do not belong to people ever, not really, people belong to them.

I went back in my memory to the early days, and decided we had more courage than sense when we bought the farm. We had faith, though. Now and then someone I meet will say, "how did you two ever decide to move to the country?"

We had, I say, a simple reason. We wanted a week-end place for our children. There were two families, Jill and her doctor husband and their son Don and daughter Dorothy lived in a big drafty city apartment around the corner from the tiny dark four-room sixth-floor apartment my husband and I had. With our daughter, Connie, and a cocker spaniel, the place was pretty crowded.

We all worked as hard as beavers, or harder. Jill was a top psychiatric social worker for the city, her husband never took an hour off from his practice which was heavy, my husband taught and I was working at Columbia hoping to get the Ph.D. degree as soon as possible.

The city schools then were not as crowded as they are now, but they were not exactly spacious. After school, the children could stand around on the sidewalk or wheel their doll carriages around the block. Or we could go to the zoo and look at the other caged animals.

All three of the children were thin and pale, no matter how we stuffed them with vitamins. Also it didn't seem to me we had much fun. Sometimes on Sundays we would all pile in one car and try to go on a picnic.

I have many memories of those picnics. Most of the time we spent sitting in traffic and breathing the fumes of the long line of stalled cars ahead. By the time we reached some fairly good picnic spot, it was time to go back again.

And everybody was cross and tired, and the conversation went like this:

"Mom, she's shoving me around."

"I am not. You stuck your elbow right in me."

"Mama, the thermos is leaking all over the floor."

We began to dream of a week-end place where we could have outdoor living in peace and comfort where vacations and holidays could be, we felt, very economical.

And so, fortified with nothing but determination and a down payment, we turned ourselves over to Stillmeadow.

I reflected in this thinking-back hour how fortunate we were. As the children grew up and went away to their various schools and colleges, they had a home to come back to, instead of a series of transient city apartments.

And when we lost our husbands, the farm was a refuge and a haven, something to hold fast to. And something we had to work for, which was a blessing.

By then we were raising all our vegetables, and we had thirty-six cockers. We were raising puppies, doing a little showing, and were really very busy.

After all, I reflected, Stillmeadow isn't a house and land, it is a way of living.

This being a week end, the children were home, grown now, but are they really ever grown? I could hear Connie in the house typing madly, writing notes to study for her orals for her Ph.D. at Columbia. As I wiped my hands on a blue dishtowel, I thought how incredible that my daughter was old enough to KNOW ALL about Anglo-Saxon. Where have the years gone?

Both Jill's children are married, the thin leggy little boy with a double cowlick in his hair is interning at a big city hospital and we call him Doctor. His wife, Anne is studying for her advanced degree in Psychology. Dorothy, at the moment, was busy warming the formula for Jill's new grandchild! Her lawyer husband was helping.

"Darling, don't get it too hot," I could hear, through the open door.

"But Darling, it isn't really hot enough yet!"

The grandchild, Betty, was telling the world that she was hungry. She was, in fact, howling. She is an utterly charming, lovely small one, with an imperative command of life. When hungry, she expects service in a big way, and immediately.

I put a cover on the pan to save the rest of the potatoes from predatory cockers and Irish, and sat a moment more, dreaming. And a strong sense of destiny came to me. For down the years, every time our finances ebbed so low as to be unnoticeable and a payment was coming due on the mortgage, either I sold a story or some old inherited stock of Jill's turned out to pay a dividend.

God moves in mysterious ways, his wonders to perform, I told Holly.

Mainly, I decided, you need faith to embark on country living.

And a willingness to work a lot. When we first moved out, we worked twelve to sixteen hours a day. Former tenants had left piles of broken glass, chipped china, old bones all around the yard. The house itself needed a shovel to clear out debris before we could scrub.

We learned to paint woodwork, to scrape floors. One

floor had a cigarette tin nailed over a hole, and we learned how to put a new floor board in.

And we loved it. The sense of achievement I had when I painted my first floor, and painted myself into a corner and hopped out on a board, was terrific. And the first old highboy that we scraped and sanded and waxed and polished, was a better thing to us than any mink coat. For we had earned it by our own hard labor.

Jill had wonderful ideas about supplementing our income with everything from asparagus to goats, but nothing ever came of these schemes. For instance, the old orchards with their sweet apples. We found that to spray them six times a year was prohibitive. So we gathered the windfalls and made applesauce. Marketing seasonal crops is a big business too, we found when we had too much asparagus.

We read bulletins about everything from goats to geese, honeybees to hens. But our subsistence farming, in the end, extended only to raising enough vegetables to feed the family, including canning and freezing enough for all winter. For fruit we have had wild raspberries and strawberries, currants and a few blueberries, wild cranberries and the windfall apples. We tried, and gave up, hens as being a luxury. It cost us more to feed the hens and take care of them than we could realize from them.

I suppose it is a comment on our whole way of life in this country that even so relatively plain and simple a thing as a hen needs professional attention. On my grandfather's farm, the hens shifted for themselves mostly, pecking away in the barnyard and laying eggs in the golden sifting light on the floor in nests of sweet hay.

But nowadays hens must have cages to live in, the eggs roll down in troughs, the lights stay on all night to keep the poor hens working overtime, incubators are electrically run, water dishes are heated in winter, and in short, the hen has become sophisticated beyond telling.

As I gathered up the pans and the paring knife and dish-towel, I took a last look at the sky, which was the color of a fire opal. The cockers were coming in, now, looking as smug as if they really had caught that rabbit. In the tender violet light under the tall pines, I could fancy I saw shadowy figures of other dogs too. Surely my Honey was there, with her dark amber eyes and shining silver-gold coat and merry cocker tail going like a whirligig. And the two lost Irish, Maeve of the high heart and lucky eyes. The great Irish. And Daphne, her sister, always following behind, with her eager adolescent look.

And the others who had no idea of heaven beyond Still-meadow. Gone now into the shadowy tide, and yet, we never really lose the ones we love, I thought.

I came into the house and began slicing the country-cured ham while the potatoes cooked pleasantly with young onions, bacon and plenty of freshly ground pepper. A good many things change with the years, but the appetites of our children remain constant.

Through the kitchen window, I could see Jill striding down the road training Tiki for his Utility Obedience degree. The small compact black and white cocker trotting along so eagerly, so earnestly, the tall straight woman with her hair blowing in the wind looking absolutely content.

And I reflected, as I popped a mint leaf in with the new peas, that the rewards of country living are measured in intangibles chiefly. Who could estimate the value of the secret places the children had in the upper woods, just when they needed secret places. Under a giant oak that has stood for a generation, a small cave is set in the cliff, and there they could set out their acorn cups for tea, leave mysterious messages for one another and generally reign in a world uncluttered by adults. Every child needs a secret place, and how few there are for city children!

The picnics we have had would stretch from here to the moon, I dare say. Spread out on sun-warmed flat grey boulders or eaten by some rush-fringed stream or cooked on the grill down by the pond, they add up to a rich store of memory.

The hot burning days when we have gone down to the pond and spent an hour swimming, the icy winter days when the children skated on clear black ice half the day, the crisp autumn days when we all went up the hill to gather butternuts and black walnuts, the spring evenings we drove around looking at the country.

No, I could never add up the riches we acquired by striking our roots firmly down into the kind earth in our little valley. Even the hard times are rewarding to a countrydweller.

There is a fine sense of pride in managing when the great storms take out the "electric" and you shovel snow, lug wood for the fireplaces, light a lantern for the chores, simmer the soup in the big kettle over the embers, and have once more conquered.

And often just as we raised our heads above the surface of our financial problems, the roof would begin to leak, or the barn start to collapse. But after we managed each crisis, we felt more faith in being able to meet the next one.

Once in a time of great stress, I asked Jill a question I had not dared to ask before.

"Do you ever regret moving to the country?" I asked.

She gave me a look of utter surprise.

"Every day," she said, "I thank God."

Which, after all, pretty well summed it up.

The baby was asleep and the girls were setting the table for supper. Don and Val were having a quick round of Scrabble. Jill was breaking lettuce in the salad bowl. A last sunset glow came in through the little-paned windows, falling on the dark old beams, the great fireplace, the trestle table.

My thinking time was over, and I was well content to be back in today in the little white house that has sheltered us for so long.

April

EARLY MORNING IS LIKE A PINK PEARL
now that April's here. The first lilacs are budding over the
white picket fence in the Quiet Garden; crocus, daffodils,
white and purple grape hyacinths repeat the magic of spring.
Surely never was spring so wonderful, such a miracle! For it
seems only yesterday that drifts piled high in the little garden
as I made my mittened and booted way to the kennel. My
heart remembers this with surprise as I examine the delicate
papery bud tips on my favorite King Alfred white daffodils.

The King Alfred has a silvery cup with a faint glow in the
heart almost like old polished ivory. I really wonder why it
was named King Alfred—not that it isn't a royal flower but
that it does not look masculine. It reminds me of a tall and
gentle mediaeval Princess robed in ivory velvet.

The early flowers have a special beauty—I always shake
with excitement when I find the first clump of snowdrops,
fragile, pearl-pure, bending their heads lightly toward the icy
dark ground. Crocus makes rainbow patches all over the
yard; scilla looks like bits of the sky snipped out and scattered
down.

George plows around the nineteenth of the month. I often
think that when we bought the farm, we had no idea that
George was going to go with it, so to speak. In fact, we
wished there was no farm across the road but rather one of
those breath-taking views of valley and blue mountains.
George finds time to run a full-going farm with a dairy herd,
and yet to come every morning to help feed dogs, run the furnace, chop firewood, lug heavy cartons. If the car doesn't

start, George gets it going. If my bed falls to pieces in the night, he puts new slats in, wires it up again.

He fixes faucets, repairs the wall can opener. If the dogs get out of the gate, he comes running from the barn to scoop them up. If he is cutting hay in his upper field and we get in trouble, we lean on the picket fence and yell.

He is my idea of a true Yankee, ingenious beyond measure, steadfast, sound. And never a day so dark but that George comes in with the sunniest smile and an air of great cheer. We lean on him, we have leaned on him shamelessly since he was a teen-ager rolling down the road on his old hay wagon.

Actually George's father fled from Lithuania to escape being drafted into the army long years ago, and he sent back for his bride as soon as he was established in the new country. The children grew up speaking Lithuanian at home, and Connecticut at school. There wasn't much school either as the three boys went to work on the farm just as soon as possible.

Frank, the oldest boy, helped us in the beginning, and when he married and moved away, Willie took over. Willie wanted more school, he went to the nearest vocational school and got through with flying flags, even though he often had to miss time during haying or butchering or rebuilding barns. He used to come over to study in the evening and talk about his dreams. When he went in the navy, I don't know who cried harder, his mother or me. But at his wedding, the family said I cried harder than anybody. I loved his bride too. A mechanical genius, Willie did not want to farm, so when he came home, he went in the toolshop in Waterbury and we sliced off a piece of our land for his house to be built on.

From then on, George swung into place as our help and comfort. And when he married, we sliced a little more off for his house. Such a snug cosy feeling to have them right down the road beyond the old apple orchard.

When George comes to plow, we stop everything and rush to watch. George loves it too, he is laughing as he wheels the great tractor around, and manages to skip the asparagus bed by the measure of a very thin dime. As the great shining blades fold the dark earth over, the long rich furrows roll out. And I think a man who plows rides the world. You can feel the great old Mother Earth being released from winter rigidity, and giving again her richness to mankind. You feel this mystery of growth which so far man has not destroyed. Plant well, says the soil, and I will nourish you once again.

All the dogs catch the excitement and dash around like dervishes, tossing leftover parsnips in the air, retrieving small stones. The Irish sweeps past. Tally ho—she says, almost knocking me flat as she flies by. I don't mind, I only wish I too could gallop over the newly turned earth at fifty miles an hour.

Meanwhile Jill rakes the yard. There is my bathing shoe that Holly made off with last August. There is a ski sock. And there is the missing part of the Christmas wreath. There is the rubber one guest left by the front door. There are the green rubber rabbits, and there are all the pieces of kindling the dogs started to carry in to the house, and decided against.

This is all historic country. When we drive out on a cool spring evening, we often go down to Ridgefield and stop to read the tablet marking the Battle of Ridgefield, which reads:

IN DEFENSE OF AMERICAN INDEPENDENCE

AT THE BATTLE OF RIDGEFIELD
APRIL 27, 1777
DIED
EIGHT PATRIOTS
WHO WERE LAID IN THIS GROUND
COMPANIONED BY
SIXTEEN BRITISH SOLDIERS
LIVING, THEIR ENEMIES, DYING, THEIR GUESTS.
IN HONOR OF SERVICE AND SACRIFICE

THIS MEMORIAL IS PLACED
FOR THE STRENGTHENING OF HEARTS.

This is a most moving memorial, it seems to me, the patriots companioned by the men they died fighting, now their guests. It is strange to think that this green peaceful valley was in the heart of the war 178 years ago.

This battle, I remember, was won because Benedict Arnold came spurring his big white horse down the winding road and flung himself into the wavering line. He was in New Haven when word came to him, and he swung as lightly to the saddle as any young Lochinvar and saved the day.

There is no doubt that Arnold was a reckless and brave man and if he had been managed with tact, the history of a traitor might never have been written.

Jill is completely occupied during the evenings, sorting seed packets. Holly, the young Irish, is a great help, filching Mayking lettuce and Crosby beets and playing tag with them. Jill tries to plan how many rows of chard to put in, how much lettuce, how many hills of corn. I am no help at all, I always advise planting everything. Just everything. For I always think how delicious the fresh young vegetables taste and after all, we can freeze the extras.

"Well, there is a limit," says Jill, "to how much I can hoe and weed. And remember the year we had a wheelbarrow load of cucumbers?"

I did remember that. Cucumbers are a wonderful vegetable, good chilled and served in sour cream, or made into pale green boats and stuffed with lobster salad—or simmered in hot cream or made into a cold soup. But you can not eat them by the dozen, so raising a thousand is a mistake. And there is, as far as I know, only one way to freeze them, minced with onion and then you must eat them fast after they come out.

While Jill sorted seeds this week, I have been reading *Poor*

Richard's Almanack. I fell to considering one wise bit:

"Doing an injury puts you below your enemy; Revenging one makes you but even with him; Forgiving it sets you above him."

I liked this, and I thought I would add, "It isn't always an enemy, it may be a friend who needs forgiving. For we are especially vulnerable to wounding by our friends, but forgiving makes for a comfortable life. Resentment is a sharp bedfellow." (My own Poor Richard saying, I felt.)

I have also been reading Edwin Way Teale's *Days Without Time.* What a treasure to have a new book by this modern Thoreau who not only writes so beautifully about nature but sparks it with humor. And expert photographs too. Like *North With The Spring*, this book enlarges one's horizon.

"I was just thinking," I said to Jill, as she put a fresh apple log on the fire, "how lucky we are nobody has yet put commercials at the head of every chapter in a book!"

"Too easy to skip," commented Jill, going back to the edible-podded peas.

I reflected that there are many fine books being written today which widen our vision, and this is a happy thought after feeling despondent over the comic book situation. Dr. Wertham's *Seduction Of The Innocent* should be required reading, but gives a grim picture. *Menaboni's Birds* or *The Sea Around Us* or *The Edge Of The Shore* or *The Shining Tides*, these I find restorative to my spirit.

About the comic books, I do agree with the experts that most of them are vicious. I do not think that even doing the classics in balloon-captioned pictures is a good way to advance literature. Nothing can take the place of a wide and varied reading of the great books by children as they grow up. But I am glad I do not have the power to wipe the comics off the map, for censorship is always dangerous. In the end, it always seems to lead to such nonsense as banning *The Merchant of*

Venice because Shylock, the Jew, is an unsympathetic character.

When the children were growing up, they read whatever they found around in the bookshelves. But we never had a comic or a Mickey Spillane type of book in the house. I suppose we established an unconscious censorship, but we never thought about it.

Don's favorite reading was, for some time, the Dictionary. He would hunch his thin leggy frame up on his bed and pore over such items as "NA-GA-NA, n. A disease of horses and other animals produced by the action of Trypanosoma brucei and carried by a variety of tsetse fly."

No doubt this foretold his later decision to become a doctor. On the other hand, we often felt he was destined to ply between some tropical islands on an old freighter, since he read everything about boats he could find.

Cicely read the romantics, from Joseph Conrad to *Wuthering Heights* and the poets from Keats to A. E. Housman.

Dorothy had one fixed goal. She wanted to read anything that had some poor underprivileged character or someone who needed help. She did not, however, want any but happy endings, or she would burst into tears and rush from the room.

Of course they all read the regular children's classics, the *Oz* books were worn to a shadow. Hans Christian Andersen, the Russian fairy tales, *Peter Pan*, and *Treasure Island* were favorites.

I am sorry to see fairy tales in such poor repute, for there is something in fairy tale and legend that is vital. No amount of factual books can replace the delight of the Snow Queen in the palace of ice, or the charm of Sleeping Beauty wakened by the Prince's kiss.

I am also sorry that reading aloud has gone out, at least in the families we know. The family now gathers, to be sure, around the television set, but that is not quite the same as gathering around an open fire and listening to the roar of the wild seas as Moby Dick bears down on Captain Ahab, or hearing the childish ghost voice of Kathy crying "let me in, let me in."

We always look ahead in the Farmer's Almanac to be sure of the weather.

"Temperature drop might kill apple crop," says the almanac, and we watch the thermometer anxiously.

"Now it clears, let's give three cheers," is a signal for the inevitable window washing.

The old bubbly small panes of glass in the windows are part of the charm of the old house, and are simply maddening to wash. Half the time we finish one window and go for fresh water and Holly jumps up and leaves a goodly layer of spring mud right on the clean window. The only time there isn't a setter looking in the window, I thought yesterday, is when we are all inside and she is on the sofa.

Only one cocker, Especially Me, is tall enough to reach the window sills, and his blond velvet muzzle is pressed into every clean pane too, his large amber eyes regard me eagerly, his golden paws smudge the white clapboards under the sill. All in good clean fun, his eyes say.

Momentarily, the freshly washed windows frame a new-born world, and crisp curtains blow in the light spring breeze. So many people ask me about housekeeping with dogs. They track in mud, they shed, they chew things up when young. When Holly was six months old, we left her in the kitchen while we went to the village. She somehow managed to open the door and get into the rest of the house. Cushions and rugs and magazines made a potpourri everywhere.

"This place looks like the town dump," said Jill, "with lights on!"

We have, at the moment, only nine dogs, eight cockers and one Irish, Hollyberry Red. And the house reflects it.

However, I feel a clean window is fine but isn't a precious memory to store away particularly, whereas the sight of a shining Irish setter and a small black and white cocker both trying to crowd on one deep window sill—well, there is something I can remember with pleasure. We can always wash the windows again another day.

An immaculate house is a wonderful and elegant thing, but it can also be an empty and a cold thing. I'll take mine with flying paws and whisking tails and eager loving looks from dark earnest eyes. When the children go away to school, and get married and move away there are so many little quiet corners in a house. A bevy of cockers and an Irish or two liven things up considerably. It is hard to be melancholy with somebody playing leapfrog around the room.

Holly is the daughter of two great champions, and somehow as she runs with graceful awkwardness across the yard, she has a royal look even at nine months. Quality shows in every line of her and shines in her dark intelligent eyes. Typically Irish, she has a fine sense of humor, is charming and intelligent, gay and always feeling the world is her own personal oyster.

Our first Irish was named for Queen Maeve because she had "a high heart and lucky eyes." Maeve was more Celtic than Holly, she could go into a deep depression suddenly and languish before our astonished eyes. And then suddenly emerge from it with a hey-nonny-nonny-oh and frisk around like a young deer.

She was a great Irish, and Jill's inseparable companion. When you saw one, the other was never far behind. It is Jill's theory that in every life there is one dog. Other dogs may come and go, but there is one grande affaire. I feel this is probably right and yet it worries me, for it might mean that I am a fickle person. For I seem able to love deeply just the dog I am looking at.

The sun rises around half past five in early April, and the mornings are so fresh and still. I like to get up and dash to the garden to see what the rhubarb is doing and then carry my breakfast tray to a sheltered sunny corner by the well. I like to eat outdoors even if I have to wear a sweater and Jill says I will eat out even if I have to wear mittens while I cut my bacon.

White clouds scud across the sky, the meadow has a faint haze of green, the wild pear is blossoming in the old orchard up the hill. The pure white blossoms give the countryside a look of having silver fountains here and there. The strange upright growth-pattern of the pear is so distinctive, somehow so proud. The apple tree is graceful and charming and poetic but the pear tree seems to have such integrity, pointing firmly to the sky.

After breakfast, I go down to look hopefully at the pond. Dogtooth violets on the slope above, skunk cabbage blazing emerald by the brook where it flows into the pond. I am anxious for the water to be warm enough for swimming, although as long as the furnace is on in the house, it is pushing things to poke my hand down in the clear dark water.

Our experience as pond builders was educational, to say the least. First the conservation bureau sent a beautiful young man to talk to us and eight of the neighbors in the valley about conservation. Farm ponds, said he, are wildlife refuges, help the land generally, keep the water table up, and help prevent bad fires. Also can be stocked with fish.

It sounded so beautifully simple when the beautiful young forester described it. You waved a wand, I thought, and there was the lovely pond, teeming with fish, loaded with herons and wild duck, replete with cardinal flowers and forget-me-nots on the bank.

We plunged blithely into almost the worst trouble we have ever had. In the first place, we wanted a pond where the brook flowed—although choked partly by swamp tangle, it was a very nice brook. Water, it seems, complicates the building of a pond terrifically. First the great steam shovel gets stuck in the swampy mud. Then it takes two pumps going like mad things to keep the water down while the steam shovel is saved. Then all the earth that comes up on the shovel starts to slide back into the hole, and there you are with one depressed steam shovel, a couple of melancholy bulldozers and the disturbed brook flowing wildly in all directions.

I was unnerved by the sight of whole trees and thickets being flung up in the air and falling like broken spaghetti. George took a different view. "That loom in there," he said gloomily, "that loom all came down from my upper fields. That's where it all came from!"

Eventually the prehistoric-looking monsters lumbered down the road again, accompanied by hysterics on the part of the cockers. The world, paraphrasing Thomas Gray, was left to darkness and to us.

But there was undeniably water in that yawning hole.

Months later, another conservation man appeared with a catalogue of proper shrubs and bushes with which to charm the wildlife. He went down to the pond with me, and stood looking out over it with a dazed expression on his face. Finally he spoke.

"Well," he said, "you sure have a g-d banked amphitheatre here!"

It came to me it did look very much like an amphitheatre for a Greek play and possibly we should put on some kind of performance to use those swooping banks. Possibly a rural aquacade—

"I love the wildlife," I said, "but I also wish to swim in this pool."

He did a little figuring on a piece of paper. "Well," he said thoughtfully, "I think you have about 200,000 gallons of water here, is that enough for you to swim in?"

He allowed brown trout was the best fish to stock it with, and we faithfully got the brown trout. Beautiful too, gleaming and iridescent. We saw them as we dumped the big milk cans out and consigned them to the water, and that, I may say, is the last time we did see them. Now and then, an occasional leap in the water at dusk assures me that they are still leading their own lives, but we have never been able to catch them to grace our breakfast table, flanked with parsley and a slice of lemon.

We learned later that the brown trout is hard to catch, wary and an individualist. I often wish we had nice simple fish of some sort that would rise to my bait.

We also learned later that we did have a nice stock of great snapping turtles.

I think of myself as an intrepid woman. I kill snakes, if necessary, I am a good mouse whacker and I never lock doors at night. But the idea of a huge unkind snapping turtle mistakenly taking me for a tasty morsel did not appeal to me.

So we undertook the battle of the snappers. First George tried to shoot the greatest and fiercest one. Then we consulted Mr. Bennett the postman, who is the top conservation expert in the valley, and he advised a turtle trap.

The turtle trap looked like a collapsible circus tent, suitable for the sheltering of elephants. It took half a day to figure out the formula for assembling it. And then we discovered we had to bait it with ancient and well-ripened fish. So Jill went to the market and brought home a respectable fish and we aged it. In a day or so, in the sun, on the window box, it ripened very well.

Then George and Jill set the trap.

And the next day George shot a turtle.

And he took him home and upended a washtub over him, because he had only winged him, so to speak, and George is really too tenderhearted to dispatch any creature he has on hand. It took him several more days to get around to doing away with the turtle.

Farm living involves a kind of acceptance of killing, I find. The hens, when they stop laying, are destined for the pot.

The pigs when fattened into sound and rugged health are definitely due to become tender hams and sugar-cured bacon. And the young calves that cannot produce tons of frothy warm milk, they are, plainly, veal.

This is one reason we have never adventured in livestock, except dogs. And George, who does run a going farm, has a hard time with his tender heart. He takes days to work himself up to butchering a hog.

I can tell when the event is imminent. George gets a look on his sunny handsome face. "Going to butcher tomorrow," he says in a low voice.

Tomorrow he puts it off. "Weather isn't quite right," he tells me.

Then he gets too busy hauling wood for someone who absolutely has to have it. Or the truck breaks down and he spends two days fixing it. Or he has to go to New Haven for a load of stale bread for the cows. If they don't get it, he says, the milk falls right off.

Eventually comes the day. A couple of farmers come in to help, and George steels himself. But it is days before his face is rosy and bright again. An interesting thing to me is that the only way he can put himself through it is by working up a rage against the hapless hog. The hog has to do some aggressive act. "Then I got mad at him," recounts George, "and I told him, I said there you are."

This, I feel, is much the way we humans are about most of life. Could a soldier in battle really cold-murder another human being, who no doubt has a wife and a ten-months-old baby, maybe a little garden, and likes to play the accordion? No, first he has to generate the killing anger even if it only lasts while the bullet pings away. He thinks of his own home, how he is saving his country, of all the things the enemy has done to upset the world. He recalls all he has ever heard of cruelty, and all he knows of it. And then he fires.

If ever I have thanked God I was born a member of the

weaker sex, it has been during the wars we have had. For I
doubt very much whether I would ever had been able to forget that the enemy might have a letter from home in his
breast pocket. And yet I could not be called a pacifist, for I
think there have been times—but how lucky for me that I was
not called to man a trench in the Battle of the Bulge or land
at Dieppe or ship out to Korea!

It is strange, I often reflect, how all of life is mirrored in a
small way in our little valley. Fear of the predator giant turtle, struggle against the enemy in the form of Japanese beetle
and potato bug, the problem of killing in the raising of livestock to feed the country. And even the uprooting of all the
trees for our pond images in a small way the changing of the
land when a big dam is put in somewhere and forests and villages are done away with.

My favorite view near New Milford is destined to go when
that gracious and green valley is flooded by the power company. I know that the old stone walls will stay there, buried
in the water, the little long-traveled roads will, for a time,
keep their journeying pattern. Old fence posts will bear
themselves firmly in the water, as if they still upheld a neat
cattle fence. But the sweep of the valley will be gone, the
hills will close down on the flat body of water, and all the
homes that were established there will be gone.

It gives one to think. For nothing is secure. Bred in the
tradition that a man's home is his castle, we now know that
is not so at all. At any door, a tall man may knock, with a
paper to sign. Or a great gas main can be laid right through
a special cherished garden. We see the denuded forest every
time we go to the village, and only a big orangey pump affair
protrudes above the ragged earth.

And when I look at my pond, won so hardly from the
swamp, and harboring the wild winged birds and the small
children on hot days and the evasive brown trout, I know I
might lose all my right to swim and fish in it, if the neighbor-

ing big city company builds one more dam and confiscates
one more section of farm land.

Eventually somebody has got to decide how to protect
the rural agricultural areas. For the big cities need tons of
milk and it takes pastures and cows for milk. You can never
pump it out of a faucet. Thanksgiving tables need fat crispy
turkeys and that means turkey farms. As the city develop-
ments move out, the farm land diminishes.

Here in New England, it will be a problem, maybe in my
time, certainly not long after. The balance must be main-
tained, particularly in this part of the country where distances
are small and so easily swallowed up. There are so many big
industrial areas and they all take produce. But the cities edge
out, the big power companies want more water, the farmer
must give way to the gas line, the reservoir (we call it the
resevoy).

The great Midwest can feed us all, I expect, but then the
problem of transportation enters in. How many freight cars,
how many refrigerated trucks needed to carry vegetables and
fruits enough—and meat—and eggs— Much of our produce
here goes to Waterbury, the arsenal of the East. The big brass
factories sing with power all night long. In New Haven,
Winchester Arms lights the sky with neon.

But all the families who work there have to buy their eggs
and cabbages and butter and milk. And it does seem better
that they should get them nearby, without extra expense of
transportation. I think it is more feasible in the long run for
the egg woman to deliver two dozen fresh eggs a week from
the next road over, than to ship eggs from Kalamazoo,
Michigan.

Economics is too complex for me. But I have instincts about
supply and demand which I believe in. And I shall always
feel a carrot next door is better than a carrot from Ames,
Iowa, all things being equal.

Now the days are longer and lovely twilight has come again into the world. In winter we seem to high-dive from day to night, but now the violet dusk folds over the valley so gently and the sky is luminous so long.

At night the peepers sing their sweet chilly song. This is my favorite music. From the dark swamp comes the sound, so brave, so intense. The cool night is filled with the singing. It is a romantic song, faintly melancholy, high and delicate. Somehow it is like all lost and lovely things; it is like walking under a spring moon with your first beau. It has the magic of that first tentative kiss. It has nothing at all in common with the robust robin's note or the busy talk of the Chickadee, but it is music. I remember when we first came, asking George what the birds were that sang all night. I had been saying, "the bird of dawning singeth all night long" as Hamlet heard.

"It's the peepers," said George, laughing at my ignorance.

I expect the earliest owners of this house woke in the night and heard this music and smiled, and said, "winter is over, spring is here," and then relaxed on their high feather beds for a little more sleep.

George says they must be frozen-in three times, and we always count. After the third time, it is going to be warm weather. Their song increases, deepens, and has more vibration.

We keep on feeding the winter birds. Jill says she spends half the day on the dogs and half on the birds and what's left she doesn't know. She is a tall woman, and as she goes out to the bird feeders, the birds circle close to her head, chattering and fluttering. The creamy suet goes in the cages, the peanut butter is stuffed in the long feeder and then she struggles with the contraption that is as fine for the birds as it is maddening to us, it has a little glass barrel thing and several screws and a little pipe and just as she gets it filled, it goes to pieces and

the seed flies in all directions. The flat wooden tea tray outside my window is more practical, you just dump in it.

A bird-lover from the far West wrote me that it was a
good idea to fill pop bottles with hot water, stopper them, and
put them out for the birds to warm their toes on. We dis-
carded this for New England as the bottles might freeze and
break any minute.

This winter we had our first lark sparrows, and we are waiting to see whether they stay or go in summer. They are odd
looking birds with white markings as if they had gone too
close to a can of white paint, and they are aggressive. I shall
never live long enough to identify all the sparrows, but I do
know the English, and the song sparrow who rocks and carols
so sweetly from the top bough of the pine tree, and now this
new sparrow. Every time we meet a new bird, and feverishly
identify him or her from three bird books and anxious looking through the binoculars, we feel as triumphant as if we had
won a blue ribbon.

I cannot remember when I first adopted my unicorn, but by
now everyone knows I have one. I have pictures of him, and

a luncheon set with him prancing on, and a good many people who see the famous white unicorn tapestry write me and send photographs of it. The line between fact and fancy has always been a tenuous one with me, and many a time I have gone out to see if my unicorn had come down to crop the Confederate violets—and how would I know he loves them especially if I did not see him lowering his silver horn and nibbling delicately?

I have no idea where he goes in winter, this puzzles me. I begin to expect him in violet time and look up the hill to see him making his way down the tender grasses with his ivory hooves falling as light as rose petals. I don't bother about whether he is a symbol, or a childish wish or a form of escape when I need it. It is a very pleasant thing to be a country-woman and not have to explain things like unicorns coming down the hill. I simply have him, and enjoy his swift delicate beauty. According to legend, to look on the unicorn is fatal, but so far, it has not been fatal to me.

And I was delighted when a couple came to visit who had read of him, and the husband said as they drove down the road, "these are the haunts of her unicorn." I often tell this story, since he was a sound and sensible businessman, but he had an eye.

I was greatly saddened when another person who had read of my unicorn sent me a clipping about a real unicorn being shot in Austria. It was a deer with a single horn—and well, it was a unicorn, and why should anyone shoot it? One has a feeling unicorns are scarcer than trumpeter swans and it is sad to destroy the few left-over ones.

A fragment of a Rupert Brooke poem, found in his note-book by a friend, is much to my liking as I ponder on the balance between ordinary reality and the extra-real in this world.

All things are written in the mind.
There the sure hills have station; and the wind
Blows   in that placeless air.
And there the white and golden birds go flying;
And the stars wheel and shine; and woods are fair.

It is true all things are written in the mind. And so I feel very easy in my mind about my unicorn. I have him, and that takes care of that!

April twilights are blue and deep. The air smells of growing things and running brooks. The pond holds the sky in it. The stars come out. If we drive to the village to pop some letters in the narrow little slot in the wall of the post office, we see all the lights on in all the little old houses on Jeremy Swamp Road, and I fully realize I am an optimist, for I always think how happy the people must be inside, bustling about with supper, father in from the barn chores, the children home from school, the family gathering around the supper table.

Grief and death come to our valley, as to all places under the wide sky, but I always find the little lights of home so snug and happy when I look at them. And on a fine spring day, I think again, as I have often thought, today is tomorrow's memory.

This day, laid in the heart, was a day of spring wind and budding lilacs and pear trees blossoming. And I would much rather think of it as such, than ponder on the speed of a jet plane or the destructive power of the little atom.

One friend of ours calls Jill "the shelter of a rock in a weary land." She has so been, in times of trouble, and illness and death down the years. But she is a sound and sturdy country-minded woman who says I am too romantic when I opine all the houses are happy.

She quotes Walpole, "it isn't life that matters, it is the courage you bring to it." Then she usually adds, "remind me to tell George there is a fifty pound sack of dog food in the station wagon, he should bring it in. And I got some special vitamins today for the two thin ones. I want to build them up."

The furnace is still chugging along, I hear it breathing as I go to bed. In New England we run the furnace until mid May usually. If we are very lucky, it goes off the first of May. Then we build big fires in all the fireplaces and in my little Franklin stove and wear sweaters at night.

I like to go out at night for a last look at the sky—this is a custom with me. The dogs race around, I stand on the terrace and look at the sky, and then at the lighted house, so steadfast, so secure. Holly and Jonquil fly off after a casual rabbit. A squirrel, very fat, very grey, very elegant of tail, departs from the peanut butter station.

I see the Thomsons' lights are still on. They are a jump down the road near the mail box and, except in summer, we can see their lights in the evening. I wonder if they are playing their high fidelity machine, and reflect that one can live in the country and still have everything. George has gone home, the cows make small movements in the barn, and a horse neighs. One of George's dogs barks that quick excited hunting bark and all our dogs echo it, not knowing what is going on but being co-operative anyway.

The April moon hangs her silvery lantern in the soft night sky, and as I turn to the house, I think the stars are brighter than they ever were. I could pick them.

May

MOST OF THE GARDEN PLANTING
comes now, and such an excitement. I sing a small tune to
myself as I watch Jill moving down the stretched string marking the row.

> Plant this when maples are in bud,
> And feel the magic in your blood,
> Plant that when maples are in leaf,
> And that's the END of winter grief!

Of course, I cannot actually compose a true tune, but I can
sing along to suit myself.

Jill follows the rows carefully, lifting the friable earth—
what a fine word that is, friable. It sounds the way the garden
feels, and it is even, curiously enough, a dark cinnamon-colored word.

Almost all words do have color and nothing is more pleasant than to utter a pink word and see someone's eyes light up
and know it is a pink word for him or her too. You can also
get into rather warm arguments over a definitely dark green
word that someone insists is beige. Also it is not a good idea
to go around explaining about the color of words in strange
company. Some people give you such a sad critical look, and
their heads shake slightly.

I can imagine that if I ever got into the witness box, my
kind of testimony might drive judge and jury mad. The prosecuting attorney would ask in the silky voice prosecuting at-
torneys are supposed to use, "and how, might I ask, are you
so sure he said the word 'murder'?"

29

"Because I noticed right away it was a slush-brown word edged with magenta," I would say. I would sit there in a quiet grey dress (it is always best to be in a quiet grey dress, or black with a neat white collar, freshly laundered and starched slightly). I would look easily at the attorney through the better part of my bifocals and say gently, "you see my ears might misunderstand but as long as I also SAW the color of the word—"

As the hard little pellets go into the earth, Jill moves down the rows, intent, earnest. Suddenly in the clear spring light, she has the look of a pioneer woman, tall and vital and dedicated. She has, I notice, gardener's hands, with firm squarish palms, long strong fingers, and sensitive enough to cope with those maddening carrot seeds that I can not even get out of the packet without disaster. Like a true gardener, she also is, in spring, red as a beet in the back of her neck and arms, but winter-pale as to face, because she is always bending down.

Planting is an act of faith. The small envelopes of minute hard particles have no slightest suggestion of the tender sweet corn, the snow peas, the dark and juicy beefsteak tomatoes that are somehow in them. They lie in this earth, secret and still, and then suddenly one morning a green mist seems to come over the garden. Fragile and delicate tiny etched lines mark those string rows where Jill moved back and forth so patiently.

Presently we go out and pull the silvery savory scallions and the rosy crisp radishes—and the miracle has begun again! As I snip the tips of the first scallions, I am always feeling that one of the most hopeful things about mankind is that we go right on planting when the season comes, despite bombs, wars, world crises. There is a basic faith in mankind that planting is a secure thing.

And how infinitely much the earth gives us for so little! Here in New England where our easiest crop is stones, and we

never see the rich steaming black loam of the Midwest, we still have only to plow and rake and maybe add a little lime or fertilizer, drop the seeds in, and be reasonably decent about weeds, and we have bountiful crops!

I note the atlas says we have a humid continental climate. This means, in my language, it rains too much here and it is damp. But how the growing things love it! Jill has to hoe out rhubarb now and then, it takes over like a giant tropical creature in a rain forest. And the shy little shrubs she put in the border a few years ago have to be cut back or we could not get in the gate at all.

This is true of the pine trees we set out after the 1938 hurricane took down our thirteen beautiful old apple trees and played jackstraws with them. We set out six small modest little pines, and now we can only get to the clothes dryer out back by hacking a path between the two most vigorous ones.

The iris—ah, the iris! Jill moved and separated, moved and

separated, gave away, moved and separated, and one desperate day flung her hands in the air and said, "I cannot take it." She dumped a basketful in the swamp, since when we have iris all over the edge of the swamp, and doing nicely.

The poet's narcissus that we naturalized under the remaining old apple trees, has really naturalized in a big way. It chokes itself. Every year or so, Jill goes out and spends a day trying to manage a million bulbs that are just rampant in the tall grass.

However, strange things happen. We used to have a whole border of primroses, with their velvety leaves and pale gold and rosy faces. All of a sudden they vanished. I said they packed up one night and just went off adventuring with their roots tucked under their arms. Jill said, nonsense, the soil is wrong.

Same soil, I said.

Doesn't make sense, said she.

I like to think our rhubarb is a heritage from the early folk who lived here. For the shining bright green leaves open like platters down by the pond, at the edge of the garden, all along the border, back of the compost heap, and at the edge of the asparagus bed. Rhubarb stalks grow tender and rosy and big all over our place.

And as I cut up the tender pieces for a pie, I think the first woman who kept house here must have done the same thing just about now. Maybe she had a pie cupboard and set her pies on the shelves, crisp and juicy from the great Dutch oven.

We have some wild asparagus too. I love eating gifts from nature. Dandelion greens are as satisfying as finding a treasure in the old jewel box. Wild blackberries, and grapes, sweet wild strawberries, and the morel mushrooms—these are rare and lovely presents.

But we had no luck with fiddlehead ferns. Perhaps we picked them too late, they tasted a little like old rubbers to me.

A friend who specializes in wild edible plants says you pick them just as they poke up, ours were older than that, I think, looking back on it.

Pokeweed shoots are supposed to be elegant, too, but we have never gathered them. The berries are poison, the stems and roots are poison, and I felt we had better not get involved with them at all.

Milkweed pods, sliced and fried are supposed to be delicious. The Indians used to eat them, and used them for thickening too, somewhat as we use arrowroot.

There must be hundreds of unsung heroes and heroines who first tasted strange things growing—and think of the men who first ate a lobster. This staggers the imagination.

I salute him every time I take my nutcracker in hand and move the melted-butter pipkin closer.

George brings in the morels, in violet time. They are shaped rather like Christmas trees, pointed firs. They are a dark bisque in color and they are what the television commercials would call "in-de-scribably delicious."

We used to have them in the upper orchard and went up with baskets to gather them. But they have moved on—or we go too late, or some other creature likes them too. George finds them when he is out on the far reaches of his farm. Sliced and fried in butter, they taste a little like steak, and exactly like morels.

They are a comfortable mushroom. No other mushroom imitates them, at least in our part of the country. You can eat a morel and forget all the stories of people dropping dead as soon as they taste a mushroom they have gathered.

The only other wild mushrooms we have eaten were the fairy rings which used to grow in our childhood in the pastures and meadows. Small creamy button mushrooms, they were delicious. With them, there was just one catch. If they had a grey underbody, you did not pick them. If pale shell pink, you stuffed.

But I admire the intrepid souls who gather mushrooms that have twins who are absolutely deadly. I would never be accurate enough not to slip just one or two death-dealers in with the rest.

George's mother, from her Lithuanian heritage, knows about other mushrooms. She used to go forth carrying a basket, her head in a bright kerchief, and come in with all she could carry. These were big pale flattish mushrooms with strong stems. She used to dry them, and save them for winter. Of late years, she has not gone afield as she is lame.

Father thought all mushrooms were poisonous. He always expected us to measure our length on the floor immediately we had taken a bite. "You can't trust them" he would say darkly.

The year Jill decided to make our fortunes via mushrooms was memorable. We learned that they had to be planted in the cellar in seasoned horse manure. This was a problem in itself. The bed had to be turned and kept warm and it had to reach a certain temperature. This was before the days of mushroom boxes which you can buy all set up and ready to go. We had a large coffinlike sturdy wooden packing case which had gone all through college with us housing pennants, pictures of our current beaus and extra blankets to keep us from catching cold (be sure you keep warm) and a vintage-model electric hot plate for cheese dreams. The box was about the size of a small grand piano and Jill and George set it up by the furnace and engaged in the planting while I stayed upstairs. I was wrestling with my aesthetic sense and very unhappy. I had always thought mushrooms grew from fern and mossy leafmold and were really poetic little things. I wasn't at all sure how this would work out and I peered doubtfully through the window as George descended the outside cellarway carrying buckets.

"You're old enough," said Jill, "to face the facts. I am only following the directions, read them yourself."

We did raise mushrooms, but pending the building of another house to live in, we decided to abandon another attempt. As the house grew more and more to resemble a stable, we realized it might be just as well to settle for morels in season and canned mushrooms the rest of the time.

As George lugged the old packing case out to the dump pile, I reflected that when we were in college I had no idea Jill had this fierce agricultural bent. She was an intellectual and if she was not winning her golf letter, had her nose in some odd German philosophy book.

My Father was a kind of emotional gardener. One summer he went into beans and we had beans by the million. Then he gave beans up, and concentrated his furious energy on tomatoes and grapes. We drowned in tomatoes and we had grapes by the tubful. Then he pruned them all wrong and that settled that. He was a gardener who wanted results, and fast. He actually kept digging things up to see how they were doing. Mama advised against this. "Rufus, give them time," she would say.

"They ought to be up by now," he would retort.

After the bean summer, she was glad, however, that he wasn't more successful in a steady sort of way. She got awfully tired of canning beans day and night.

Father liked things in good amounts anyway, at all times. Sent to the store for a can of peas and a loaf of bread, he would come staggering in the door with a full case of asparagus, a case of corn, go back and unload a case of tomatoes. He might have forgotten the peas, but he had lots of other things. He liked the feeling that we were well equipped in case anything happened. "You never can tell," he would say.

I often wish he could have lived to see a good Deep Freeze, he would have had the largest made and absolutely jammed. Then he could have arranged for half a pig, half a beef and half a lamb and really felt satisfied.

We did have one of the first electric refrigerators in town, and Father would come in after his last class at college was over, having stopped at the butcher's and laid in four steaks, three pounds of calf's liver (expensive by then at twenty-five cents a pound). His rosy face always looked boyish, his blue eyes were bright and excited, his curly hair in its usual rebellion against any constraint by brush or hat.

Mama would look up from the apple pie she was trimming and her brown eyes, so wise, so deeply dark, would smile. She would wave a small floury hand at him. "Oh Rufus, there just isn't an inch of space—"

"Well, let's get the Trevors and Farley and Yutzes over—it's early yet."

Father liked to have company, and the house was always full. But he was too restless to sit still long, and when we were at the table, he always bounced up and went off to hunt something right in the middle of the meat course. During dessert, he might fly down cellar for some rock specimen he had brought in from a field trip.

In my early childhood, I remember his playing the violin and singing for the company (he had earned his way through Johns Hopkins by his music) but after the death of Grandpa he laid his violin away and played no more, although he would sing now and then in what was to me the most beautiful tenor in the world.

Ours was a violent and tempestuous life with Mama as a firm long-suffering buffer between Father and me. He could be severe in the same manner as his ancestor Cotton Mather, like all the Mathers down the generations, he was always right and never quiet about it. He could be soft as a mourning dove's note and charm the hide right off an alligator.

Father was a mining engineer, but Mama finally persuaded him to settle down as a professor so we could have a home. Not that Father ever really settled down but at least we had a house and I could stay in one school more than a month or so.

He had one of the most brilliant minds I have ever been exposed to, and this combined with his childlike unstable emotional reactions, made living with him pretty arduous.

I have always said his attitude toward traffic signals was some kind of symbol. Since he opposed them, he never obeyed them. He felt his judgment was far superior to the turning on and off of any lights. Stop signs were highly unnecessary if you looked where you were going. He said he looked. Speed limit signs stimulated him to drive on like a madman. He drove like an automobile racer and people we took for a quiet little ride on Sunday afternoons often emerged from the old sedan rather pale and shaky. Mama said the angels looked after him, for the only bad accident he was ever in appeared to be the fault of the other driver who came out of a side road NOT observing the stop sign! Father was full of virtue about this. It was a woman driver, he said, and she didn't look where she was going.

As a teacher, he was followed faithfully through every course he gave by those students who were strong enough to stand up under the field trips. He somehow had a way of making the pre-Cambrian era breathlessly exciting. And I still remember the one that began, "we shall now walk across the bottom of the ocean!"

Now and then when we were out hunting Indian arrows, he would stop and point to a boulder by the edge of the cornfield we were quartering. "See there, that is the way the great glacier came moving across this whole area—" and as he waved his arm, the air grew colder.

I could see a great advancing white cloudy mass of something like the sugar snow at circuses but infinitely cold and overwhelming.

Our little village is a combination of past and present that is peculiarly New England. In 1732 the Congregational Church went up, and around 1800 the Methodist Church was erected half a block down the road. Eventually, a few years before we settled in at Stillmeadow, the two tiny congregations finally joined and a Federated Church was formed. A few extra Episcopalians came into the fold, and possibly an odd Presbyterian or two and some unorthodox Jews.

Half the time the services were held in the Methodist Church, half in the Congregational. Communion in the Congregational Church involved individual communion cups passed around, in the Methodist, kneeling at the altar. When it was very cold, the service was moved to the church with the better furnace. During Easter, the bigger church was used.

And then suddenly, in our day, it was discovered that some change had to be made. The church was GROWING as the town grew. The new young minister sparked the Sunday-school program, more members came to church. In over a hundred years the beautiful little buildings had stood firmly, and with repainting, had kept on. Now, it seemed, there was an urgent need for Sunday-school space, for heating, for restroom facilities for the increasing Sunday-school group. The choir needed a corner for robing. And the kitchen needed a good sink and a few shelves and a range—in short, just lugging water and working on a deal table were not sufficient for the faithful Women's Guild. The kindergarteners were set up in the parsonage.

The teen-agers had Sunday school in the basement of the Methodist Church. Then the main service might be in the Congregational Church. For families with several children, Sunday was a merry-go-round of putting down and gathering up children, of racing from parsonage to churches, then back again.

After a year and a half of committee meetings, the building committee drew up recommendations. It was proposed that we move the smaller Methodist building in back of the larger church and at right angles, join them with a small connecting link and get everything under one roof, and by raising the foundations for the Methodist Church, add a whole story for Sunday-school groups, a parson's study and so on.

And here the interesting study of a historic community was illustrated. There were those who wished no change at all, under any circumstances. As the churches had been built, so they should stay. The small back lot where the horse-and-buggy congregation had parked was good enough for the founders of the church, and for the current members, let them park on the highway or wherever. There was the problem of the Methodists wanting to move their church back some day if the Federation ever was done away with.

There was also the problem of raising the money for the whole project.

When the church membership gathered to vote on the question, I was impressed with the way the young business-men who had done the planning undertook to iron out all the objections. I felt the church was a growing proposition and might better serve the community with adequate physical equipment.

But the high point of the evening for me was when the oldest deacon raised his voice and said, "I would like to ask, Mr. Moderator, whether the heirs of the Browns were paid off when we bought the parsonage in 1842."

The head of the Congregational Ecclesiastical Society rose to answer and said soberly, "we have five deeds of the twenty-three heirs of the Brown family, but I haven't at hand the rest, I would have to look them up. However," he said slowly, "this is not possibly pertinent to the matter at hand."

It is one of the most delightful things to me to live with the past going along currently. I remembered, as they spoke, the friend of ours who told all about the fire in their house and when I asked, in shocked tones, what night that was, she said, "it was in 1850, and we lost almost all the furniture."

And another friend who told me that her best china had been dumped in the Pomperaug. I asked about that, and it turned out her great-grandfather had remarried, and one of the children had carted all the best china out and tossed it, in resentment. This was possibly not more than eighty years ago, but gives one a nice sense of continuity about life in our valley.

I think this sort of thing is peculiar to New England, at least in America, for many of the families have roots which have never been disturbed. The names of a good many are the names of the original group that came over from Stratford and made a thrifty deal with the Pomperaug Indians for land in return for a couple of kettles and a few beads. I may do them an injustice, perhaps they also gave a gun or two and a few hunting knives.

Be that as it may, the Indians were friendly hereabouts, and none of our doors have tomahawk gashes in them such as the houses in Old Deerfield farther up, in Massachusetts. As nearly as I can figure, these Indians were rather quiet peaceful folk, addicted to a rough form of agriculture and less warlike than some of the tribes.

The arrows which we have turned up from time to time are delicate bird arrows, well shaped and usually of white quartz. Most of them are so small I cannot see how any marksman could shoot them and strike the prey, but they must have been phenomenal hunters.

The camp must have been where our pond now is, for the brook would be rushing and big then, flashing with trout and fringed with water cress. Pleasant for little copper-colored boys and girls to play in. One feels the Indians were a grave race, but I know the small ones played some. And I love to think they lived on our land, and the little Indian dogs hunted just where our merry cockers hunt.

During the Revolution, Woodbury, our neighboring village had a Tory section, and tempers boiled all along the road that Rochambeau and the French troops marched. After all, the small controversy over moving the Methodist Church behind the Congregational for a community congregation is as nothing compared to those days.

For a time the first Episcopal bishop of Connecticut held forth in the Glebe house on Sundays, and then popped into a secret tunnel from behind the woodbox in the fireplace and crept to a neighbor's house for the week. The Church of England had a rough time during those days.

I never tire of the story of the doughty husband who locked his wife in the secret closet back of the chimney when the French came down, so no French officer would cast a roving eye at her beauty. I think she must have been divided between rage at missing the ball and pride that her own husband thought she was too beautiful to hazard in public!

I like to see the old great chest which Major Bull's Negro slave carried behind him during the Revolution for it brings such a picture of the changes of time. In those days men went to war with all their personal goods and servants too.

And there was more than one battle which was suspended temporarily while both sides had tea.

Nathan Hale's birthplace is not far from here and I often think of this young patriot schoolmaster who combined ardor and loyalty with a rather astounding lack of shrewdness, being so easily caught.

It probably shows the academic dreamer should not essay practical plotting.

I note from my reading that Connecticut was one state which turned in supplies for the army without fail during the Revolution, delivered its quota of soldiers, and always responded to any appeal. Sometimes, I gather, men would disappear and go home for the plowing and the haying but generally they came back in due time. One wonders how Washington ever won this war with such a casual roster. Half the time nobody got paid either, and the food was limited to what happened to be around. Clothing was negligible, ammunition was always short.

I suspect if ever one man did win a war, it was Washington, for few leaders have ever had so little for so long. And one wonders at his great heart when after it was over and he expected to go to his beloved Mount Vernon and raise his fancy fruits and vegetables and hunt with the fox hounds which I think Lafayette imported for him—anyhow they came from abroad—and then he had to begin all over again to pull a sorry, tired, impoverished band together and make a nation grow.

It used to be popular to debunk all heroes. But nobody could ever debunk Washington for me. It seems to me he pin-pointed the whole struggle for Independence, and I am heartily pleased every time I cross the Sandy Hook bridge to think that General Washington forded the river here.

I never was too much in favor of the debunking school anyway. While there is a curious excitement about discovering odd weaknesses in great figures, it is too much like peering through a hole in the parlor curtains.

I would rather concentrate on the great things a man can do than on the sins he has committed. Whether Abraham Lincoln had a satisfactory love life is not, in the end, our business. He established a dream for America, fought for it, and died for it, and that is surely enough to measure a man by.

My special love is the lilac. I suppose if I ever came back to this world as any kind of plant, it would be a lilac. Either a Lincoln, or a white lilac with lacy white-jade blossoms against the deep-green leaves. I am sure heaven is bounded by a white picket fence that never needs repainting, and with lilacs always in bloom hanging deep clusters over it.

When the lilacs are in bloom and the apple blossoms and the white narcissus, New England is an experience in rapture. I love the lilacs too because they are a faithful flower, they

grow around old blackened chimneys where houses once stood, they mark out abandoned gardens. When I cut the clusters and bring them in the house, their sweetness is pure and singing as young love. White lilacs belong in old blue sugar bowls, purple in milk-glass vases.

Pale gold tulips, white narcissus, smoky black tulips (the new variety) and white lilacs from the bush by the well-house make a bouquet to remember.

The texture of spring flowers is especially lovely, the feel of a tulip petal is like lustrous old porcelain.

Apple blossoms mist the air with white and soft pink. We

drive along the winding country roads to see the old orchards when they are in full glory. The apple is one of the most beautiful of trees, because the shape of the tree itself is so gracious. The silvery grey trunk usually has a slight angle, and the branches bend in a design of beauty. If I could paint, I would first of all paint an old, very old apple tree in an old abandoned orchard with blossoms not fully out, just pinky and in bud. With a spring sky softened overhead and young grass below.

Even though we cannot spray our old apple trees, we can fully enjoy their blooming, and the gentle silvery green leaves coming out, and the nice shade, designed for a hammock swung underneath, and then in autumn, we can gather wind-falls for spicy applesauce.

The old abandoned orchards are home for the birds, too. Every knothole has a busy little family cheeping in it. In winter, nuthatches and woodpeckers whip up and down knock-knocking and darting bills for nice juicy morsels of all the little things that attack old apple trees.

In our early ambitious days, we planted what is known as a vest-pocket apple tree, with five varieties of apples grafted on one trunk. It is a pleasant and good tree but we have never had an apronful of apples from it. It is a nice idea, though. It was a small tree when we got it, and Jill slung a shoulder sprayer over her shoulder and sprayed it diligently and hard. Nothing came of it but more leaves and more branches.

One year we did get four small apples of indeterminate origin from one branch.

That year the untended wild trees had hundreds of good rosy apples.

I was thinking about spring flowers as I came back from the village the other day and I saw what seemed to me a very nice example of flowering springtime. Our young neighbor,

Bibi Thomson was out in her garden wheeling a barrowful of fertilizer for her border. Bibi is one of those girls you think must have been cut out from a Vogue ad, in the first place. She wore, this morning, lilac shorts and a lilac sleeveless sweater and a lilac jacket (what Connie used to call an up-top). She looked incredibly lovely and as if you might pick her and put her in a vase and have a bouquet of her.

As far as I was concerned, I mused, the wheelbarrow load added to the charm. For I like women who are not afraid of work, who work hard, who can be gay while mopping their brows and who can hang out the laundry in the morning and run a blood bank in the afternoon as Bibi's kind of woman does.

It is a reassuring thing about life in our valley that so many young families manage to have charming homes, keep up with world politics, help with everything from a church steeple to the League of Women Voters, raise sturdy rosy-cheeked children with a kind of easy grace, and yet live on a reasonable income. I find it a very hopeful sign that our American heritage is not lost.

Bibi is rather extraordinary, I thought, as few young mothers could look so extremely decorative while doing as much work as she does.

Her husband is just as special for he manages not only to do a full time job in a neighboring town but to be active in the Firemen's Association, the Church, and a dozen other activities. With time left over for his hi-fi collection and for cooking a steak to perfection over an open fire.

If I ever get discouraged reading too many articles about what's wrong with the world from the divorce rate to juvenile delinquency and from atom bombs to dope rings, I look up the hill and see the lights of the Thomsons' little red house shining in the night, and think of Phil spending his Saturday mornings in summer laying a stone wall for the terrace, and both of them hauling the sled out and sliding down the road in winter with their daughter and I say, they are not statistics, nobody has ever interviewed them, but they are a very real part of this country and they are not alone. There are many such families.

I used to be a stupendous mouse-killer. Our Connecticut mice eat anything at all from my best wooden stirring spoon to a down cushion. They shred everything. But, on the other hand, there is a kind of look in the eye of a frightened mouse that arouses odd feeling in me. The beady, shiny eyes look out, so aware, so desperately aware. The small polished nose quivers. The tiny delicate paws tuck under, for defense.

I wonder suddenly who gave me the right to kill this creature? If he or she chewed up a box of crackers, was it not for sustenance? Who set me over this tiny one, anyway, to judge and say I should whack out the breath and still the little beating heart?

My worst experience mouse-wise was with Aladdin, the Abyssinian cat. We keep the dehydrated dog food in a big galvanized container in the back kitchen in a cupboard. Came the day the lid was left off and Aladdin jumped right into the can. It was a big jump for the can was half empty. I rushed to retrieve my kitten and found a mouse was there too. Aladdin and the mouse began whirling around and around the can at a dizzying pace. The sides of the can vibrated with the speed of the two of them, dry dog food flew up, and Aladdin's tail was just long enough so that the chase looked like Little Black Sambo and the Tigers. It looked as if the mouse and his tail were merging part of the time.

"Oh, me," I said to Aladdin, "this can't go on! I must TAKE STEPS."

I fished him out and he swayed dizzily to the floor, his head going round and round. He tried to raise a tired paw and wash his face. But as soon as his head stopped whirling, he popped back in the can.

I went to the fence and yelled for George.

Cats are very special people. It is strange how controversial they are, for non-cat people are violent on the subject. Cat people are equally violent. If you love both cats and dogs, as I do, you are always riding two horses in mid-stream. Speak of the wonders of a dog's love and loyalty and a cat person looks icily at you and says, "I see you don't fully appreciate cats."

Speak of the wonders of a cat—from Siamese to plain alley, and a dog fanatic sniffs, you don't fully appreciate the superiority of dogs.

I think this goes along with our American passion for firsts. We want the best seller, the top movie star, the awards. We want the hit show, the best rated TV show; we are a competitive and anxious people. I, however, do not belong to this national fever. I relax and love dogs for their own richness of personality and cats for theirs. I never go into a pantod wondering if I were on a desert island and had to choose would I choose a cat or dog? Why worry? I can't get cast away on a desert island as long as I stay right here on my forty acres of New England soil.

I haven't been in any boat except a canoe for years and am not likely to be, and nobody gets as far as a desert island in a canoe.

One could argue a long time on the relative merits of dog and cat companions on a desert island. The dog—at least my dog, would sit and snuggle and say, what's for supper? The cat would flick an eyelash at me and get her own supper somehow and come back licking whiskers.

The dog would be dependent, the cat would walk on her own. I am glad I don't have to solve this, I just go along loving dogs and cats.

Everybody toys with this desert island idea, I think. It would be hazardous nowadays to try one, as somebody might be using it as a testing ground for some new explosive. I used to lie awake in the night and make lists of what I would have to have, aside from a dog and a cat.

Maybe if one book, I might take the Bible, although I would worry over some of the interpretations and wish to talk them over with an informed person. Well, assume the Bible is there. Mine would not be the modern understandable version but the old poetic rolling one. Phrases singing along. Much more encouraging if living on bananas and crayfish.

I would probably settle for the complete works of Johnny Keats. Because there would be a lift in "some shape of beauty lifts the pall from our dark spirits," even while I was lugging palm fronds to weave a shelter.

Most people who have been cast on desert islands in fiction have the right knife, the rope, the tinned stuff, and all goes well. They salvage from the sea everything they have to have.

Desert islands will soon be impossible in any case. There will be radar, and army and air-force personnel on them all.

In the future, anyone cast on a desert island will meet a sergeant at the water's edge and will have to sign papers before he or she can emerge, just in case of communist spying.

It is sad, in a way, to see our whole world encompassed and taken over. The only pioneering left is in the stratosphere, even the deeps of the sea are submarine-inhabited. Man needs an unknown horizon somewhere, I think, and it makes trouble when none is left.

It might be one trouble with this world now is that we have been everywhere.

But I hope, in my day, we don't get involved with Venus and Mars. They must have their own troubles and let us leave it to them to solve them.

Jill says she is declaring a moratorium on peanut butter for the birds. It melts, she says darkly, coming in with the jar and the spreader. She says the peanut butter our birds ate this past winter, if spread out, would encircle the globe. We keep on feeding the birds, come spring, come summer, come autumn, but at least the peanut butter struggle has to end with warmer weather except for a gobbet on the flat tray.

Mid-spring is such a hopeful time. As I think about the world situation and listen to all the reports, I think of all the constructive forces at work along with the destructive ones. There are so many earnest organizations seeking for world peace, and there are so many people looking to the end of controversy, the resolution of conflict. I can't help believing, being perhaps an optimist, that the forces for peace will prevail.

I follow all the reports of preparedness and non-preparedness and wonder whether we should undergo all this at all, in any event. A friend writes me her son is dropped in northern Alaska to live a week in an igloo on K rations and I wonder whether he should not be at home as a bank cashier with a wife and a baby to worry over. I cannot solve this question, but I still feel we have to trust our government and depend on the democratic ideal paying off. We have lived by it too long to retrace our steps.

As I walk out in the violet dusk to stand under the biggest lilacs, I can only pray that love will prevail over hate in this embattled old world. "Perfect love casteth out fear," says the Bible. We of this generation have a stupendous job, possibly bigger than the pioneers, than the ragged Revolutionary horde, but I see no reason to abandon hope.

The stars are like apple blossoms and I can smell the apple blossoms themselves in the moonlit night. The green valley is still, except for George's cows mooing now and then.

The whole land has a changed look now that the winter etching is gone, everything is sweet and blossoming under the May moon.

When I go out at bedtime, Little Sister, a small black and

white cocker figure, follows me at a hopping run, cocker ears afloat behind her.

The Irish flies to the back of the yard where an errant rabbit is nibbling unconcernedly. The rabbit lifts an ear and lopes into the swamp, he knows about the fence.

Now if I walk softly, I may see my unicorn stepping from the green wood, ready to nibble the white lilacs.

White lilacs in the moonlight, white fire of moonlight over blossoming apple trees, white little house under the great sugar maples—and Little Sister and Holly waiting by the door— we are deep in spring!

June

THIS IS THE SINGING MONTH. RAMbler roses everywhere, over white picket fences, over grey stone walls, climbing old well-houses, blooming on lattices in old-fashioned gardens. The whole green countryside is laced with shell pink, ivory white and rose red. The sky sings, too, such a deep tranquil blue. I think I can hear the horns of elfland faintly blowing as I go out to the Quiet Garden to shell peas.

The gentle charm of old white houses is enhanced by the riot of roses, as well as by the tall pale amethyst iris and the shorter pale gold. Most of the old houses have borders of iris around the yard, or flanking the walk to the front door. I like to bring iris in the house and set it in the milk-glass swan compote where the light from the window falls on it, the petals are translucent and the color a pure and lovely note.

Faith Baldwin does not wish any flowers arranged in orthodox flower arrangements. She likes flowers as is, just put in water and left to their own devices. She is very firm about this, and for a tiny exquisite small person she is firmer than almost anybody. If she comes for tea, I am careful NOT to make arrangements. My own feeling is that flowers come into their own in the house if they are properly arranged as to mass and color and design, and related to the container, and that it is an art much like painting with living color to be able to make fine bouquets.

I think the beautiful mass arrangements in Williamsburg add greatly to the atmosphere of that enchanting place. They are traditional, and they are made with flowers grown in the same way as they were when Williamsburg was young.

I saw the Wythe house by candlelight once when I was in Williamsburg, and I remember the polished beautiful furniture and the muted tones of the rugs but most of all the way the candlelight shone on the massed roses in silver bowls.

It is strange that the human eye finds beauty in certain forms. Why does a circle seem satisfying and a pyramid shape inspiring? The crescent may be fine because of a connection with the moon, and the moon has played a great part in our life always. In that case, the circle might be the sun. In flower arrangements I find the triangle a happy design, for the apex gives a sense of height and uplift and the lower points help relate the bouquet to the container and give stability to it all. If the deeper colors in the flowers are kept toward the base of the arrangement, it is more pleasing, and the lighter values are right at the top. The main thing is to cut the flower stems in varying lengths, and to give each blossom room enough in the bouquet to look comfortable. Some bouquets one sees are stifling.

On the whole, I like bouquets in containers that are not formal vases. Don says that with a whole closetful of vases, I am always making bouquets in old bread tins of pie plates. I do have a hand-hammered silvery grey aluminum casserole which is beautiful with purple lilacs, white lilacs and tulips in it! Old flowing blue sugar bowls are lovely for pale pink roses and delphinium and milk-glass saltcellars look charming on a coffee table filled with Tom Thumb rosebuds and forget-me-nots.

The autumn flowers, such as zinnias and marigolds take on added glory in old copper bowls or wooden mortars, and winter bouquets are admirably suited to antique pewter tea or coffeepots or mellow waxed wooden bread-mixing bowls (what they call trows in Williamsburg).

One of the loveliest table arrangements I ever saw was

shown at the Southern Connecticut African Violet Show, for a member had used a piece of curved and weathered grey driftwood, tucked delicate mosses and lichen in the hollowed out parts and where the root formed a niche, tucked a Romany African violet in. The fluted pale lilac of the blossoms in the setting of grey and woodsy green was lovely. And actually you might say a piece of old wood and a little wild moss and a potted plant weren't much to work with.

Strawberries are for June. A big blue bowl heaped with freshly picked richly ripe strawberries and a subsidiary bowl of powdered sugar is as handsome a centerpiece as one could ask for. So is a strawberry shortcake, made the proper way. Not a spongecake dotted with small berries and topped with a fluff of whipped cream, not a cake at all, but a rich old-fashioned baking-powder biscuit enriched with sugar and baked until the top is golden. Baked in a pie tin, then split and buttered, yes, buttered and never mind the calories. And then the berries—which have been partly crushed and set to warm a little on the back of the stove to bring out the full flavor. The berries are ladled well over both layers of the shortcake.

With this, a comfortable-sized pitcher of thick Jersey cream, not whipped, just at hand to pour over as is, so little creamy brooks of cream make their way to the ruby sea of juice below. Ah, that is fine fare for a June night supper.

It is best to give yourself up to it and not add anything else to the meal except pots of boiling-hot black coffee.

We temporarily added another member to the household this week when Hollyberry Red loped onto the terrace with a very wee rabbit. No bigger than a thimble, bright-eyed, incredibly soft, the rabbit was not injured by the sudden trip. The soft mouth of an Irish setter is always a surprise, it is really true an egg can be retrieved unbroken provided you want to play games with eggs.

Connie was home for the week end and she spent two hours at a stretch with a baby nursing bottle trying to get the tiny thing to take some nourishment. Finally she got down a few drops of warm evaporated milk via a dropper. She kept working every little while.

In four days the small one had developed personality, waggling his ears bravely, putting a paw out, giving great shiny looks when milk was in the offing. He also made small gestures toward fixing the grass up in his shoebox.

By the time we learned from my naturalist-cousin Rob that rabbits have front teeth so designed that they must nurse sideways, so to speak, the baby was doing very well. His will to live was astonishing.

He fitted inside Connie's small palm at first, and then he seemed to begin growing. And then we gave him to a little girl whose rabbit had been run over, partly because she needed a rabbit and partly because it didn't seem practical to raise a rabbit with eight lively cockers and a livelier Irish setter romping around. Jill said everybody would get complexes.

But I hated to see him go. The way this very small, very wild youngling adjusted to circumstance was amazing. Lugged from the nest by a fierce huge creature full of great teeth, dumped in the midst of people, he nevertheless gathered his small forces together and made up his mind to manage.

A good lesson, I thought, for people who might have troubles, a good example of courage.

Holly was patient with her odd humans. After all, this was her own rabbit, she discovered and brought him home, only to have him pried away from her before she hardly had a good smell of his fur. And then she never got him back either.

I am always surprised at how very patient our dogs are

with us. We take so many things away from them—sunny little Jonquil bounces up with a huge hunk of creamy fresh suet which has dropped from the bird feeder, for example, and I pounce on her and open her eager mouth and take it right away. She looks wistfully at me, but her tail keeps wagging to show she loves me, no hard feelings.

Or Tiki manages to acquire a murderous steak bone and he loses that. Or Especially Me finds a loose vacuum-cleaner brush.

Dogs forgive you so much. For shutting them up when you go away, for leaving them in the first place, for having various needles stuck in them (for what, they wonder), for pills thrust down their throats, for baths, for thistle removing, for a hundred odd actions every day. And still they look up with love, stick to us like burrs.

Some breeds have more independence than cockers and Irish. There are some dogs that lead their own lives from time to time. But not cockers or Irish. It is not enough to be under the same roof, or in the same house, no, nor in the same room. When I sit at my desk, a fringe of recumbent figures is so close I can barely move my feet. Little Sister, the small black and white, is usually right under my feet, actually. The rest sleep dreamily as long as I stay where I am, but let me go out of the room for a drink of water and the sleeping beauties erupt into terrific activity, leaping after, wagging, making hopeful hops toward the refrigerator.

The Irish is more determined in character than the cockers. If Holly decides to be fed, she bangs her feeding dish firmly on the floor. If she wants a fresh drink, she starts climbing right into the sink. If she is outdoors and wants to come in, she stands on tiptoe and bashes the window loudly, at the same time uttering an odd squeaky wail. She is as stubborn as she is charming, and it seems odd that there is something so utterly vulnerable about her at the same time.

I believe all Irish owners agree with this, at least all those

I know do, that an Irish heart can break all too easily. When Jill is training Holly in Obedience, if she speaks sharply to her, Holly may turn to jelly and collapse. Our other two Irishers did the same thing, and it is not easy to re-establish a fifty-pound dog on four feet when you have to scoop her up and support her at the same time. Holly weighs around sixty-five, I should think, being more robust than our lost dears.

She really loves training, except for the command to SIT. She does not like to sit. She will stand indefinitely, waving her lovely red plume, and smiling pleasantly, but to sit—ah, not that, says she. I have noticed in my long experience with dogs that the Irish generally lie flat, or run, or stand, they seldom sit any more than a pony does. The cockers characteristically sit with neat paws under, and head always lifted. I have watched at dog shows the way poodles, the breed that goes on tiptoe, sit sharply down, their forepaws barely in touch with earth. Basset hounds, on the other hand, cannot sit like other people at all, they sag on one hip. And great Danes go down in a sort of sliding jerk. With dachshunds nobody can tell whether they are sitting or standing. Looks the same anyway.

The toy dogs mostly have an arrogant prancing gait as if to indicate they may be small but they are of consequence. The Pekingese, called the sleeve dogs because they were originally carried in the Chinese mandarins' sleeves, trip along with a regal manner, the Afghan braces his straight front legs and abandons all hope for his hind legs and gets himself .together afterward with a look of great surprise.

If we ever have to go away for a few days and leave the dogs, I apologize to them a week beforehand and make all sorts of explanations. The day we leave Jill has on her list to say good-bye to the dogs, but I simply scramble in the car and hide my face and never, never look back, for if I saw all those faces, the eager bright eyes, I just would not be able to drive off down the winding road. Sometimes we have gotten all ready to go, and told George just who would be in which kennel run, and who should have the extra feeding, and who the pills, and then at the last minute Little Sister flies to the door and begs so earnestly because I am putting a hat on. If it is not something like a day's shopping trip to New York, I turn back, and scoop her up, and off we go.

We have done quite a lot of wayfaring with dogs, from the days when we carried a litter of six in a carton back and forth from New York week-ending, to the days we traveled around with two very jealous cockers who had to be kept one in front, one in back. Once we went to Cape Cod with mother and family, six puppies and one anxious little mother. We have driven to dog shows with two Irish setters and an odd cocker or so, and we took many trips with Maeve who always rode standing up and drove by resting her muzzle on the back of Jill's neck and really guiding everything!

Dogs are so easy to travel with, they will put up with long trips, or short ones. Early ones or late all-night deals.

But my travel with my cats has been a little different. We have transported one Manx, one Siamese, one Abyssinian at various times, and although I know some cats love riding, and now and then I have seen cats riding as relaxed and happy as dogs, ours just never were.

The jungle wail the Manx gave on his solo trip was deafening and continuous. He not only sounded like a single tiger or leopard or lion but like a bevy. It was unfortunate that we had to park outside the motor vehicle bureau for twenty minutes while Jill went in on the business of legalizing us as drivers. When she came out, I had crouched down, to be as inconspicuous as possible, and Tigger stood glaring and screaming at the window. We said nothing as we sped home, for we could hardly have heard ourselves speak.

Esmé, the fabulous Siamese, gave forth with a constant howl, rather low in pitch, but carrying. She always knew she was just commuting but she did not cotton to the idea, and wished us to know it.

When we got home, she would stand and blaze at me with her heavenly sapphire-blue eyes bigger than soup plates and curse violently for ten minutes. Then, regally, she would forgive me, and come and land in my lap clinging with her long seal-brown velvet gloves and uttering a last regal pronouncement.

The Abyssinian, possibly, of all cats comes closer to being like a dog in adapting to his humans instead of properly expecting them to adapt to him. One hesitates to make any statement about cats, at all. Dog people may be lax and indolent about their pets, but the red flag is always flying with cat-lovers.

I personally believe this is a heritage from the days when witches were associated with cats and cat-lovers are still defending their own. Cats were persecuted off and on down the centuries and yet man could not do without them, and had to come to the realization. It may be that mankind at times resents the superior ability of a cat to wrest a living from the most adverse circumstances, to hold its head up, and never to be defeated. No cat I ever knew would curry favor, only accept favors given, and this is a wonderful quality.

You can train a dog to refuse fresh hamburger offered by a stranger, a cat would sniff and decide personally whether it was good meat or poisoned.

A cat can do almost any kind of trick, if feeling in the mood. But I cannot imagine a cat in an Obedience ring, running around in the hot sun and doing things on command. For it would not make sense. Whereas a dog is tolerant of your not making sense and only wants to fix things so you are happy.

People are always asking me if I prefer dogs to cats. I consider this an unnecessary question. I appreciate both for their own personality and charm and intelligence, I just happen to think they are different in their approach to life and I like both.

I would wish to be as willing as a dog to undergo trials for my loved ones and as unregimented as a cat. I would wish to be as easy to manage as a dog and yet as marvelously adequate to face any situation on my own as a Siamese.

And I love both the way a dog looks up to me and a cat condescends to me.

I respect grocery cats and theatre cats and alley cats beyond measure.

I respect solid barn mousers such as George has, who keep rats and mice from ruining the grain. I respected the wild little grey pussy who raised a family in a stone wall nearby and would not truckle to humans but would come out at night and eat the food they laid down. Millions for defense and not one cent for tribute fitted her perfectly.

A well-rounded household needs both, and dogs and cats do very well together if properly introduced.

Esmé, the fierce, the independent, used to snuggle down in the wing chair with Honey, the big blond cocker, and push a paw at her to make her move a little. The little wedge-shaped face would go down on Honey's golden lovely fur, the sapphire eyes would close, Honey's dark amber eyes closed too, they both slept, quite unaware that they were hereditary enemies.

Cats are knowing personalities. Dogs may advance on some guest who is absolutely terrified of anything with four paws, just because of a pleasant perfume and a quiet voice. Cats never. I have friends who insist that cats jump in their laps for sheer persecution because they know they loathe them. I do not believe this. I think a cat picks a person with a reasonably level lap, soft comfortable clothes, and a cat just assumes conferring privileges will be appreciated. If not, never mind. Both dogs and cats estimate a guest as he comes in the door, and decide whether he is a nice person. Dogs assume the best, cats figure it better work out, or else.

I would venture to say a dog can be understood quite wholly, but a cat is forever a mystery. And who doesn't need a little mystery?

In June, the house begins to fill up with week-end guests. The children feel the urge to come out, friends and relatives who have been "long in city pent" as Milton says, now come out.

We keep the sunburn lotions on the shelf in the back kitchen. People cannot resist burning themselves to a crisp as a salute to a country week end. Warning does no good. "Oh, I never burn," the guest says airily.

We hand out the cream as they come in from the pond and the Quiet Garden. Jill, meanwhile, goes about her garden chores. She cannot afford to make a career, says she, of "evening herself up." The golden coppery tones are fine, if you have nothing to do but turn and toast and toast and turn. She is busy.

I think this is true of all real countryfolk. City people vacation, and get a warm golden tone ALL OVER. Country people are always spotty. It is never an even color. I think I could tell country from city by this alone. Forearms get cinnamon in countrydwellers, backs of necks are copper, but the front stays relatively pale because most outdoor work requires bending. George gets brown when haying begins, as the reflected heat simmers on him, but even George does not tan like a city person who lies flat and bakes, turns, and bakes again, shifts slightly, bakes some more. Tanning is an art and you cannot follow this art if you are busy.

I sometimes look at guests prone in the chaise longue and feel a twinge of envy. Frying chicken gives no glow to the skin. I frequently urge Jill, who is a child of sun, to lie down and even up, but she is always too busy. Weeding something, or picking peas, or hoeing.

In all the years we have been countrywomen, I have seldom known her to go out and lie down in one of the chaises just to get tanned. Once I drove her to it, and she was cross all day. Said she got nothing accomplished.

We eat most of our meals outdoors now, down by the pond, or in the Quiet Garden, or on the back terrace. We can cook on any of three arrangements. We have the big barbecue which Smiley Burnette, the Western-movie star built while he was resting here one week end. Or we can wheel the movable grill up to the little garden if it is too hot by the pond. Or we can use the portable round grill which you carry in one hand and plunk down by the trays.

I was amazed when we had as honored guests the head of the Netherlands House of Representatives—they call it something different there, of course—and his utterly charming wife. We had a picnic by the pond with grilled frankfurters and rolls and a big salad and a typical American dessert of ice cream with fresh strawberries. They both said they had never eaten out of doors before and what a pity! They were going to institute outdoor meals when they got home. They had never had hot dogs either.

Eating by the pond, with the sun deep in the clear water, and the charcoal sizzling, and the rolls crispy brown, represented American home living quite adequately, I felt. And our talk was as easy and satisfying as if they had just dropped in from down the road. The great statesman and his lady talked about their children, their home, the world situation, all with grace and ease and it was as if we had always been close neighbors. After the Washington merry-go-round and all the banquets and speeches, I thought it might seem dull. It did not.

As I kissed them both soundly when they left, I reflected that what makes neighbors is a common feeling for home and family and a common zeal for world peace. And somehow our little American picnic was a very happy time for all of us.

They came to present a carillon to this country for our having rendered assistance to the Netherlands, but for me, they came to represent the natural closeness of people who love their homes and children and the cause of world understanding.

I could not help feeling, also, that if a few Russians came to see us, and passed the mustard and adventured with a hot dog, world troubles might ease up.

Often in the night, I think of the stresses and strains of this troubled world. I wonder why we have to build destructive machines to outproduce other nations. The people of the world want to have their homes, to give their children better education, better lives. If only we could so persuade a few power-mad dictators—if only we could!

Foreign exchange students are a means of promoting understanding between nations which can hardly be overestimated. I have seen at Columbia, Japanese, Turkish, Finnish, Latin American, Swedish, students all gathered together getting to be friends over tea and sandwiches while discussing quaint American customs. The atmosphere produced by mutual study is always a leveler, people who take examinations together have a common bond. I would like to see the foreign exchange program expanded so a large proportion of young people from all countries would mingle. It does cost the government money, but this is one place that it is not wise to economize.

I like to think of the busload of foreign students that drove through our valley on a trip to see rural America. The Japanese were madly taking pictures through the bus windows, greatly excited. What they were photographing was washday, for in the back yards the washings were being hung out and to their great amazement they saw MEN helping. Husbands and wives were both doing the same job in a casual way together. This was the most remarkable sight they had seen!

We seldom really realize the difference in attitude toward the sexes which obtains in other countries. Now and then it does come to us as when a perfectly respectable ruler of one certain country would have been kept from visiting our shores because we seem to have a little rule about admitting more than one wife to America. Obviously he couldn't discriminate, I thought, and leave ONE of the two wives behind. His life would have been very unpleasant, I feel sure. I was glad to read that in the end the State Department juggled the rules a bit so the three of them could come if they wished.

Old houses have a special charm for me. They have a special lived-in quality, the sense of time having passed over them, they are steadfast. Fireplaces that have warmed generations have something a brand-new fireplace does not have.

Often in the flickering light from my own fire, I can see hand-made shoes on the hearth being warmed, or copper-toed boots. Or possibly now and then satin slippers. The satin slippers would be very special since the folk who built Stillmeadow were simple folk, and worked the land.

This was a house of homespun living, but one has the feeling it was happy living. It is strange how houses affect one. Some houses, old or new, seem to breathe a serene air. Some, for no good reason at all, seem depressing. Now and then I go into a house that suddenly makes me feel chilled, and I know several houses which give me a sense of brightness even if I am melancholy when I enter.

There is no reason to think houses cannot have their own personality, and they do. In an old house, the living that has gone on within the walls adds character, in a modern ranch house, it might be the reflection of the architect's mood, I suppose.

Old houses were built soundly, built to endure. But now and then things happen to them. Our friends Lois and Burt Klakring were about to buy an old house not long ago. They were just ready to close the deal when the real-estate agent took them down cellar to see the furnace.

"And one thing you can be sure of," he said proudly, "these old beams are as sound as ever." He took a penknife from his pocket and stuck it in one of the great foundation beams.

Whereupon the knife sank to the hilt, soft powder began to drift out, and the beam ominously cracked open. They all ran for their lives, Lois said. They made it, but it was a near thing.

So they got a modern house in the end.

With a modern house you begin the traditions, I feel, but with an old house, you inherit them.

Old furniture has its personality too. I think it is fine to create new designs, to change. That is, in theory, I think so. But when it comes to my own furniture, I would take one combback Windsor for all the black iron-legged chairs there are. The sofas that are so low they hang to the floor and so deep that you have to sprawl to sit in them are not for me. And an antique maple blanket chest with heart hinges is more beautiful than any sheer-faced bleached piece.

And I like my furniture to seem solid, not as if it might fly off any minute and circle the house waving an aluminum arm in passing. Mr. Robsjohn-Gibbings' *Goodbye Mr. Chippendale* I enjoyed very much, and I read it comfortably sitting in my Early-American wing chair by my nice 1690 fireplace. It amused me without changing my mind at all.

Furniture fashions come and go, and I remember well the days when antiques were moved into most of the attics in our town and golden oak took over. Lovely drop-leaf cherry and pine tables were used on back porches for chores, and parlors went Victorian.

Doing over antiques is a hard but rewarding task. We have tried most methods from scraping with a piece of broken glass, and cursing as we scraped ourselves, to sloshing on paint-remover and getting a gluey mass all over us and the yard. We now begin with remover, and when the old paint or varnish is well soaked up, we use a putty knife to push the mess to the edge of the piece, then wipe with paper towels. If, however, the piece has the old casein paint on it, we first wash it with a solution of washing soda and hot water.

After the first few layers are off, we begin the sanding with finest grade sandpaper, sanding with the grain or with fine steel wool or both.

This takes a good deal of patience and is best done in a sunny yard on a summer's day not too hot, not too humid.

To refinish the piece we usually use the French method, of six to eight coats of shellac (diluted fifty percent with alcohol for the first three) rubbed down slightly between each coat. For tables or pieces with hard use coming up, we finish with a coat of dull-finish varnish, and then wax.

Country auctions still offer the prospective buyer good values in old sleigh beds and pine blanket chests although one seldom gets a museum piece for a few dollars any more. The museum pieces are snapped up by the antique dealers and that is that.

Country auctions are fun, with all the people gathering and the Ladies' Aid serving lunch and the auctioneer exercising his wit, and yet they can be sad too. When the contents of a house are piled on the veranda to close out an estate, there is something bitterly mournful about the broken rockinghorse whose rider has gone away and the great rubber plant in the brown urn that nobody tends.

The dusty piles of books have more stories about them than in any table of contents and browsing among them, one can piece out the life of the house. *The Poems of Whittier* in faded green presented to Arabella respectfully by Edward and *The Young Man's Book Of Elegant Poetry* from Arabella to Edward. Later on, a well-worn book of household hints. In another pile *The Sunbonnet Babies* and *Black Beauty* and *Little Joe.*

The day of buying sets of books just to seem correct is over, as far as I know. Sets of Dickens, sets of Shakespeare, sets of Sir Walter Scott, sets of Kipling are not often the chief literary furnishing of a living room.

Possibly we tend to buy books singly as we read them nowadays. Possibly we like to vary our reading, skipping from books on *How To Raise Guppies* to *Out Of Africa* and back again. However, one should not generalize on this any more than on anything under the arc of the sky.

I know some experts feel we are quite over the age of fiction and that the decline of the novel is not only imminent but a fact; that short stories are on the way out, since even the popular magazines are now stuffing the pages with nonfiction articles.

I would think it might be more difficult in this era to write

good fiction, since the actual happenings around us out-Herod
Herod, as it were. Adventure fiction has been outdone by *I
Escaped From the Soviets* or *My Life Behind The Iron Curtain*. While James Ramsey Ullman's *The White Tower* can
hold its own with *Annapurna* for mountain climbing, few sea
stories could hold the interest as tightly as *Kon-tiki*.

But I think novels and short stories will probably be around
as long as men can read at all. And there is a satisfaction to a
writer in creating characters which no amount of good report-
ing could duplicate. I venture to say also that great fiction
illuminates life in a way no other form can do.

The informal essay seems to be coming back, and this is a
fine thing. There is a personal directness, an immediacy of
contact between author and reader which is rewarding to
both. I find John Crosby's daily piece in the *Herald Tribune*
not really a review of radio and television but a sharp and wise
essay on us and our times. John Mason Brown is a superb
essayist, and there are many others.

Mysteries probably will always be in demand and the lure
of a detective story cannot really be explained. Some people
say they like to puzzle out the problem, it is an exercise like a
game, others say it is restful. Jill simply says she likes them.

She prefers Dorothy Sayers's *The Nine Tailors* to all others,
rereads this fairly often, and her tastes run also to Joseph
Shearing and Josephine Tey rather than to the tough school.
One of her favories is Tey's, *The Daughter Of Time*, in
which Detective Grant proves that the little princes in the
tower were not murdered by Richard the Third at all. Richard was neither a villain nor a hunchback, and this is proved
as clearly as any current fact could be.

She believes there should be a law against Mickey Spillane,
but cannot decide how to pass it.

The untimely death of Josephine Tey was a great loss.
Miss Pym Disposes, in 1948 began the brief career, and Jill

has been saving the Tey books, for their literary quality makes them a real and permanent addition to her library.

We like to drive around the country roads in the early evening when the violet light is coming from the hills. One night last week we came slowly along Jeremy Swamp Road and suddenly met a possum.

He was in the exact middle of the road. Jill stopped the car short. He stopped short. He turned his pointed, salt-and-pepper face toward us, his beady eyes shone in the light from the car, and his incredible tail snaked into a straight line behind him as he froze.

After a few minutes, he gave us a last look—was it contempt? Then he moved into the shadow of the roadside thicket. Such an odd, silent little neighbor, I thought, living his mysterious life in the night.

It is a comfortable thought that we have so much wildlife around us. For as houses go up along the country roads more and more, the wild ones tend to fall back into the forest. Where once we saw four deer crossing the road, we are lucky now to see a print of delicate hoof now and then. But all winter Jill lugged corn and bread for the ruffled grouse that live in the meadow just below the kennels, and one winter we had to take care of three hen pheasants who simply CAME TO STAY. Jill finally got a barrel and put straw in it and turned it on its side for shelter from the blizzards and they moved right in. They would come early every morning and perch on the fence and look toward the house waiting for food.

They went back into the swamp when nesting time came, and we wished them well.

A red fox running along the thicket is a beautiful sight to see, the pointed face and the plume of tail—I don't know why they call it a brush, it does not look like a brush—and the swiftly graceful gait all give a moment of complete beauty

to me if I happen to be up in the meadow when he goes by.

And a pair of young rabbits playing on the lawn on a dewy morning is a charming sight. They spring so lightly in the air, their long ears quiver, they look like creatures out of an ancient fairy tale. They seem to make a ritual game, bounding and leaping in a pattern of delicate movement.

And down by the pond, we often see the blue heron fishing. The grace of the long slender neck and long slim legs makes him a spectacular bird. The strike for a minnow is sudden and arrowy, now and then he stands on one leg absolutely motionless for a time. Then when he moves to another fishing spot, each leg folds up in a dramatic sweep and slowly lowers, almost as if he went on stilts along the dusty shallows.

As twilight deepens into night, the soft strange dark little bats swoop over the pond, and whatever one's opinion of bats may be, their falling and rising rhythm is lovely to watch.

How strange they are, these nocturnal creatures who fly and yet are not birds, who are mammals and yet make free of the sky. Now and then we used to find one in the house, possibly come down the chimney or in through an unmended clapboard at the attic level.

I know of nothing short of a rattlesnake that throws such consternation among a roomful of guests as a visiting bat. I suspect it is some subconscious memory of vampires from our legendary past. Women scream and throw pillows or sweaters over their heads. Men look brave but are slow in acquiring the technique of grabbing a bat. I have never really met anyone who did get a bat in her hair which never came out, nor anyone ever bitten by a bat who came to spend the night.

I do admit a bat is an unexpected sort of guest and makes such erratic courses around the bric-a-brac and the corner cupboards that it is very hard to get him out. A whole bevy of the braver adults can spend half an evening batting, so to speak and get exactly nowhere. My theory is that a bath towel swung at the bat may deflect him toward a door, if it is managed with the skill of a matador with his cape.

A broom is not so good for it may mash the bat and always brings down the standing lamps and the milk glass from the mantel. Once after a bout with a bat, we had the tiny morsel in a large towel and as we carried him to the door and a better world for bats, I had a peek at him, terrified, panting, folded up on himself. He seemed a small thing to cause such to-do.

However, animal and wildlife lover though I be, I would not want to sleep with a bat circling over me.

The moral universe is a fine phrase and I sometimes wonder what, exactly, they mean by it. Ordered it must be for the seasons go in perfect order, the roses come in order and the migratory birds even migrate in order. When the thermometer drops a degree at a certain point, rain must become snow. This is order. As far as mankind is concerned, it is debatable about moral universe or no. Morals are a sometime thing. To be moral in Connecticut has nothing in common with being moral in the communal life of the jungle. Morality consists in following the pattern you are brought up to follow. And it changes so. It was moral in the Pilgrims' time to cheat the Indians, to lie to them, steal from them, ambush them and take their own land from them. We respect the Pilgrims for their bravery, their fleeing to America and many other things but not for their moral relationship to the natives.

Today in my valley it is not moral to gain advantage through trickery over anybody. We even have ideas about traps and how many fishhooks should go on a line.

As far as wildlife is concerned, I cannot feel there are either bad or good, moral or immoral birds and/or animals. I think this is perfectly silly.

The predatory blue jay who snatches the best suet is only following the blue-jay pattern. The cowbird lays her eggs in other birds' nests, but maybe it is because she cannot figure out how to make a nest for herself, who knows? Or she is dilatory and doesn't get to nest-making in time when all the good apartments are already taken?

I always end my thinking in confusion and decide to make a cheese soufflé for supper, as I understand that very well.

It must be a terrible responsibility to be a logical, great thinker. Fortunately nobody has ever expected this from me. Jill says I operate very well on feeling and instinct and not to worry over it. And Connie gives me a tolerant smile and says, "now Mama, you know you don't really believe that! Why you said only yesterday—"

Ah, but that was yesterday!

And *that* may be anything from an idea we ought to provide free puppies to all orphan children, something their very own, to taking a firm stand with the Russians and getting results.

The moral universe was no problem to Father. The laws of God were the laws of geology, the creation of the world and the evolution of species fitted in very well with his interpretation of the old Methodist Bible. He explained the six days God was creating the world, were really six aeons of time. And when God said let there be light, it was a thing about the constellations changing positions or something, and that was very simple to Father. As for a moral universe, it meant simply that you did what your father told you to and were a good girl, and that was that.

The one thing that ever, I think, troubled Father was the business of Jonah and the whale. That gave him pause. Scientifically he found it hard to believe a man could live inside a whale forty days or however long it was, and hard to believe the whale got along all right if Jonah was banging around inside.

I said the whale swallowed Jonah and got upset and just threw up, but Father was never sure.

My friend Hazel, who lives with Ted Key, sent me a picture of herself this week with four dogs. I sometimes think the reason I love Ted Key so much is that Hazel is so much like me. More dynamic, true, this stocky arbiter of the house, but Hazel and I are kin just the same. I would never ask Ted how he dreamed Hazel up for the cartoons that have enchanted the country for so long in the *Post* and in books, for that would be to admit Hazel is invented and this I could never admit. When I get a letter from Hazel, it is from Hazel and no other. If I have anything to say to Ted, I write it on another piece of paper and address ic to him. Now and then he himself sends me a note. But usually just a message through Hazel, or a postscript saying simply. "Me too. Ted."

We have a lovely three-way friendship and we are all perfectly happy with it, but I can well imagine some people might find it a little odd. For one thing, neither Ted nor Hazel has ever visited me nor I them. And if Ted came with his family, wife and boys, how would he ever explain to me that Hazel had been left at home? I dare say it is bad enough when one artist has an alter ego but when someone else gets the same one too, it is quite strange. Anyhow, I noted that Hazel's latest picture to me was of her, foursquare and solid, with a cocker in her lap and an Irish peering over her shoulder and two more just dogs around her lap too.

My dogs, really.

Recently Ted had a *Post* cartoon with a little frustrated man looking dismally at a very large dog, obviously Irish, sitting on a sofa. Fresh paint all over sofa, dog and all chairs in the room.

I flew to the post office to send an urgent message to Hazel that I could not live without that picture. And Hazel wrote back that she was sending the jerk right over to the magazine office to get the original back, OR ELSE. When it came, a small note by Ted on the bottom said, "better just paint everything the same yellow!"

Yellow was, of course, the color the Irish had tracked over everything.

I now have quite a gallery of Hazel, via Ted. Including the one with a whole house jammed with Easter chicks and Hazel saying firmly, "Watch Your Step!"

I suppose the reason Ted Key is such a fine artist is that he has a warm heart, a sensitivity combined with his feeling that life is pretty funny if you look at it from the right angle. I do not know if he feels this, as my letters to Hazel are on a different plane, naturally. Hazel isn't interested in art, just in running that family.

But since Helen Hokinson died, I do not find anyone with the quiet rich humor that is gentle as well as acute, that Ted Key has.

And when the *Post* comes, Jill stops everything and says, "What's Key doing now?"

Certainly I cannot imagine what I would do without Hazel! Hazel, of course, could do without anybody, she is a woman who can manage.

Alice and Margaret for a swim and supper. Their Florida tan has hardly faded. I sit and think while Jill bastes the roast, that I wish I could write a whole book about them, not for their brilliant minds at all, but for their rich warmth of personality. Many people are brilliant, few are also unselfish and giving, deeply loyal and belonging to the grand tradition of honesty and faith and kindliness we were brought up to believe in.

When one falls to thinking of life and its various vicissitudes, one realizes that friends are the bulwark of the whole edifice. With Alice and Margaret, all they need to know is that someone needs them, someone is ill or in trouble. They gear their lives to it without a thought of any sacrifice involved personally.

This is a fine and comforting thought. Selfishly we also know, were we in trouble, we would say, "call Alice and Margaret."

Steve and Olive are like that too, in fact, I feel we are blessed with friends who would give willingly. And in what I term a kind of cut-and-come-again civilization, that cannot be overestimated.

June is filled with guests who just need to get out of the city. But there is always time to sit outside a few moments and watch night flow softly down the hills, see the stars brighten and the white moon lift her casual silver sail on the deep, deep sea of the sky.

Little Sister and Jonquil give over digging after moles.

Hollyberry is relatively quiet and stands dreaming by the white roses.

The rest of the cockers drift about the yard, still eager, but in a muted sort of way. They have had a busy day and feel less barky.

The Quiet Garden smells of lemon thyme and apple mint, and the faint cool spiny smell of roses lingers in the air.

Jill is on the road again, working with Tiki, her patient figure dimly seen in the sweet shadowy dusk. I think of Tiki the night he was born, I held him in my palm, rubbing him with a warm cloth, rubbing the breath into his rather squashed lungs while Sister trembled and shook.

Sister had never been to any classes on the new Read method and she found having a puppy quite puzzling. Jill warmed the olive oil and we gave Tiki a drop of it, his infinitely small red tongue lapped when the oil went in his mouth.

What a miracle, this drive to live! As breath labored into his lungs, he began to move his tiny legs and squirm with his morsel of a body. And then he uttered a faint but demanding cry, thin as a strand of silk, but powerful enough to move mountains.

He was, he said, hungry!

Now here he rushes down the road with Jill, about ready to graduate from cocker college. An extremely masculine, upstanding cocker, but he still has the funny little lopsided white star under his chin that Sister has.

When the gate latch clicks, I can hear him bounce with joy. He has been a good boy, and now where is the snack? The rest of the dogs fall on him with bitter sounds, he has been OUT in the world, and being trained and it just is not FAIR.

The magic of June is a very special magic, I think, as I start the chops broiling for supper. It is compounded of much beauty and kindliness on nature's part, it really leaves nothing to be desired.

It is the deep heart of New England beating to a rhythm that never grows old, that is forever young, forever fair.

Surely the petals will never fall from the rose this time, surely it will be always June!

July

A GOOD PLACE FOR THE FOURTH OF July picnic is right in your own back yard, I feel. More and more, America has turned to the outdoors, and this is a fine thing, but on a big holiday those folk who have a back yard would be well advised to enjoy it.

There has been a terrific change in the eating equipment since I was a little girl. In those days, Mama would fry the chicken over the old sputtering gas stove that had an odd way of zooming up in a great flame and then dying right down to nothing.

While the chicken fried, Mama heated the round soapstone fireless-cooker stones over the fire. Then the chicken was packed in the big fireless kettle and one stone hung down in the lid. The other stone, wrapped in brown paper went in a carton and the kettle rested warmly on that during the wild dash to the picnic spot. We had the rest of the picnic in a big wicker hamper, and we had the kindling for the fire. We had white enamel eating utensils with dark-blue edges, very fancy, and tin forks and knives (at least I thought they were tin). We had fringed napkins and usually a checked tablecloth.

Father always built a fire big enough to roast an ox on. Eventually it died down enough for the big enamel coffeepot to go on, the coffee boiled richly, Mama dropped in an eggshell or two, and the picnic was served forth. By the time Father had his apple pie and Wisconsin cheese, he was booted and spurred and ready to start home.

So I never thought of a picnic as a leisurely affair until I was long grown.

Today a picnic is so easy. Portable grills to cook on, folding neatly. Or a round charcoal bucket-shaped affair that cooks like a dream. Thermos jugs, thermos bottles. Colored paper plates and paper cups with handles for hot drinks. And paper napkins in every shade of the color spectrum. Plastic knives and forks and spoons, weightless, easy to use. Instead of chopping down saplings as Father always did, we may unwrap a small package of charcoal briquettes, add a dash of a lighter fuel—

It almost makes me wonder if we are getting too soft! And when the picnic is over, we make our hydromatic power-steered way home—and never once stop to fill the radiator at a farmhouse.

If we wish, we can turn on the portable radio too, and I dare say it won't be long before television goes along. On the whole, I am glad nature isn't as geared up as we are, and that the same old ants turn up right under the chicken, going about their business in the same old-fashioned way.

Naturally I wouldn't go back to the great fire-building and lugging days. I love the modern efficiency gadgets as well as anybody. I am just inconsistent enough to look back and forward at the same time. I like to use my old black iron spider, for instance, and then turn to my electric frying pan for the next round. Gives added spice to life.

Actually in an old house like Stillmeadow, you always live both in the past and the present. The electric dishwasher purrs along while I wrestle with one of the windows which has to be propped open with a hickory stick, and which, once up, has to be hit with a hammer rested on a folded washcloth to get it back down. The vacuum cleaner swishes along an erratic course over those old wide black-oak floors with the wide unfillable cracks.

Jill tried everything known to man or invented by woman to fill those cracks when we came here, sawdust and shellac, plastic wood, caulking compound, wood filler. But the great beautiful boards shift in winter, shift again in summer. The stuffing comes out and that is that. And when Holly gets bored, she spends a little time prying out odd leftover bits of plastic wood and tossing chunks in the air.

I used to feel there were advantages to the situation for we could always tell if the cellar light had been left on by mistake. But then Jill had an underfloor put in from the cellar side, and now I can't see down to the cellar any more.

There are some drawbacks to being a decent citizen. It can be a nuisance, as I discovered last week. We were going on a brief trip to Cape Cod and for once, we did really get ready for one of those early starts. We had the dogs in the car, at least three of them who had been elected for the tour, we had the picnic packed and IN, and the suitcases were loaded the night before with masterly planning on Jill's part. The camera equipment was tucked away from the wandering paws, and the dark-glasses were in the front seat.

As she started the motor, Jill said casually, "did you put the license paper in the glove compartment?"

"It's already there," I said, peering like a dark owl through my glasses. But what I picked up was a receipted bill for dog food from last April. "It's right here," I said, "I know it is."

The dogs, anxious to go, began breathing down my neck. I extracted a bottle of Bufferin, a first-aid kit, a bar of soap, a bottle of hand lotion, one cotton glove, two old lipsticks, a compact, a bottle of cough medicine and a dog leash.

"Well, it must be in your desk," said Jill, with great restraint.

So we rushed back to unlock the house and put in a feverish half hour hunting for the thing. We dumped drawers, shook out papers from files, scrambled through old purses. Our well-timed starting hour passed into oblivion.

"Well," said Jill, "we'll just go by way of the motor bureau in Waterbury and get them to fill out a duplicate. They'll charge fifty cents, no doubt, but then you'll not get nervous."

So we drove to the Waterbury Motor Vehicle Bureau and I skipped in and told my story to the first girl at the long counter. She called a second girl, and I repeated it. After some thought, she called a third girl and I told it again. Finally the third girl gave me a long blank to fill out, which took me some time because I am not a good filler-out of blanks. I invariably get the answers on the line above, or the line below.

Meanwhile the girls called a man from a back desk and a conference ensued. Evidently this was a totally new happening to the motor vehicle staff. I handed the blank in and the man gave me another, which I filled out, getting very hot and bothered by this time.

By now there were seven standing on the other side of the counter staring at me and talking in low tones. And after I signed the last paper, the girl I talked to in the first place, came over and handed me two little metal clips and a bill.

"Nine dollars," she said, "pay over at the far desk."

"But I already have these," I said, handing back the clips, "right on the car. I HAVE the license, I only just lost the—" I got a grip on myself. "I only want," I said, "just one of those little papers—I have merely mislaid the little paper—but I can't put on another license—there isn't any ROOM."

She went back into the huddle and fast conversation ensued. I gathered half of them were for me, half against.

"Nine dollars," said the girl, in the end.

So I crept out, nine dollars poorer but completely legal. We were about three hours behind our schedule and not in a happy frame of mind. We went to the Cape, and came back, with nobody paying any attention to us at all.

Two days later, I got a third official paper from the state I have sworn to love and cherish saying the second license paper had been incorrectly filled out at the bureau so please substitute the enclosed. I then realized that I was probably the only citizen of the state who had (a) paid eighteen dollars for one year's license and (b) now had three licenses. For of course, by then, the original paper had turned up under my desk blotter.

Sometimes I wonder where lost things go. Sometimes things disappear that we absolutely know were in a certain place and could not have been moved by ANYBODY. I had a leopard neckpiece that simply took off, and Jill missed a favorite sweater. Now and then a book I especially want to reread has GONE AWAY.

I believe there is a place somewhere, where all the lost things go, and the people who live between the worlds must need them and magic them away. I would dearly love, I think, to go there and see the tall strange one wearing my Knox hat and leopard neckpiece. And they must do a mort of gardening in that land of lost things, for they have a goodly number of rakes and saws and hoes and clippers of ours.

But the very oddest thing they willed away was a dog door, which I ordered for Jill for Christmas—not for her own personal exit and entrance, to be sure, but for her to install in the back door so four paws could patter in and out without being waited on every ten minutes. In and out, out and in, they all go all nine of them, and we felt tired of it.

The dog door came in a huge carton, by express. It was half the size of a house door, naturally, with a frame, the swinging-door part and so on. It came, it was put in the back kitchen until time to install it. We never saw it again.

So I deduced that the people between worlds had a dog

that wanted a dog door to pass in and out by instead of just dissolving himself from one side to the other.

Hot still days come now, with heat simmering over the fields, crackling in the long corn rows. The Farmer's Almanac says quietly, "Hot, sultry, bit of a drought, but let's not pout or shout."

This should settle the pronunciation of that word drought anyway. I have always rhymed it with south.

The hottest time of the year in New England it is, the heat is actually dramatic in its intensity. We like to sit down by the pond at suppertime where the cooling air rises from the water. With Alice and Margaret, neighbors from down the line, and Steve and Olive from the old red house by the water-cress brook, we wait for the hamburgers to broil and the buns to toast while we talk, idly and with long pauses.

The real art of conversation implies an ability to sit quietly now and then, I think, without any sense of strain. Even brilliant talk with no intervals gets wearing. Also it implies listening as well as talking.

I was highly flattered when Mary Margaret McBride, in her newspaper column, called me an outstanding conversationalist along with Faith Baldwin (and there is no doubt about Faith, she sparkles) and John Mason Brown and a few others. I was especially flattered because I couldn't imagine it.

I can be absolutely mute in any strange group, I am timid and doubtful of my opinions. I can, at times, if sparked by people like Alice and Margaret and Steve and Olive, make a fair conversation, but I am absolutely dependent on the atmosphere, the people around me, the time of day, and the weather. With Mary Margaret McBride, almost anyone could converse well, for she has a genius for bringing out hidden thoughts, feelings, and ideas and she flies from subject to subject in a breathless free-association that somehow manages to make a great deal of sense.

It is hard to analyze brilliance in conversation, for it isn't intellect, nor sharpness of wit, nor earnest beliefs, it is more, I think, an attitude of receptivity to what the other people are thinking and feeling and a quickness to respond to it.

I have known people who deliver brilliant monologues but conversation takes at least two.

Yankees are traditionally close-mouthed and this is a good quality.

It is not true, however, that Yankees are dour. Not Connecticut Yankees at any rate. A passing farmer will stop and chat at any time, and in the social center of the store, conversation can be had always.

Victor Borge is a near neighbor of ours, and the radio repairman converses with him amiably and then tells all the village about the state of the Borge radios and television sets. We know how many and where his aerials are and just when he will be on with Ed Murrow and what trouble they had setting up the tower for it—and all to be taken down the next day, says the radio man with a little sigh.

The chicken woman, young and breathless and very pretty, delivers the new-laid eggs on a Wednesday and chats in her soft voice before she darts out into the night. She lives on Ed Sullivan's road and I think it is somehow heartening that the elegant confines of such a big star are near a chicken farm where a young couple works so hard for a family living.

Actually we view with alarm the gradual implement of the famous in our rural valley. Victor Borge is satisfactory because he raises Cornish rock hens, and not as a hobby, but a going concern. So even though he makes his living doing a one-man show in New York, everyone concedes he is a real resident. But the idea of our countryside turning into a Colony appalls us and we hope that with no railroad, bus or taxi service, it will not seem desirable for the outside world to move in.

I should always prefer the great farm wagons lumbering down the road heavy with sweet hay to pastel convertibles flashing by. I can sympathize with the attitude of the typical Cape Codder who on one hand makes a good thing of summer people and on the other sighs relief when the season is over.

We have few summer people as such here in our valley. It is still primarily an agricultural community and the stony fields produce quantities of crops: Milk and eggs, apples and grapes and peaches and cabbage and corn flow into the cities.

We keep our *Field Book of Eastern Birds* right on the old trestle table, so we can rush to identify any wandering bird that stops at the feeding stations. We keep grain in all summer, although the peanut butter is retired when melting weather arrives. Grain and sunflower seeds and bits of old cake and bread are acceptable any season.

The *Field Book* is a kind of Bible for birders. Other books we love, such as *Menaboni's Birds*, which is almost poetry, and the John Kieran book for beginners which has so much charm, and several others. But Hausman is a standard at Stillmeadow. Roger Tory Peterson's bird book belongs with it and is excellent.

I have a feeling for Hausman when I read about the robin: "Field Marks—Upper parts a slaty brown—but no, we will not insult our readers! Field Description—but have you noticed, dear reader, that the male robin's head is very dark—"

This gives me a very cosy feeling about robins and Mr. Hausman both. Seldom nowadays does dear reader get a personal message from an author, and such a sly little chuckle along with it. Anyhow, I gather Mr. H thinks any dolt knows a robin, but I could tell him it is not so. We *have* had guests from the big city who asked innocently, "what is that pretty bird?" That pretty bird is a buxom robin who has just latched onto a long, strong worm, has both legs braced, and is hauling away like a mad thing.

Something about a robin makes me feel he/she would be very good on committees.

The purple finch is one of my favorite birds—but Jill says any bird I happen to look at is my favorite bird.

The purple finch is no more purple than I am, but is a charming rosy color and a most exquisite bird. Mr. Hausman calls it a crushed-raspberry red but I somehow don't like the association of crushed berries with my little feathered lovely one. The song is a melodious warble, but I admit that I do not feel anybody really describes a birdsong accurately enough to be identifiable.

With one exception. I asked a bird expert what person it was that kept incessantly repeating *Wichity wichity wichety* around the yard. Could only be a yellowthroat, said my expert. I have not seen the yellowthroat but I hear the sound now with an easy conscience for I know him.

In winter, my favorite bird is undoubtedly the chickadee, for this is a brave and merry bird and small and charming. The dee comes to my window sill not three feet from where I bang away at the typewriter, and cocks a shining dark eye at me as he gobbles the sunflower seeds. My special pet, with the one bent wing has been here over two years. The chickadee has such a jet-black cap and neat black throatpiece tucked in, and the grey top is cloud-soft. The under part is supposed to be white but since I have seen my chicks so close, I have discovered there is a glow to the white, almost a faint apricot tinge. As they cling with their tiny jet feet, they tilt their black-capped heads down with a swift darting movement. And the sound of their cheerful *Dee deee deee* is always pleasant to hear. Also now and then they say *Phoebee*. For no good reason.

One falls into bird talk easily, we find. One morning last

winter I looked out and saw three brilliant strange visitors at the feeding station. The upper parts were olive-brown and the under parts a glowing yellow. The wings were black and white and the tail black. I called Jill and she came running.

"It's an accidental," she said firmly. "Must be evening grosbeaks."

Accidental or no, the birds were laying away a good meal. They stayed for some time, then flew off in the pines as the blue jays and sparrows came winging in.

Watching the birds gives me much thinking about the universe we inhabit. For the birds are a whole world, all by themselves. Nobody could compass all of the birdlife there is on this planet, understand all the migrations, interpret all the ways. But how it extends our lives to observe what small bits we can of these mysterious winged folk, and how wonderful a world is which is furnished with birds!

Once when we visited Alice and Margaret on their Florida

island, we went in a boat along the bayous in the dreamy still hot air, and the white egrets rose and sailed over. I shall not forget this ever. It had all the lyric precision of a sonnet.

I always wonder, when Jill brings in a basket of sweet corn, whether maybe the Indians had their corn patch in the self-same spot. Our fancy hybrid does not much resemble their maize, but it is still corn.

Whenever we drive down Kettletown Road, I wonder whether the kettle was a good one that was traded for the land. A kettle must have been a mystery to the Indians. Their clay pots were all they had.

When I was growing up in Wisconsin, my Father often took me to the site of an old Indian village on Lake Winnebago and we used to turn up shards of Indian pots, bedded in piles of shell. I always dreamed of finding a piece big enough to hold something, and I never did. But there they were, strange little bits from long ago, within tossing distance of a row of lumber-catalogue bungalows!

A friend sent me a copy of Keats which belonged originally to a John Mitford, Esquire, in 1845. This is a precious book, 1841 edition, and came enclosed in a special box to preserve it. Clergyman John Mitford was the son of a John Mitford who was in the navy and mentioned in Nelson's dispatches (as an "insane rogue"). My Mitford had a bookplate with a plump cherub enveloped in waving forked tails of a sea creature or maybe more creatures. Could he have been a son of Triton? The sea is quite agitated around it, in any case. In the flyleaf, Mitford notes in a spidery hand that for Keats' death see Shelley etc.

The ivoried pages are marked now and then by a respectful pencil. I think I should have liked this John Mitford, Esquire.

Now the little cinnamon-colored volume lies on my desk,

and although the singer is gone, the song still sounds in my New England ears.

When Faith Baldwin went round the world, I made only one request, "go to see how Hampstead Heath is, where Keats lived." She went, with an Englishwoman who had never been there. The plum tree where the nightingale sang—"thou wast not born for death, immortal bird"—is gone, but another plum is planted. The wallpaper is different, but that is because when they did some repair work, they found a small piece of the original and copied it. It has a green feathery design, says Faith.

"No hungry generations tread thee down," wrote Keats. So many hungry generations tread so many things down, I thought. But it is good to think the little house in Hampstead has withstood the bombing, and has a new plum tree and has the wallpaper restored.

For who of us does not need a shrine? Even people who never heard of Keats have in some way profited by his outpouring of lyric ecstasy. For I think all beauty adds to our heritage, whether it be the flawless purity of the Greek in the Parthenon or the rich and lavish splendor of Dylan Thomas. So my Johnny Keats saying "Beauty is truth, truth beauty," gives a lift to us today in an uneasy age.

In the letters I find a great deal worth remembering. I wonder, sometimes, whether he realized as he dashed them off to this one and that, that one day long after he was laid in the Italian soil in Rome, readers would reread his letters.

"My prime object's a refuge as well as a passion," is memorable. For this is so true of most of us. Work we love, work we struggle hard at, is at once an easement of the spirit and an excitement. This is true of our George, who only farms the rocky Connecticut soil, but finds in the filled silo that his prime object is a refuge as well as a passion.

What a profound truth for this twenty-odd-year-old Englishman to utter! For those of us who, as the natives say "live mostly by our heads" it is doubly true. One can work steadily and hard at catching the exact phrase, the real and true expression, the nuance of a smile—and be wearied and discouraged. And yet, our prime objects are a refuge—we go back and try again to really express the bits of truth we have in us! And feel better for it.

Struggling with poverty, ruled by a highly unsympathetic guardian—and one must feel sorry for him, too, as this wild young poet must have seemed out of all reason—hopelessly in love with a rather shallow young girl, and already seeing the bright dark spots of blood on his handkerchief when he coughed, this young Keats still could write in his letters "I must think that difficulties nerve the spirit of a man."

As he went off to Italy to die in the little apartment on the Spanish Stairs, tended by Severn, and looked back at his loved England and penciled the lines of his last great sonnet "Bright star, would I were steadfast as thou art," one wonders whether he had some prescience of his place in the world of letters. He had in his earlier days a strong sense of destiny, but it may have faded then, with exile and illness and doom upon him, and weakness from the incessant bleedings which were the remedy for tuberculosis in that day.

I have never made my mind up about Severn. In the passionate disturbed Keats Circle some thought Severn was a climber, a hanger-on to glory, but nevertheless, he was the one who took that last terrible journey, and I wonder how many of the others would have.

When I plucked a laurel leaf from the grave in Rome, I could almost see Severn standing in the shadows seeing the end of the story, and if he plumed himself on standing near greatness, who shall blame him?

We no longer live in an age of poetry, that is certain. I suspect the roar of the big guns in our day has muffled its rhythms. But there will always be people who find a quickening in poetry that nothing else gives, for poetry is a more

direct communication than prose. Music may be the closest
approach to the soul, but poetry is music in a different tone
and because it uses the word as its medium, may be more
clearly understood than, say, a Bach fugue. For the truly
great poetry, one needs no technical training, no understanding of counterpoint or symphonic themes. One needs to be
able to read, and to think it over, and that is it.

As to who are the greatest poets, I would not venture to
say. Many poets have great lines, many have even a line or
two. If you read poetry as often as I do, you find certain
lines sing back in your mind. These, I feel, are probably
great for they create their own immortality.

"The grave's a fine and quiet place, But none, I think, do
there embrace," I find myself saying on a starless night when
my pulse is beating rather slowly.

Or "I shall die, But that is all I shall ever do for death." I
have so many lines of Miss Millay that sing in odd moments
to me. "I know I am but summer to your heart, and not the
full four seasons of the year—"

Dylan Thomas, who died so young, so pitifully, seems to
me to have the quality of sensuous exuberance that I love in
poetry. As if words could not contain the burning images in
his mind, they pour out, tumbled, almost incoherent. I am
just beginning to know him, coming in by the back door,
as it were, via *Quite Early One Morning*, which purports to
be prose.

"The sea that was lying down still and green as grass after
a night of tar-black howling and rolling," says Mr. Dylan,
and for me, that is poetry enough.

Having been raised with poetry, I am astounded at the lack
of it in young people nowadays. Although we began in
school reciting "The snow had begun in the gloaming—and
bus-ily all the night—" and went on to "Lars Porsena of
Clusium by the nine Gods he swore," still we did learn that

words went in form and pattern sometimes. But recently a young man asked me, "just what is a sonnet anyway?"

"A sonnet is a moment's monument," said I, quoting Rossetti rapidly, "Memorial to the soul's eternity"—and then I wondered—is that Rossetti and then I saw the blank stare on my listener's face and I sat down and folded my hands and said meekly, "a sonnet is a poem of fourteen lines, and it has to be fourteen lines, and it has a definite rhyme scheme, either English or Italian— Now the Elizabethan—" But he wasn't listening any more. Quatrains and sestets meant nothing to him, he was pulling a bur out of the Irish ear nearest him, and I thought, well, that is practical and constructive anyway and Dante is still Dante and Shakespeare is still Shakespeare and always someone—as long as we are on this odd little planet—someone will read "When in disgrace with fortune and men's eyes, I all alone bewail my outcast state." Or "Life has no friend; her converts late or soon, Slide back to feed the dragon with the moon."

The sky is wonderful in July, it seems deeper and farther off someway than at any other time, a silken, burning blue. The thermometer jumps like a jumping mouse, and the beans ripen like mad. Butterflies flicker over the pale blue and dark blue delphinium, a hummingbird flickers also, in a different rhythm in the border. At night the nicotiana sends a heady tropical sweetness in the air. Flowers that smell sweet only at night are very special, they live a life of moon and stars, and are always mysterious, it seems to me.

I always remember one July night when a very tired man who was visiting us, suddenly disappeared. We finally got to wondering and went out to look him up. He was lying flat on the lemon thyme in the Quiet Garden, and he said he was just smelling. Let him alone. The nicotiana was opening deep bells then, and the stars were opening out in the sky, and he was just taking it all in lying down!

I think of this as the salad month, for we have salads for everything except breakfast. Almost any fresh vegetable, cleaned and crisped with ice cubes, goes in the big wooden bowl and with slivers of mild cheese and fresh sugar-cured country ham is not to be sneered at as a main dish. We finally found an Italian double cruet which holds red wine vinegar on one side and pale greeny olive oil on the other and you can pour at will. It was odd that after all our hunting, we found this cruet in a Vermont country store featuring handcrafts from Vermont, and we were asking directions for a dog show. It just is the way things happen to us.

It is also the freezing month and the Deep Freeze is a most demanding item but also pays off in those bleak winter months. I like to remember the early colonial folk who froze pies in the winter, they were the first Deep-Freezer folk. And pie cupboards were in almost every house. Now country living has been completely revolutionized by this freezer proposition. The fresh dewy vegetables are picked and rushed to the freezer after a whisk in a blanching bath, and there they are, bringing summer food to the December table.

What a change in our whole diet! In my childhood we ate cabbage and turnips and Hubbard squash in winter, later on we had canned corn and peas. But now we can have anything from strawberries to asparagus just by bringing out a box from the cellar!

What it really means is the end of seasonal food. We eat whatever we feel like eating. If we want oysters in July, we get out a package of oysters frozen in an R month. This is very practical and helpful to the homemaker but also takes some of the excitement out of life. We no longer eat asparagus like mad, on toast for breakfast, creamed with a slice of ham under it for lunch and with hollandaise at night during asparagus season. Not at all. We eat it when we feel like asparagus. On a hot July night we may have asparagus which we picked in the early days of May. Modern ingenuity has licked seasonal eating. We can have a rhubarb pie, crusty and simmering with rich juice on a picnic by the pool.

We can have shad roe, fresh as a daisy, broiled and tipped with lemon wedges, and all miles and miles from shad roe territory or season. Our fish man brings the roe when he has it and we just wrap and pop in the icy depths and there it is.

This is the dry month in New England, so when it rains, we are grateful. It is the only time in the year we are grateful for rain, rain being our chief product come summer, come winter. But in July how sweetly sounds the patter on the old roof, and how grateful is the lawn. You can see things turn greener after a rain. Bean pods plump up. Chard stands more erect. Lettuce looks brisker.

The pond shines darkly clear, the scum disappears. We swim without sweeping motions of our arms to clear the way. And such a lovely pale light comes after the rain is over, like a lovesong in sweetness.

Jill is what I call a sometime swimmer. It means that if she is busy training Holly to do the Long Sit or Tiki to take the jumps, she says, "you go on, I'm busy."

Then I give up waiting and swim. Maybe she will get around to it, maybe not, but hot weather means nothing to her, she was raised in the hottest corn-growing Illinois territory and she rather likes to steam. I do not. I like to be cool. I like to sink slowly to my chin and feel the cool gentle water all around me, and if the small fish whisk past, I do not mind. Connie says they nibble her toes, but I wear large heavy tennis shoes anyway, as I do not like mud on my feet and the bottom of our pond is plain Connecticut mud. I wear my glasses too so I can see where I am. I suppose the sight of a woman in tennis shoes and an old suit and bifocals wheeling dreamily along the pond is fairly amusing, if anybody came by to look. All I can say is I do *not* wear a garden hat, as one of my friends does, to protect her complexion. She wears a scarf first, then the large straw hat and as she swims, it does look like a misplaced garden party but it has a very nice effect nonetheless. Especially when the hat has flowers on it. The sight of a flat circle of pinks floating around is very interesting.

Water is not man's natural element, but it is strange to think how the deep green seas have always lured us. From the early divers who plunged down after pearl and gold and silver in ancient galleons manned by what Father used to call the "denisons of the deep" to today when frogmen slide down to adventure in the glimmering depths, man has always felt a strange kinship with the sea. Does it perhaps go back into time when all life was seaborne?

In any case, when I first saw the ocean, I felt a quickening such as I never had felt before, a sense that all mysteries were immediately mine, rather the way I suppose a mystic feels at certain times. The rhythms of tide on shining sand are basic rhythms, they speak of God and eternity and peace that passeth understanding.

Our own small sweet-water pond has a small echo of this too. The brook tumbles in down the ferny hill, the sky and the clouds are in it and on clear nights the moon and stars shimmer there. Although it covers about a third of an acre, it is nine feet deep and it has a life of its own with skimming waterbugs, darting fish, polished emerald frogs, and the blue heron and his family. It is actually teeming with life and one wonders whence it came, since before we dug it out this was just a swamp.

Summer is so brief, so packed with living, I hate to see each day end. The long twilights are like separate amethysts strung on a silver chain. The Farmer's Almanac says "Days are hot, nights are not." This about sums up July in New England for it is hot and humid and you can feel the corn growing and the cherries ripening, and yet at night a cooling air blows in from woods and streams. If we sit by the pond, we need sweaters, and as far as I am concerned, I never take the winter blankets off my bed all summer long. I like to be sure.

Connie, home for vacation, has been off with me picking currants. The currants are shining, redder than a maharajah's rubies, and much more useful, I say. I pick the lazy way, I carry an aluminum arm chair and put it by the biggest bush. Connie skips around lightly, keeping a wary eye for wasps.

It was nice of the Lord to invent one fruit that can be picked without standing on your head or climbing a rickety ladder, I tell her.

The polished scarlet berries fall in the pail, juice stains our fingers, we talk in a comfortable desultory way.

Currant jelly, made the minute we get the pails in, is about as close to perfection as anything can be. It seems to catch the light and keep it, and the rich, slightly spicy smell fills the kitchen. Connie is busy making toast so we can spread the frothy part on it immediately, and I lick up the testing drops from the saucer as fast as I put them in. Comes a winter night, how good that essence of summer will taste with roast duckling or a savory paper-thin slice of ham!

The raspberries grow in the upper field, trailing casual canes along the edge of the swamp and it is definitely hotter there than any place on the farm. It is very still, there is a kind of quiet wildness there, and one speaks very low or not at all when raspberrying. Even the dogs vanish in the shimmering air and only soft rustles mark their hunting.

Raspberry shortcake was my Mother's favorite, and is mine. Lightly sugared, lightly mashed, warmed a little, the rich rosy berries poured between layers of golden rich shortcake, and then a pitcher of warm heavy cream added—well, it makes July memorable.

Jill never seems to appear now without a spraying outfit

slung over her shoulder. Bordeaux mixture for the cucumbers, potatoes, tomatoes, spray for the roses, dust for the
squash. What a mort of pests we do inherit. The Japanese
beetle arrives at the wrong time always, that hideous vora-
cious glittering creature is a nightmare. For the beetle we
have tried almost everything from planting milky spore to
hand-picking in a coffee can of kerosene.

But nothing matters to the beetle. For they can always
breed on the next forty acres and COME OVER any time.
For the Japanese beetle and for poison ivy, a Federal Program
is needed. As I see the garden vegetable leaves turn to a dry
brown lace, I feel such a fury rise in me. Or when I go out
to pick a bouquet of the ivory-white Frau Karl Druschki
rose and find the heart of each flawless bloom packed with
coppery green metallic beetles, I turn green too. My philosophy tells me everything belongs in the pattern somewhere,
but I have to work hard at it to adjust to the Japanese beetle.
He doesn't even make good bird food, no self-respecting bird
will snap up a beetle if there is any other food around.

As for what hereabouts we call "poison ivory," Jill has
sprayed and struggled for over twenty years and every year
fresh little gleaming three-leaved plants spring up here, there,
everywhere. The trees along our roadsides all through Connecticut bear heavy climbing bounty of ivy, old grey stone
fences are deep with it. It mushrooms up in secluded glades
and lines driftways. Inevitably it gets in bouquets picked by
the unknowing. Children are laid up, screaming with its fiery
itching poison.

I would like to know what it would cost the state to do
away with it. And what it would save in man-hours (which
is what everything seems to be measured by) to have no
more poison ivory knocking people out.

Holly has a terrific passion for ice cubes. The instant the
little click of the ice tray comes, the Irish is also there, eyes

eager, tail waving wildly. Any guest mixing a tall cold drink
may find a velvet mahogany nose in the glass unless he hands
out a nice plump cube immediately. Holly has a very sensitive mouth, she feels the cold and drops the cube, then turns
it over with a delicate paw, picks it up again, and *crunches*
with a sigh of pure delight. She crunches it fast enough to
get another before the tray goes back to the refrigerator.

With an Irish setter, there is a special excitement in following the darting flash of mind that means Irish. Holly can
take one look at a pan and begin to figure how to get at what
is in it fast. If someone else has a bone, she plots on sneaking
up and letting a loud Celtic voice out to intimidate said bone-
chewer so she can then nimbly take over. If you want her
to do something she is not IN the mood for, she collapses,
paws folded over tummy, and eyes languorous and melancholy. If she wants something you don't give her, she sparkles
like a night club, so gay, so winning, and her eyes are three-
cornered, shining and deep. I then call her the girl with the
three-cornered eyes.

"I just love Holly," said Nancy, with whom we left her
when we went on a brief trip, "I just love that dog, she is so
mushy."

Thinking over my life with dogs, which has been a twenty-
four year stretch—well, even more as I had an American water
spaniel when I was about eleven, I consider that if I did not
have a dog or several dogs to wait on, I would feel rather
odd. The gay and gentle cockers and the wild and enchanting Irish make for a very good household.

I do not resent non-dog-lovers, I feel sorry for them. I
think how much they miss, of rich loyalty and love and warm
welcome home when they go away and the cosy feeling of
a soft velvet nose pressed in the palm if one feels sad. Nine
dogs isn't many, I decide as I wash the pans and let four in
and five out.

A July night has a special quality, the hot air is ebbing over the meadow and a faint cool breath steals in, delicious and exciting. Mist brims the meadow now, and a silvery look is about the world.

In George's barn, a cow gives forth a soft mooing, and one of the Kelloggs' dogs bays in the distance. How still it is, here in the little fold of the valley on a hot summer night! I feel the world revolving around me, I hear in an inner ear the troubled voice of the times, but the stars come so bright and clear upon the sky, and the moon rises so slow and steady that I cannot feel the turbulence of life, only the steadfastness of the seasons.

Suddenly I feel I am everywhere, this is a strange feeling. I am in the rose garden of my Bombay India friend, whom I have never seen, who writes that her son has married a "decent Parsi." I am in an igloo on the deep green-black ice-cap with the son of my friend in Washington, living on K rations just to see if this be possible. And I am in the desert with the mountains rising so purple and violet above the golden sand while Smiley Burnette strums his guitar and sings cowboy songs.

I am in the eighteenth-century bakery in Williamsburg talking to Parker Crutchfield as he bakes the gentleman's bread and the household bread in the great ovens. Candles flare, the night is hot, and the life of yesterday moves against the life of today.

But I am actually right on the worn doorstep of the old white farmhouse, and I call the dogs in and close the door. I may have been a thousand miles away in five minutes, but I am, after all, at home.

And the moon is right over my apple tree, and this is July in New England. The mind makes many journeys, but the heart stays home.

August

COUNTRY LIFE IS ALWAYS FILLED
with surprise. George has several young calves, very pretty
with their black-and-white markings, and awkward leggy
gait. They look just like normal young calves, but they will
not lie down out of doors. They stand up all day long, and
George has been trying to persuade them to lie down now
and then. I keep hanging out of the window to watch George
persuading a calf to lie down, and I am full of wonder at the
infinite mystery of the world. These calves lie down in the
barn at night. But outdoors, no. What goes through their

funny heads that makes them so different? One seldom thinks of a cow as an individualist!

George once had a wild cow, too. Secretly I know both George and I felt proud of that cow who would not give in to routine. She stayed just out of reach in the woods after breaking down the fence. He could see her, could chase her, but she was a young and agile female, and she kept free for a long time. George in his wise country voice said, "and Gladys, once a cow is wild, you can never tame her again."

I couldn't help wondering whether some of us if we once kicked over the traces would be tame again? On the whole, better not try, for the independent cow wasn't really very practical in her approach to life. The end of a wild life for a heifer is the butcher.

This morning a postcard from the young man who was to come and clean up the yard. "Tried to call," he wrote, "line busy. Company stayed late. Car refused to start, and ducks caused accident. Will be over Thursday. Joe."

Trying to decide how the ducks caused an accident took our minds right off the state of the yard. It is probably a mystery that we shall never clear up, a kind of James Thurber situation.

Our Quiet Garden definitely sags in August. Jill says she can never keep things blooming in all seasons. Time gets the best of her, she says mournfully. Before we ever get all the spring bulbs tended to, the roses are all over everything and the Japanese beetles are there, and then my white pansies give up in the heat and the ivy border springs out over the flagstones and then the weeds come in where the lemon thyme is struggling. Succession bloom, she feels, would be a joy, but she needs four more hands and a couple of extra backs.

When we eat supper in the garden, I look at the pale white clematis climbing the fence and admire it as we cook the hamburgers and dish up the cucumber mousse. But Jill darts to her feet and whips up a clump of weeds from the edge of the border. She takes a bite of her toasted bun, darts over again to the far side and wrenches a tuft of something else up from the lavender bed.

"Just relax," I say, "such a lovely evening—"

Jill sets her plate down and gets on her hands and knees and begins to weed the thyme. "Just a minute," she mutters, "this is in terrible shape—"

The true gardener's eye, I think, is always focusing on the needs of the garden, the state of the soil, the moisture problem, the pests, the pruning, the thinning—if you really add it all up, you wonder any soul is staunch enough to attempt to grow a single rose!

In the vegetable garden, the blessing of the hot still days is manifold. The rosy ripening globes of the tomatoes, the amber silk on the sweet-corn ears, the lucent emerald peppers, and the royal purple of the eggplant—the color and richness and textures in a vegetable garden are a recurrent miracle. When I walk down the bean rows, I think of Yeats and his "Lake Isle of Innisfree."

> I will arise and go now, and go to Innisfree,
> And a small cabin build there, of clay and wattles made;
> Nine bean rows will I have there, a hive for the honey bee,
> And live alone in the bee-loud glade.

Somehow there is a magic in the number nine. However, if he were to live alone in the bee-loud glade, I wonder what he would do with nine bean rows? Maybe they were very short rows? Or maybe the faery folk would gather in the bright of the moon to pick and eat beans? Otherwise, I think Mr. Yeats would have had little time for his golden singing, at least in summer. He would just pick beans!

The shape of a bean is a lovely thing to see. When very young, it curves like a small scimitar, later it lengthens to a lance size. And the color is beautiful, the golden wax has a glimmering tone and the green is a rich blue-green like an agate.

To really savor beans, they must be eaten when young, young, tender and butter-sweet. Therefore it follows you must grow your own and pick them your very own self. Nobody, but nobody, ever picks beans young enough. Those large robust things like chopped-up bits of garden hose which are labelled frozen string beans, are barely edible. The limp piles in markets have lost their goodness long since and were too elderly when gathered in the first place.

But picked when delicate and young, cooked quickly and not long from suppertime, dressed with warm butter and a sprinkle of rosemary and served in warm bowls—this is fare for the gods. Sometimes I add a spoonful of sweet cream at the last moment, if not too involved in dieting.

Cooking is an art easy to practice when you have a garden. For instance, a salad. Instead of planning it and making a list, you wander idly along the rows carrying a rush basket and a sharp knife. Three kinds of lettuce, young onions, pencil-slim carrots, a couple of young tomatoes, a sprig of dill—and how good fresh dill is in a green salad!

On the subject of salad dressings, many a friendship has foundered, I suspect. Some gourmet cooks want nothing but a cruet of the best greeny-pale Italian olive oil and a cruet of the finest red wine-vinegar, freshly ground pepper and freshly ground salt.

Some respectable people like a dressing with garlic, and sour cream, and mustard—some prefer a dressing so heavy it sinks the salad. And there are dozens and dozens of commercial dressings with and without herbs and spices and egg yolks and Worcestershire sauce.

As for me, I am sure it indicates the weakness of my entire character. I yearn over the wine and olive oil added to a crisp and lovely bowlful of greens. On the other hand, I do

like a dressing with everything in the world in it. The way
I make such a dressing means it is never, never repeated, it
is a once-in-a-lifetime affair. All it has in common with other
times is the bowl. I use the same old wooden bowl, mellowed
by time, dented by explorative knives here and there, and
darkening gradually to a deep autumnal shade.

When Johannes, our Viennese friend, comes for a week
end, he makes the dressing for all the salads, and he too begins
with the bowl.

Then he opens the refrigerator door and begins taking out
bits of this and that. The dressing is stirred in the bowl, the
vegetables added in the end. A dash of sour cream is likely
to be there, and a grating of cheese, lemon juice and oil, and
a sliver or two of left-over rosy ham. He lifts and turns the
salad gently with the wooden salad-servers, never "tossing"
as the books say.

It is strange, I muse, as I watch him, that a world war
brought him to this little kitchen to mix salads. Certainly as
a budding young actor in Vienna, he could never have
dreamed of even coming to this country. And the mad flight
to England just ahead of Hitler must have seemed like part
of a drama he had not expected to act in. In the American
Army, he had a varied career. Part of the time he was taken
for a German spy, part of the time he was in trouble because
he could not master the art of firing guns.

I first met him when I was teaching short-story-writing at
Columbia—traveling in once a week on the poky little train
that ran doubtfully on the Seymour line and coming back
running for my life through Grand Central to catch the last
train!

The class was almost entirely ex-army, navy and air men.
A few privates, some lieutenants, one lieutenant-commander
in the British Navy and an army major and some assorted
corporals. There was one WAC and there were two or three

ordinary civilian women who also thought they could write. Even if they had not been on the front.

They wrote fiercely, with burning eagerness, they were all excited and tense, and the class crackled. Fortunately we met on a top floor in one of the less-used halls and I closed the door and let the racket go on. They shouted, they slammed fists on manuscripts. The army and navy had terrific battles over almost any old plot. They wrote like mad, and most of them wrote amazingly well. For they were young men who had been lifted out of the normal world and hurled at disaster and madness, and they were full of it.

They were brutal critics, inspired authors, and we all had the time of our lives. Now and then the head of my department would meet me as I staggered into the office with ninety-six short stories and/or articles under my arm and say calmly, "well, how are you getting on with the army, navy and air force?"

"Fine," I always said, "now you take this one pilot—" and I was off.

Johannes always came in late. He just could never get in to class on time. This became part of it, too, and as he gently opened the door and slipped in with his dark cape flying behind him, some officer would turn and say, "welcome back."

Then we were back again with the marine who "did not believe in style, Mrs. Taber."

It was my theory then, and is now, that a group of battle-scarred men who had been winning a war could not come right down to a student's desk and behave like high-school boys. As long as they worked, and how they worked, and learned as much as I knew about the craft of writing, and felt they were getting something of the marrow of literature, I let them shout as much as they felt like.

Now and then Johannes, one book and an advertising job later, reminisces about those early days. "We were all a little mad," he says. "But it was wonderful."

In his black turtle-neck sweater and black trousers and silver medal at the belt, he has the same young dark look that he had during those early days. So I decide as the salad goes on the table, just not to count back to when that was!

It fell to Jill's lot to get him his driver's license one summer when he was going to puppy-sit for us while we went away. He had driven, he admitted, an army truck sometime around the Battle of the Bulge, but no good came of it. They would go out early in the morning and practice. Come back briefly for lunch, Johannes with a pale wild look, Jill very Scotch and determined. "He's so impulsive," she said once.

The night before he took his driving test, he stayed up all night studying the booklet and appeared deathly pale and heavy-eyed and quite frantic the next morning. He flung his jacket slant-wise over his shoulder, clapped his hat on at an angle, and he looked as if he might just have stepped out of a Bavarian fairy tale. He did not look like a Connecticut Yankee getting a driver's license. I watched them jerk away and sat down weakly with a fourth cup of black coffee.

He got it, however. And practiced by going to the dump every day with the dog-food cans. He also went for the mail, and only the first time ran into the telephone pole.

The last time he came out, Connie met him. She was visiting with some neighbors on the platform as the train pulled in. Travelers disgorged themselves, and the neighbors said, "where is the man you are meeting?"

"I can't see him," said Connie, "I can't see him at all. He should have a black-and-white cocker with him. And he is a Viennese."

As if that explained everything, said she afterward. Well, possibly it did.

I am always amazed at the way we New Englanders are proud of our weather. When we get a January blizzard, it is the worst blizzard in history, and now in August, we feel it is much hotter than anywhere else in the world.

All our thermometers play a game, no two ever get the same answer. "Right by the barn door it was a hundred," says one neighbor at the store. "Ninety-eight is all I made it," says another, very conservative. "Over a hundred when I went to the hayfield," says George.

Weather in New England is always dramatic, and always personal. I myself am in a constant conflict. Shall I peer every half hour to see just how high it is climbing, or shall I ignore the whole thing?

This is the season to be careful that dogs have plenty of fresh water and are as cool as possible. I am naturally a mild woman, but when I see a dog shut in a car with the windows closed, I tremble with rage. After all, nobody *has* to have a dog. There is no law. If one chooses to have one, some decent kindliness is obligatory. That is all there is to it.

At Stillmeadow we refill the water dishes every little while all day, and if it is a scorcher, we sponge the faces of the old ladies now and then, and encourage them to stay inside on the damp cool stones of the hearth. We do not encourage ball-chasing. For we have learned that hot weather is more lethal to dogs than cold. If the very old ones pull through the heavy humid heat of August, they face the blizzards with equanimity.

Holly keeps jumping around, nothing quenches the Irish. She likes to lie on a snowbank in February and in the broiling sun in August equally well. Her shining coat seems to insulate her in a strange way. Just as it sheds water. Giving Holly a bath is quite a thing, for the suds just slide off and drip down in the tub. And when you have sixty-five pounds of dog to get over, it makes quite a problem.

Jill says I am such a fiend for cleanliness, she is rather surprised I don't whip the chickadees in in winter for a quick shampoo!

But of all bathing, the bathing of a Siamese takes the primary prize. I seldom speak of it, for many cat experts feel it is murder ever to wash a cat.

It is as controversial a subject as recognizing Red China. However, our cats have always had occasional baths. They have lived to ripe and happy old ages, they have had no skin diseases, no fleas, no mites, no hairballs. When the air gets full of flying leftover fur, and a tentative paw begins to scratch an ear delicately, I say, this is it. Jill gets out an orange sack. Pussy goes in. A good mild dunk follows, and a rubbing with a warm bath towel.

A brushing with a soft brush afterward makes the fur look so shining and fine, and a nice clean kitten curls up by the fire, only making a gesture at washing one paw which she opines we left over.

I know cats scrub themselves endlessly, but I don't see why they shouldn't get a little help. I know cats, have loved cats too, that leave a sooty mark when they lie down because they cannot with one small tongue really *get at* the whole works. This tedious business of licking a paw and scrubbing can be pretty discouraging to a clean-minded cat. And everyone agrees that a cat does not like to be dirty. A cat will work to exhaustion trying to clean up after a mouse hunt in the coalbin.

George always has a dozen or so cats and when he goes to the barn to milk, they follow him in a stately procession. There seems to be some order of their going, they stay in line, and each cat stays in the right place in the line. The several dogs go along on the side, slightly behind. George has the typical farmer's gait, one who began heavy work so young and works so long, a kind of rolling, slightly slanting gait. It would mark a farmer anywhere. It seems to me, as I watch, that the cats and dogs have the same way of rolling along, but this must be just my imagination. Still—it looks as if—

I like Katherine Mansfield's saying, "Life should be like a steady, visible light." Here in our green valley men have worked the farmland and made the earth yield good crops, have established homes, and raised children, and worshipped God in the little white churches. Patriots came from here in the early days, lawyers and doctors have gone out from the little villages, a few have come to stage and radio and television stardom. But the actual quality of living has not changed so much. Instead of the pie cupboard we have the farm freezer, but the parents who work so hard on the school lunches and the Cub Scouts and the Junior Choir in the Federated Church are in the tradition, it seems to me, of the first little band that struggled over the crest of the hills and knelt and thanked God this was to be their home. I would hope that always life in this place would have honor and integrity and good faith, I would hope we avoid intolerance and hatred which are so acid-deadly to the soul and mind.

As we drive along the Pomperaug at dusk, I see the supper lights shining from all the old white houses and the few newer ranch-type homes. I know in this house a child has just died, in this house a family faces a hard financial struggle, in another a gentle little woman goes for an operation of the gravest kind next morning. I think of them all, my neighbors, with their sorrows and struggles, and the hazards of living we all meet. And in spite of all, it seems to me a happy land, and I think of various simple countryfolk I know whose lives are certain and sure "a steady, visible light."

What someone has called my gentle philosophy of living comes from the warm sense of the good there is around me. I can read the direst news in the papers and then go down the road and find some man or woman doing a very fine sacrificial deed for someone else. I think of George with a twenty-four hour day, taking on the chores of a neighbor who has illness in the family and thinking nothing at all of so doing.

I think of the volunteer firemen who work all day at hard jobs on farm, in factory, in white-collar jobs in the city and leap out at three in the morning to help save someone's house and barn. If lucky, they get thanked, if not, then not!

As George says, "we have to be neighbors anyhow."

Democracy always seems to move ahead crabwise which is backward and yet goes ahead too. The little crabs I see on the beach when we go to Cape Cod seem always to go in the wrong direction and then suddenly there they are. I think we operate in much the same way, scuttling back and then sidling forward, and in the end, we are a little ahead of where we were before.

August is for hammock reading, the books all say. The *Saturday Review* even lets down the austere bars and suggests books one can get through without a mental marathon. I, however, just read anything in summer that I can find to read. Of late, it has been household management—*Management In the Home*, by the famed Mrs. Gilbreth and colleagues.

I am a little hampered by not being able, ever, to understand charts, or read tabulated figures or do percentages. However, with this limitation in mind, I launched forth on home management and, skipping the charts, found a good deal of fine advice. It is not in me to make a notebook of my motions as I make coffee, I faced that right away. I would be a gibbering idiot were I to try to list the steps I take in making a cheese omelet. My motion-mindedness is confined to moving fast.

However, I found the book fascinating. I began by falling with cries of joy on the scientific bed-making. I took position A. I whipped the sheets, blankets and spread around on that half of the bed. I moved to position B, and found I couldn't reach the left-over stuff from position A so I sneaked into position C and grabbed everything and heaved.

I set my teeth and tried again. I have been running around a bed making it as a squirrel runs around a cage for years. Now I was going to save strength and time. I took position A again. Moved to position B. Looked at the book again.

Finally decided I was too short to reach that far and keep the things level amidships but would keep on trying.

Next I fell on the ironing advice. I knew where I belonged on that one. I belonged on the one who got all tired out and flustered and nothing came out wrinkle-free anyway. I was definitely not the slow easy relaxed ironer I should be. This was a losing battle.

Then I got to the kitchen reorganization and I decided that was it. Splendid, I said, after the manner of an English novelist. This resulted in the retirement of two cookie pans and one extra can opener. Jill said that was something, if not much.

I still think everyone should read this book and if he can do charts, do them, by all means. So far, in my limited way, I have managed to improve my orange-squeezing by taking the steak board and putting it by the squeezer and cutting the oranges on it instead of running across the kitchen with each and every severed and dripping half. I know Mrs. G would feel a glow that such a backward person as I could go this far.

The only real doubt I have is when Mrs. G says never do a job any better than it has to be done. Now this is contrary to my whole childhood upbringing and I cannot feel I should subscribe to it. I was raised to feel that whatever one did from brushing teeth to sweeping the kitchen floor one did it with all the fervor of one's being. If a job is worth doing at all, it is worth doing well, my parents always said.

I am aware that Mrs. Gilbreth is cannonading against the over-meticulous housewife, the one that scours the ash trays after a single ash has fallen. At least, so I interpret her. But the very words astounded me. And now as I run the vacuum cleaner and begin to push aside the sofa, the tricky little thought comes that if I skip those under-sections—who is to know and I shall have more free time—never do a job any better, I say to myself skipping past those dark corners.

This could revolutionize a household. But it is such a challenging idea, and the book does show up so many shortcomings on the part of us average homemakers, that it ought to make anyone manage better—time to read more, if she isn't making charts of some new activity instead!

Jill says soundly that the main thing about such a study is that you re-evaluate your own activity. For instance, our telephone is in the most remote corner of the front living room, which is definitely wrong. To answer it, we hurdle over two sofas, around three chairs, past a few tables, dodge the firescreen and knock over the woodbasket. At night, this goes on in the dark, since there is no way to turn on a light *before* you get to the phone. Mrs. G would think nothing of this. But, says Jill, it is a 1690 house and it wasn't made for phones and a phone is an anachronism in it. The phone went where the house cables could come in without any sawing through of a massive chestnut hand-hewn beam, and that is it. Also we have light plugs where they could be inserted and nowhere else. Short of building a new house around the phone, our phone stays where it is.

Actually our lives are guided by the house itself, or by special considerations that would never rate on any kind of chart. For instance I moved my little rosewood sofa to the bedroom when Honey was a puppy so she could nap there while I was typing. The room was very crowded what with my bed, a chest, a Franklin stove, two doors, four windows, one easy chair and a bedside stand big enough for both books and the radio. But the sofa went in under the windows, just as a temporary measure. It is right there now.

For in the latter part of those brief fourteen years that my dark Honey spent with me, she found the sofa just the right height to get into easily. And although she went into that mysterious next room longer ago than I will ever count up now, I keep the little sofa right there. Often I look up from my desk and think I see her sitting there, those great dark amber eyes looking at me with such love, and the deep velvet muzzle quivering. The other dogs jump around on it considerably and by now the aura of favorite bones definitely rises above the aura of Mary Chess' White Lilac I spray around my room, but never mind, it is Honey's sofa. Even Hollyberry Red spreading her magnificence all across its length does not diminish the little golden ghost.

Jill's bedroom is across the landing from the keeping room, up and down steps, and was the "borning room." Here the babies and mothers stayed in the early days, close enough to get some of the heat from the great giant of a fireplace in the keeping room, near enough to hear what was going on. No place for the phone there either as practically the whole of the American Revolution dwells there in Jill's collection of historical books.

So the telephone, we think, is lucky it is not finding itself in the back woodshed with the fishing tackle, the firewood, the flower vases and the turtle trap.

We continue to do our broken-field running when the phone rings. And quite often we do get there before central rings off.

I have no confidence in a telephone anyway. The ring always sounds fiercely ominous, although it often is just the express company saying there is a box for us in Woodbury which is marked perishable.

On the whole, reconsidering the book on home management, I think the author, and her colleagues, are after all trying to make every homemaker more efficient—in short, do a better job. So deep down in their hearts they do not feel you should never do a job any better than it has to be done. Certainly by the time a woman charts her every household chore, she is going to be efficient or ELSE.

Mr. B. Altman has finally sent back my Severn miniature of Keats re-framed in a solid-silver, sound frame. Holly crashed against the old one and smashed it completely. I had almost lost faith in my favorite New York store, since Mr. Keats stayed there about two months. I could have, said I, dug up the silver, beaten it out, cut the glass and done it myself in a week. I wonder if the framer recognized Johnny Keats or only thought, while trimming the support, well, there is a handsome young man—but what an odd jacket he has on—and that deep collar must be something new at Brooks Brothers. From the haircut, he might decide this was an actor or possibly a musician. But certainly nothing from out Hollywood way!

Some people feel we are out of the cultural flow here in the country, but we never feel that way at all. Bill Hirsch, our plumber in Woodbury, came to fix a leak in the sink this week. I felt the sink was gradually going on down into the watery deeps like a lost Lyonnesse. Bill had just come back from his brief vacation. What he did was to take his family and tour the Civil War battlefields as far as possible. For the Civil War is his chief interest. He sat down after the water stopped gurgling and we had a fine talk about the campaigns, including a complete going-over of the Battle of Gettysburg, and I may say, after we were through, we felt the South *must* have won the war.

Our good friend who does the yard work is writing a novel and when he pauses for a smoke after a bout in the beets and carrots, we discuss the current articles in The *Saturday Review*, as well as the trends in fiction and biography.

It is very pleasant, when I am Frenching beans to have him poke his head in the door and say, "by the way, I brought the Stonewall Jackson, will get it in a minute."

The postman, George Bennett, is an expert naturalist and conservationist. He has been awarded all kinds of medals for his services to the state. Instead of delivering the mail, I often think he should be giving a course to everyone in the valley about nature and wildlife, spreading the richness of his study and experience in plain view for less knowledgeable folk.

He reminds me of my Virginia friend who says, "put down your bucket where you are." For he has put down his bucket in this small locality and persuaded almost everyone to plant, and plant, and foster wildlife, conserve, build ponds. The year he made us all graft things was a strenuous one, for grafting is not easy and it often does not take. But out of the hundreds of flowering twigs grafted in woodland and orchard lanes, enough survived to make it memorable.

He is a firm taskmaster too. "Now you get these planted AT ONCE," he says, "not stand around in a pail all day. Get them RIGHT IN."

We drop everything and get them in.

We seldom have a really hot night, even in August. But there is something very special about it when we do. It is rare to be able to sit in the Quiet Garden without even a scarf or sweater and feel the moonlight. A silvery mist rises from the meadow, and the scent of the nicotiana is unbearably sweet in the still air. Voices are soft, and pauses come often. It is always pleasant to me when friends are content to just think together, and not talk incessantly.

The moon has a special beauty on such a night, it is the color of the pearl-white nicotiana flowers. It is Shakespeare's moon that "tips with silver all these fruit-tree tops."

The shadows of the old apple trees are plain on the cut lawn, a delicate lacy pattern. The cockers and Irish give over the rabbit-chasing and dream in the moonlight of greater hunts tomorrow.

We cannot see our neighbors' lights for the trees are so heavy with leaves. So we are in our own green mysterious world, quite separate. There is no sound except a single hound baying on the hill, a far-off lonely sound.

Now I can begin to think of my unicorn coming on silver hooves down the slope by the pond, bending his head with the single ivory horn as he dips a velvet muzzle in the cool water. He has been deep in ferns all the hot day in that part of the woods where nobody ever goes. Now the dark water ripples over his hooves as he walks over the forget-me-nots and drinks his evening thirst away.

After he has gone, we may take a dip ourselves, carrying a lantern to set at the edge of the steps. The pond has a warm surface from the heat, but the underneath area is cold from the springs that bubble up endlessly.

I always decide, as I swim thoughtfully across the moonlit water that August is far too short after all. It is a beautiful month, I tell Jill, no matter if the thermometer does climb around 100 much of the time.

Jill says she must pick more beans tomorrow.

If the children are at home for the week end, as they are likely to be when it is really hot, they dive and swim and toss the big rubber ball and chase themselves around with the rubber float and could be easily ten years old instead of grown-up working adults. It is a delightful regression and we all enjoy it thoroughly.

When they come in, dripping and scrambling for towels, they always suggest a snack. If it has been a couple of hours since supper, there is no reason for them not to be starving again! "Is there anything to eat?" is a kind of echo that sounds all over the house.

They settle for cold sliced-chicken sandwiches and big glasses of frosty cool milk topped off with a few butternut cookies or a wedge of angelfood cake.

Silence settles gently down in the old house after they go to bed with their various versions of light summer reading. Psychoanalytic texts, a world history, a law book, and something pertaining to the fourteenth century see them off, while Jill takes up the latest Josephine Tey book, and I pop off with a glass of milk and Dylan Thomas' *Quite Early In The Morning*.

There is something really wonderful about a hot summer night, I think, as I turn the light out and the moon comes in, steeping the room with silver.

August is a fine month.

September

I DROVE TO THE VILLAGE YESTERDAY along the golden country road. At every farmhouse a group of children stood waiting for the school bus. Hair brushed, shoes polished, pencil cases clutched in tight clean hands, they looked so earnest, so vulnerable to the world. As I passed, I waved at them, and they waved back. It is hard to remember back to the days when schoolchildren went to school in a world that seemed very safe and steady.

Now we live in such tension that any strange object in the sky is possibly the end of the world. Anxiety is the keynote as we go on building more destructive weapons. It is no longer possible to assume that if we learn our lessons and are good girls and boys, all will be well. We have learned that the innocent and young are thoroughly expendable.

But musing on this, I thought it is a very fine thing that the children do go to school in a free school. That we are coming more and more in America to see to it that all children, all races, all religions, all colors shall have the same basic educational opportunities.

What an encouraging thought this is, I said, as I turned to the post office. For instance, take the hot lunch program alone. When I was in grade school, children who could not go home for lunch, or whose parents did not pack them one, could slip out and buy a couple of lethal sinkers at the little Greek stand, drink some pop, and face their lessons with large greasy lumps in their stomachs. Charity baskets at Christmas and Thanksgiving went to all poor families, and they were elegant. Coal was delivered to the needy, and the little town was a kind town, no doubt of it.

But the idea of a general balanced feeding of the school-children had not been heard of. At least not in my part of the country.

Now and then I would sneak over and indulge in a sinker myself. But I had to ride my bicycle home a couple of miles for lunch so I could have a hot meal. Mama didn't know anything about vitamins because they hadn't been invented yet, but she was a very sound dietician by instinct.

The sinkers were very large and very heavy, very dark and extremely greasy. If you bit in with valor, you came on a gelid lump of red stuff, supposed to be real jelly. The dough inside had a pale chewy texture. After consuming a couple of these, I went back to my arithmetic class with a very queasy stomach.

Just when thermos bottles came in, I cannot remember. I do recall our first one was a kind of squat jug made of some kind of clay material. We just adored it. But it was not to carry to school, any more than a gallon gas tank.

I went on thinking about the advances in our way of life for the young. We now have, in our village, a school doctor. We have eye examinations, and dental care—we have balanced sport programs for those who need therapy. And our principal arranges fascinating trips through brass works and hotels and plastic factories and trips to Washington—it seems like a dream when you add it all up.

So after all is said, our children are inheriting many fine things along with that hydrogen menace. And with so much good, I wonder whether we should fear annihilation?

There are still all too many places in the world where children do not stand rosy and confident waiting for the school bus to take them to a free school with a curriculum that is independent of dictatorships. But we can hope to help with foreign children projects of which there are many, and this is a heartening thing to consider.

We are a kind of Aladdin's lamp country, too, I thought further, as Miss Evangeline looked up the postage to Bombay, India.

We love rubbing lamps. For a good many years, I have been interested in the Piney Woods School, in Piney Woods, Mississippi where "in the joy of spraying a human orchard" as they say quaintly, they do just that. This little colored school takes in the orphans, the underprivileged, the children down from the cotton patches, and teaches them as much as they can learn. A desire to learn seems to be the chief requirement.

When they need a dormitory, the boys build it. The girls cook and do the laundry. When they need books, their friends like me comb the shelves and ship cartons of miscellany off. One year they took clothes, any clothes at all, and the girls in the sewing classes remade them for serviceable wear. Their budget list is phenomenal. They ask for so many pounds of flour, so many dried beans, so much salt pork—

Some from this little school have gone on to careers as lawyers or doctors or nurses or whatever. Some merely learn skills to make a better life for themselves and their children.

And then suddenly somehow the little man who dreamed this dream for his people was discovered by television. I did not see the hour, but some critics said his dignity and character were a revelation in the rather honky-tonk air of the program.

But I did hear the announcement a week later "and for the little school in Piney Woods, so far 400,000 dollars have come in, and they are still counting."

"Why, that's MY school!" I cried, leaping up and upsetting my tray. "My Piney Woods. Oh me!"

Yes, we are an Aladdin Lamp kind of people.

The whole countryside is bright with color now. Not the tender colors of spring, but the vital tones of coming autumn. Goldenrod follows the line of the fences with its feathery spikes of minted gold, the chicory sets deep blue stars adrift on every lane. The gardens are like a Mexican fiesta with countless shades of zinnias.

My favorite zinnia color is the soft pale salmon, and I love to mass the blossoms in an old dark-blue sugar bowl. For the sharper oranges and reds, I use an old wooden bucket or a copper container, just right with the brilliant shades.

Zinnias are the most independent flowers! You get them all arranged so nicely in a bouquet and an hour later they are standing up stiff as ramrods and facing in the wrong direction. I have given up doing a good arrangement with them, I just pop them in and leave them to their own devices.

Jill has been down in the lower meadow looking at the wild cranberries. They are paler in color than the tame ones, big waxy ovals, very delicate and spicy. We do not know whether some former owner had a cranberry bog there, or

whether they just grew by themselves. They seem very plump and big for a wild berry, but there they are, and when we get them before the frost does, they make a clear and rosy sauce which is special. We have to practically lie down to pick them, having no cranberry picker and plenty of tangled weeds to battle. The neat bogs on Cape Cod are a different matter altogether.

There they look as if you could slice them and spread them on a sandwich, so neat, so even. And in the autumn it is a fine sight to see the Portuguese pickers bent over and moving in rhythm across the bogs, scooping the rich jewel-red berries into the pickers.

We are a long way from the days when cranberry sauce was served with Thanksgiving turkey and that was that. It is equally delicious with ham, and excellent with cold slices of chicken or goose. And the clear, shining ruby juice makes a lovely breakfast drink as a change from the oranges and grapefruit. Lately it is even featured in cocktails, the cranberry mix being very friendly to gin. Cranberry-and-orange relish was a delight in my childhood, now there is cranberry upside-down cake and all sorts of other variations.

When you pick them, the berries feel as if they had been dipped in wax. They fall in the pail with an odd little hollow plop, very pleasant. No other berry sounds the same at all. It is almost as if they were faery drums beating a magic note.

I really think it is a fine art to be a well-dressed woman. The ones in the fashion plates don't affect me much, for I can't imagine anyone with no mid-section at all, just a long neck and a pair of lovely long legs. Most women do have a different frame, even the shad-thin ones. And I am not proud of the way women follow the lead, like sheep after the bell-wether. Even Connie, who is an individualist in many ways, says she never did want to wear those skirts to the floor and found herself doing it. Currently she deplores the return to the ugly long-waisted packaged look but she expects to follow it although it won't, as the saying goes, "do anything" for her size nine, tiny-waisted shape. Ed Shenton says she looks like something out of the Renaissance and certainly her delicate coloring and fine slim hands and oval face do suggest it. However, she must dress in the moment, although she advised me firmly, "Mama, you better hurry fast and buy all the clothes you need for the next three years because these new styles are just *not for you.*"

We are improving as a nation in the use of practical materials, however, and the beach and sport clothes, when not noticeable by their absence of material, are a big improvement. In summer, the coppery-bronzed young girls in sundresses of fine charcoal or coral cottons or in Bermuda shorts with soft little pearl-colored sweaters are a far cry from the days of full skirts and ruching around the necks of starched shirtwaists.

And the clothes for the very young make me sigh, for when Connie was young there were no such delectable mint green and jonquil-colored playsuits. No little aqua corduroy bathrobes with a ragdoll to match. Children wore silk dresses with smocking and bonnets of lace, hand-whipped in rows and rows. Later on, little boys graduated to linen suits which wrinkled every time they squirmed. Also there were so many layers! As Jill's enchanting grandchild staggers around in a brief pumpkin-colored outfit with rosy bare toes and *no* petticoat at all, I am amazed. When Connie was that age, I reflect, it was a wonder she could breathe and move, I had her so swaddled in wrappings like a precious ivory carving.

So despite the fashion race—up one year, down the next, in one year, out the next, I think we have progressed considerably.

There are always women like Faith Baldwin, too, who man-

age to dress exquisitely no matter what the style is. However,
I often think how Faith would look in a belted gunnysack and
decide she would still be exquisite.

This is a quality of personality above and beyond clothes,
I feel sure. Faith can put on a pinky simply-tailored little
frock and run a comb through her crisp short hair, step into a
pair of size three haymakers and look like an illustration
from *Vogue*. But far less artificial. She uses very little make-
up, no nail polish, wears just a little perfect jewelry and
manages to convey at the same time an air of complete sim-
plicity and extreme sophistication such I have never observed
in any other well-dressed woman. She could, I reflect, wear a
clump of orchids and make them look like a small bouquet
she had happened to pick in the fields while filling her big
bird feeder, and lugging suet for the wire cage.

She also has a touching quality of wanting everyone to feel
comfortable. She once wrote an article to the effect that a
woman ought to be caught dead wearing slacks. Women
should dress neatly and smartly and in dresses or suits, said
Miss Baldwin. So all the first years of our ripening friendship, Jill and I dressed feverishly if Faith was coming for tea
or to spend the night. Until the day she dropped in without
warning and there we were in our corduroy slacks and sweat-
shirts after washing a bunch of cockers. The next time she
came, she wore slacks.

And when she visited us, she came with grey-flannel slacks,
plaid slacks, checked shirts, and flat little shoes. The fact
that she, in these, looked like a perfectly exquisite portrait of
a lady and we still looked like farmhands did not detract at all
from the fact that she was going to fit into our pattern. We
found it very moving.

A further revelation was when we all went to the Cape and
Faith and I went fishing for flounder. She wore galoshes that
day, as we had to wade to get the canoe out. And one of our
fishing hats. I hesitated to admit that, ardent as I am about

fishing, I cannot put the worms on, nor take off the gasping fish.

"Think nothing of it," said Faith airily, "I put 'em on, I take 'em off."

Silently we fished. As the flounder came in, Faith whipped them off the hook, thrust them in the creel, re-wormed the hook, tossed it back.

"This one is Reginald," she said, "he looks like a Reginald."

The next morning we ate Reginald, dipped in seasoned flour, lightly browned in butter and garnished with lemon wedges.

"He came to a good end," said Faith.

For me, September is a nostalgic month. I always think back to the football games and the late picnics when I was growing up. In the little college town, the ivy on the grey-stone buildings was tinged with red, the sun shone on the campus, woodsmoke drifted in the air. The professors hurried along the crosswalk with their lecture notes under their arms and a dreamy smile on their academic faces. The tensions of mid-year had not yet appeared, the faculty was as placid as a faculty can ever be. There was a kind of fiesta air as the team jogged out on the field on Saturday afternoons and the band blared the Alma Mater "and the elms on the campus softly whis—per— Lawrence is our *dear* old Ho—ome."

As a faculty child, I was everywhere, at the games, at the rallies, at the drama productions. I just really did feel Lawrence was my dear old home and it was years before it came to me I was not indigenous to those halls of ivy.

Actually a faculty child has a very odd position. Neither the right age for the students nor belonging to the adult world that teaches them, it is a sad and wistful state. At faculty teas, you pass things. But no matter how much you may know of the affairs of the college from hearing them at breakfast, noon, and night at home, nobody ever asks you anything.

At football games, basketball games, hockey games, you are welcome to cheer like a five-alarm siren, but nobody is going to ask you for a dance that night because you are TOO YOUNG.

As for your own contemporaries, they think you know too much. Having spent so much time in an academic atmosphere, your language is not the same and you begin by not knowing the right slang. This clears up if you work at it, and the day when the gang decides you don't know much after all is the day of great triumph.

The battle of education goes on incessantly. Regional schools divide men as sharply now as anti-slavery divided them earlier. Little towns are apt to prefer spending much more for less and being on their own, and this seems very silly but is human and natural. But I do get a little tired of the people who say, "I went to school in a one-room schoolhouse, and what was good enough for me is good enough for my son—"

I always feel like rising and saying, "why aren't you using kerosene lamps and carrying water from the old well? That was good enough for *your* father, so why are you involved with electricity and plumbing and heating and so on?"

But what I loathe even more is the attitude of some city people who feel in a rural area such as ours, a school does not need too much by way of modernization in equipment and teaching. "After all, few of them go on to college, most of them are farmers in the end—" this is a gauntlet thrown down to me every time.

The intelligence of our rural population needs no apology. And as for the ultimate goal of education, just what is it? Is it to enlarge the horizon and train one to think with steadiness and wisdom, or is it to separate society into little channels with needle-threading for the future homemakers and economics only for the future bank presidents?

I realize the liberal arts are under fire, and have been since

I was a college student. There were those then that said Latin and Greek and Ancient History and Elizabethan Literature were a pretty futile way to spend time. For women, if they married, little could be learned to help in child-raising and homemaking. If they went into a career, they should have vocational courses pointing toward their career.

It would be very, very nice if there were time enough in one's life to learn everything. But there just isn't. So there will always be a conflict in the educational ranks as to what is basic, according to one's own sense of values. For me, I wish I had had more Latin and some Greek. I couldn't fit Greek in because I had to take so many required courses—I could have done without Advanced Algebra and heaven knows Advanced Algebra could have done without me! I could have given up Reading and Speaking as it was called very easily. I had been acting in plays all through my grade-school and high-school life and debating and speaking, and that time could have been well spent in learning enough French to read the great French literature in its own tongue.

I also would have enjoyed a course in home economics. And landscape gardening. And interior decoration. And then there is astronomy.

Perhaps it is a good thing I have no influence on the curriculum anywhere. Chaos might result. However, I am sure of one thing, the subject is of little account if the teacher be inspired.

An inspired teacher not only teaches the subject, but rouses intellectual curiosity about a hundred other things. Gives glimpses of immortality in the most mundane of lessons. And how tragic it is that we pay our teachers so little that they have to feel that poverty is to be desired or they give up their teaching and enter some field where they can decently and comfortably live and support their families.

Some people think teaching is such an easy job, it doesn't

deserve the pay of say a bricklayer. Or a laundry delivery-man. Besides, look at those long vacations!

If there be a more arduous job than teaching well, I cannot think what it might be, except to be president of this torn and confused country. In the first place, teaching has to be crea-tive, it has to deal with the countries of the mind which are always difficult, unpredictable, illimitable. It has at once to encourage the dull and slow to their highest understanding and satisfy and ease the burning hunger of the natural scholar. It has to be profound and yet not tedious for the young are impatient. It has to challenge the spirit, it has, within reason, to pack a few basic facts into a mind for future reference. Train in techniques of scientific research.

I am horrified when I think how much depends, for in-stance, on the first teacher who teaches a child to read. This may be the beginning of a lifetime of love of books. And whether rich or poor, well or ill, happy or sad, books can be a refuge, they do not change with changing circumstance, they are the open highway to yesterday, today and tomorrow, wherever you will to travel.

Now if a child begins with feeling reading is a heavy chore, this will hang like a miasma in the background. "I hate read-ing," is the saddest utterance. The first teacher who makes the arrangement of words on a page an exciting affair is giving a child a better gift than a gold mine.

We could hardly overpay the teacher.

Now this long vacation is another thing. This is the time when teachers should be studying and doing research and refilling the well of inspiration. Instead of that, many teachers work. I know of men teachers who do carpentry, hire out as painters. Some clerk in grocery stores. Women tutor or do secretarial work or act as companions to elderly folk.

Blessed are the students of history whose teacher has an outside income so he or she can go to Rome in that long vaca-tion, dig around in the libraries, savor the essence of the past, look at the political situation today and come back to that class to discuss the fall of the Roman civilization with side notes about the moonlight on the Colosseum and the sunlight on the Spanish Stairs.

The teacher who has to be gainfully employed in an alien field during the summer to keep the bills paid, loses some richness in his teaching. To be a teacher is a year-round job, and has nothing to do with the hours in the classroom or correcting papers. A dedicated teacher is always working at his job provided he has just enough money to pay for the tonsils coming out when Jimmy has had too many sore throats.

There are other hazards to education these days, aside from the low salary debilitating the teaching. When I read about the inter-collegiate debates and that several colleges withdrew their teams as soon as the subject was stated "We should recognize Red China," I was too shocked to speak. One president said quite plainly that he feared if his team drew the positive side, fifteen years hence one or more of its members might be investigated as subversive. He was more right than courageous. For it is the function of college debating teams to bang any subject around just for the mental exercise and that a subject can be dangerous is a new and frightening symptom of our confusion.

I was heartened that so many colleges refused to change the subject. If we are afraid of argument, we are done for anyway, I told Jill. And if the college youngsters can't debate on anything under the sun, it is a sorry comment on our land of liberty. In this instance, it was all the more curious, as half the arguments for recognizing Red China had nothing to do with communism and its value, if any, but were on other bases entirely.

This kind of attitude, persisted in, would debilitate our educational life and we would, in effect, move toward the Kremlin quite rapidly. The next step is to follow Russia and make even the music slant toward a governmental attitude.

Here in our peaceful green valley, we are not preoccupied with remodeling the church and adding to the school and getting good crops. We feel the surges of national emotion, we are concerned. We may be in a way isolated but we are not insulated.

As the hay wagons lumber down the roads, so heavy with hay, so sweet-smelling, we are glad the crop is good. But we have an eye to the world situation nonetheless and we are deeply concerned with the people in arid countries who do not have enough. We never discuss the possibility of anyone being a communist, no witch-hunts go on. A poster in the window of the post office brings out cartons of clothes to ship for needy children or pints of blood for the blood bank, but we do not say much about it.

I suspect we are typical of small communities all over the country. And I feel this is a national reserve that might be tapped to help the world, if only someone intelligent enough made a plan. If the world were well fed, it would be time to consider policies and politics. And while it is not a rich agricultural breadbasket, I know that right from our little area much could be spared. If transportation could be managed, and a central station set up as in New Haven, I can see the produce that would pour in. "Sure," George would say. "I can spare a couple of loads of cabbages and potatoes and squash." The lumber dealer would say, "I can send a truckload of good roofing material easy or not." The coal supply would contribute coal enough to warm the fires of a lot of cold families. Grain and seed and fertilizer would be hauled over, while the schoolchildren collected everything from stationery to socks. I would think a town would collect some of everything it used, and just lay it aside to be sent to some suitable town in a far-off country. I suppose it labels me as a complete romantic to dream of such a thing, but anyway I can dream.

The line storm, as we call it, usually comes in September. Rain falls with a clean, driving force. It makes a tangible wall of dark silver. George looks like a deep-sea fisherman as he splashes in from the kennel, his sou'wester pouring with water.

The pond brims to the top of the spill-over, cascades into George's brook. The air is incredibly fresh as we dash out for the mail. Beautiful is the color of the countryside, dove grey of sky, charcoal of tree trunks, silver of rain blending into a kind of twilight for the world.

The hearth fire seems especially snug and the teakettle whistles merrily. I actually don't think a teakettle should whistle right out loud—I always jump at the piercing note— but that is the modern way of telling me the water is exactly boiling. And tea must be made with freshly boiling water, in a freshly scalded teapot. We like ours steeped not quite four minutes, strong and comforting.

Very, very thin-sliced bread and butter is the best accompaniment for tea. For company, however, we may have a sugary teacake fresh from the oven or cinnamon toast bubbly with butter and cinnamon—or tiny hot thumb-size biscuits spread with white-clover honey.

Conversation at teatime should be tranquil, I think. Not the time for world problems or controversial issues, but a time to rest the spirit, remember pleasant things. Everyone needs such a time, and tea goes well with it.

After the storm, the world is polished and shining. The light is so golden, we feel we have never seen the sun before. The battered zinnias shout with color, the asters, flat on the dark earth make little pools of violet and deep rose. We are in for a spell of perfect weather now, every day luminous, every night brimmed with stars. Picnics at noon, supper by the applewood fire at night, a walk in the cool moonlight before bed.

The fall chores go on apace. We are electric with energy.
Jill works at the pine chest we got from our Indian friend
Grey Fox, for she says it is pleasanter to do over furniture in
the sun outdoors and let the chips fall on the grass. The chest
has faded blue casein paint on it, which is murderous to get
off. A decorator neighbor advised washing with a solution of
washing soda as a first step, and this is a fine idea. Soda seems
to dissolve the casein. I told Jill she could leave a little of the
slaty blue, because in the Metropolitan all the pieces have left-
over paint on them, or nearly all. Makes them more authentic,
I think, as do the wormholes.

I dare say Jill and I seem very odd at times, and possibly
we are. When Jill bought white wool yarn in the spring, the
clerk wanted to give her a heavy twist. "No," said Jill, "the
birds won't like it." The clerk gave her a very odd look. As

Jill went out, she turned and called back, "Nests" and thought that settled it, but she said the girl still looked odd.

Then when she bought the butterfish, the man wanted to clean them and she said casually, "Thank you no, it's for the turtles."

That time she got out, and went back to say, "Turtle trap, you see."

The boys at the market were so surprised at the jars and jars and jars of peanut butter we kept buying that finally George turned his beautiful blue eyes on her and said, "would it be too personal if I asked you how you and Mrs. Taber eat so *much* peanut butter?"

"Birds," said Jill.

Since then, the boys at the market go in for peanut butter by the case themselves. Joe has built a feeder and reports on how many birds they have—

So now we shall have to explain that the boxes and boxes of washing soda are for one recalcitrant pine chest.

As summer wanes, we cherish every mild dreamy day. I love the soft blue haze, I know summer still walks the lanes, but the frosty slipper of autumn is just behind. We now get up early—or what the books call betimes—for dog shows, as the last outdoor shows are being held within striking distance.

Being involved for a long time with Obedience training, we have a routine. We get the dumbells and box of fifteen scent-discrimination objects and the leashes and the bench chains in the car the night before. We put the entrance papers and the show directions in, too, as often we have gone many a mile and found they were at home in my desk drawer.

Groggily, we get up early and Jill pops dogs in the kennel who are NOT going to the show. I pack a lunch. We locate the sun glasses, in case it is hot, as it may well be. I explain to Sister that she is a Utility Dog and all through and can't go now, and she sits looking sloe-eyed at me saying I betray her every time I set forth with this paraphernalia.

The current dogs, Tiki and Holly, jump around in the back seat as we take the long road.

"I really think we should give this up," says Jill. "Look at the map, please, for that route number."

"Yes, we should," I agree, "after all we have twenty-four Obedience degrees, that is enough."

We drive on. Eventually we get to a heavy brush of traffic on some side road. We pass station wagons loaded with collies, poodles. A dreamy old English sheepdog leans a shaggy head out of a sedan and *eyes us* solemnly. We begin to feel the excitement of the show.

We invariably get lost. So do other show travelers. We line up, back and fill, lean out and ask directions. Some brave soul leads. We are off.

Comes the show ground. We fumble for our entry cards. We park. It may be a mile from the ring, it may be in a poison-ivy nook. But we park, and we now go forward with at least two dogs, sometimes three, winding themselves around our legs as they get excited and forget to *heel*. We carry also the lunch, a collapsible canvas seat, all the Obedience articles, two purses filled with Bufferin and salt tablets. Plus a comb and brush for the dogs. We acquire a catalogue, which I may carry in my teeth, having no other way left.

The sun is hot, unless it is pouring rain, in which case it is very, very cold. We find the ring, we set up the folding chair and we find that the judge has not arrived. If it is hot, we try to make a little shade for the dogs under the chair, which is too small. If it is raining, we drip. And wait.

In the end, our special darling lopes into the ring, looking askance at judge, stewards, spectators, and our hearts jump into our eyebrows. Maybe this is it, and maybe it isn't. Some small boy whistling at the ringside may call our dog to a happy reunion, quite outside of the rules.

Perhaps we do the exercises correctly, and then the day is lit up with glory. The blue ribbon and the silver ash tray mean a great deal. They mean days of heeling and sitting and staying and retrieving and work for both dog and handler and no silver mink could ever be as precious.

During the lunch-intermission everybody sits around and tells just how well Timmy does at home. What he does in the ring is a dog of a different color, but at home—my dear, you should see how he takes those jumps!

Finally we load ourselves and all the junk, and by now it is all junk, into the car and start the long drive home. The sun goes down, the dogs sleep on the back seat. I nibble a stale sandwich.

"Now the next time," says Jill, "I am going to give Tiki more of a workout before we get in the ring."

And so we begin again.

Smiley Burnette's little girl is a kindred spirit of mine. The Burnette cook says, "That Becky is sure sometimey. Sometime she like to be with folks, and sometime she like to be alone."

I am a sometimey person too. Sometime I like to be alone and listen to the sound of leaves about to fall, which is the sound of September. After the richness of the summer, the harvesting of the hay and sweet corn and the first of the cabbages, there is a strange feeling in the air, a sense of waiting. Now the plump cattle drift in from summer meadows, and all the kittens are half grown and the spring chickens look fat and matronly as they scratch around in that silly way they have.

Now I like to wander down to the pond and just do some thinking in my sometimey way. My usual thoughts about people and animals and politics and plays, about music and poetry and God and the stars.

And what life is all adding up to anyway, which is, I think the great cry of mankind.

Walking in the pale shadowy edge of a September evening, I feel the stars moving in a divine order, and I sense suddenly that we are all children of God. "I will lift up mine eyes unto the hills, from whence cometh my help. My help cometh from the Lord"—these are old words and words of deep security to a troubled heart.

Why there must be such suffering in the world, we know not. The good and happy, the young and the old are struck down suddenly. The old question of Why, Why—Why—rises again and again. A lovely young mother dies, leaving her husband and children desolate, and a psychotic criminal rises from his bed and goes out on parole to kill one more cop. We cannot solve this problem, at least I cannot and nobody I have ever asked has a ready answer. I asked our young minister and he said he did not know either.

I should ask him another time, when I am not badgering him about Naaman and Elijah, because that is a poser too. Naaman got cured of leprosy because he bathed in the Jordan on the prophet's orders, but only after his servants had urged him to just try it. So I got to wondering if it was the servants' faith that cured him, or his trust in the servants, or was the prophet just doing a sort of test case or what? Because I couldn't get around the fact that Naaman himself had *no* faith. So it wasn't his faith that cured him! There are a great many puzzling things in the Old Testament, if you come to figure them out, I decided.

The little white house looks peaceful in the last light. I like to think the builder was building for time to come, the staunch beams and hand-hewn stones were for enduring, not for a day. He had a long view. He built for his children's children.

The night is full of dreams, as only a September night can

be. I feel as if I could hold life in my hand, distilled and crystallized like a special jewel. Here is all the loveliness there is, all the peace, all the joy, all at once realized. Such moments come rarely and come completely. I could, I feel, gather a bouquet of stars and put them in a milk-glass swan compote and they would be there forever.

However, what I really do is to go in with a whirl of dogs and start a good steaming corn chowder for whoever is around. With bits of crispy bacon and a drift of paprika and a goodly savoring of onion, and plenty of cream, a corn chowder is a fine salute to September.

Hollyberry Red allows she will help with any leftover bacon fat for she does adore bacon and she says it is excellent for an Irish. She has to keep her strength up, says she and I tell her her strength is as the strength of ten anyway.

This daughter of International Champion Red Star Of Hollywood Hills, C. D. X. and Champion Redlog Strawberry Blonde, C. D. X., does not bother about her royalty or her beauty or her possible career in the ring. She bothers about the bacon fat in the skillet and the little crispy bits left over, and also suggests a bowl of corn chowder is most acceptable when you are growing and hungry.

The soft September twilight folds over the land and all the valley folk are at supper. Cats lap warm milk in the kitchens, dogs finish their own bowls and get the table scraps afterward.

Early to bed, for tomorrow will be a busy day while the weather holds so warm and bright. But we can see the stars blossoming in the sugar maples as we turn the lights out.

For the stars, it is enough to be.

October

BLANKETS BLOWING ON THE LINE give me such a nice feeling as the October sun and wind give lovely freshness to them, preparing for the stuffy winter rooms. All our blankets have stories about them. There are the two fragile homespun ones which Grandma Raybold had. They are a pale honey color, and invading moths have nibbled the edges at some pre-moth-spray day. They remind me of my little precisely garbed quiet grandmother with her gentle voice and wise eyes. As I hang them on the line, I am minded of my Uncle Walter, her son and Mama's brother. He was the one man I ever knew of whom it could be said he "saw life steadily, and saw it whole."

He was a quiet man, self-educated, and in the paper business. Nothing glamorous or spectacular at all. And yet every life he touched had a glow from his touching it. When he died, even the Pullman porters who had been on the run he frequented on business trips made a personal grief of his going.

What I remember most is that when my Mother died and a number of personal difficulties outside were crushing me, Uncle Walter took me for a walk after supper. The street lamps cast a pale lemon glow on his erect figure, his careful hat, his impeccable shoes. All he said was so simple and so short. We walked, and the light fell on him, and the shadows moved. The new-cut grass on the lawns smelled sweet. A little dog nosed along the curb and vanished.

"The Raybolds have always been heavy burden-bearers," he said quietly and as if that were quite to be expected and accounted for.

At that moment I felt myself one of a dim line stretching back and back and back, of people who went about their business and just bore their burdens. He never said another word to me about mine, he just let me assume I was to bear mine in the family tradition.

It is strange how that simple statement has sustained me down the years. Thereafter, every time I felt crushed by events, I stiffened my spine and said softly, "well, the Raybolds have always been heavy burden-bearers."

This, I think, is the chief heritage any child could get from the past, a feeling that to endure is the expected thing. And it was so valuable that he did not discuss my particular burdens, give lengthy advice, he just walked beside me in the latticed light of the street lamps and said that one quiet sentence.

Often I have wished to give my child such a password to serenity. But I never have been able to phrase the words. In this modern day, one is seldom able to speak the telling word to one's children. We have so many words nowadays but all trivial.

We live so much on the surface, like the waterbugs that skim the pond. And yet one would wish to utter a sentence or two that would be a permanent testament to life. When I get to thinking, on a bright October day, of my message, I get quite speechless. I would say, "love people. Give your best to whoever needs it. Share all you can of your experiences." But I never do. I only say, "isn't this weather heavenly? I hope it will last."

And then I go out and make a nice casserole of chili and rice and hope it may convey something to those gathered around the trestle table to eat it.

The blankets are still being hung up—after Grandma Raybold's come the angry green numbers, relics of Jill's son's camp years.

The nametapes are still on them, and as I pin them on the line, I remember the feverish sewing on of tapes when he first

went to camp. Such a timid, small, leggy boy; and as we drove him the eighty miles to the seashore, it seemed like a horrid mistake. True, he had allergies for hay and *would* ride on the hay wagon with George and we would stay up all night with the steam kettle in consequence, but still—he was so little! And as for social consciousness, never mind that, we thought.

And then that first week end when we visited and he dashed from the surf to say he was a natural swimmer—water held him up—and he was really too busy to bother with us. These blankets bring back memories of those camp days, and I am glad he had them.

Then there is the purple blanket which I cannot figure out. Where it came from, what its history, I do not know. It has always been here, all twenty-odd years. It is a purple blanket and there it is. It doesn't go with any decorating scheme we have, but it is a good blanket and there it is!

I like things that wear well, from cooking pots and pans to friends. No matter how many new shining utensils I get, I always reach for the old wooden spoon that has been through so much stirring with me. And I often pass over the elegant white and blue casserole for an old cracked brown one. It takes living with things to love them. And somehow the aura of happy meals when the children were little and we were full of energy clings to those old things.

"One should never get attached to things," said Ed the other day as he polished the wide black-oak floor to a glow. "I think it should always be so that you could go out the front door, turn the key, and never come back at all, and never miss a thing." This is a good stern philosophy, I thought, but not for me.

In fact, I have often told Jill that if we ever had to move I would just go away and huddle in a rented room somewhere while she gave everything away. I love to give things away, it is not that. Anything anybody needs, I am glad to part with. But things like Mama's monkey pitcher and the deep green goblets from the captain's attic in Maine—these have a value for me, I admit, far beyond any value they should have.

The monkey pitcher happens to be valuable, experts say, but the reason I love it is not so much the soft smoke-blue color and the odd little figures capering on it—monkeys they are, I know—nor the graceful flowing lines. But it was one of the first objects I noticed as I was growing up, and I can look at it any time and see Mama's face as she dusted it.

Mama was a plump small person, rosy and smiling. I think she was beautiful, but of this I cannot be sure. She had the deepest clearest wisest brown eyes and the softest most uncontrollable brown flying hair and the kind of voice that sings in the memory. Her mouth was notable not so much for the Raybold firmly modeled lips as for the way it lifted in a thoughtful private smile when life was either funny or should have been. Her little hands were almost always reddened from scrubbing and washing and cooking, and her figure was certainly nothing to startle the fashion experts. Plump as a partridge always.

She was the kind of woman that people in trouble always came to. Perhaps when I have said this, I have said everything.

So that monkey pitcher, which evokes her image is a great treasure to me, and I would never want to close the door on it and go away. This is a very sentimental attitude, but I never have worried about being sentimental, I accept it, I am!

All the recent furor over "Momism" never bothered me at all. Whatever equipment I have had to meet life with came from this gentle little woman, and I doubt whether I would have been a stronger or better person without the security she gave me. In all the wild, tempestuous atmosphere of life with Father, she created a small island of quiet. And this is all the more remarkable when I consider how like my Father I was, stormy and passionate and unpredictable and leaping from emotional crag to emotional crag. Mama would say, "now Gladys—"

And things smoothed out.

The day of the home dressmaker seems to have gone in most places. This is a pity for the town dressmaker was a grand institution. When ours came, it was a gala day. The sound of the sewing machine humming all day and the laughter from the sewing room as Mama and Alma chattered away was a pleasant thing. The smell of chicken simmering on the gas range was fine, and I was usually in a dither over whether my dark-blue corduroy trimmed with fur would get done for the Saturday night football dance.

Alma never used a pattern. She would riffle the pages of a fashion book and say "I think I'll make the neck like this— and the skirt like this—and how about raglan sleeves?"

Then her long slim shining scissors went snip, snip—and the material divided like the Red Sea when the Israelites crossed.

My favorite dress was a rose satin, caught up with rosebuds and garnished with lace. I must have looked pretty awful in it as I teetered off on my first high-heeled white satin pointed pumps. But I felt like a Queen. Walking down Main Street with my beau—in those days we usually walked—I felt so elegant and so cherished. And with a burst of astounding eloquence, my beau said, "you know you look like a rose—not an open rose, but a bud about to open—"

I decided then and there he should be a poet. Eventually he grew to be a top insurance man, and that probably was just as suitable. For it surely takes imagination to sell people the idea of spending money on things that haven't yet happened, just in case they *might* happen!

Every season has its own glory in New England, for every month has its separate identity, different personality. October is the dramatic month, everyone knows about autumn in New England. More and more tourists come during October and eager travelers stop all along the roads taking dozens of pictures.

The air is cool as an old coin teaspoon, and a faint tang of blue woodsmoke spices the wind. The color of the great sugar maples is so dazzling it seems I must have dreamed it. The maples give forth light, like closer suns. The oaks glow with a garnet fire, and all the thickets blaze with scarlets and pale gold and cinnamon. It is like the music of a trumpet.

After the black frost, a few flowers bloom again, spikes of goldenrod gleam by a split-rail fence, a spray of hardy clematis shines white in the garden, and now and then one finds a rose, smelling of summer and warmth.

Poking around in the vegetable garden, Jill always unearths some tomatoes which have been sheltered by ragged growths of weeds. She says it is a lesson not to weed too much in late summer. Broccoli is still there, and of course the cabbage and acorn squash and carrots go on happily. The chard tends to toughen, bracing for more cold weather, but is still edible. Some lettuce can be had, but most of it is gone.

I note that we appreciate more the few leftovers in the garden than we do the riotous plenty of summer. Perhaps there is a lesson in this!

It seems very exciting to get a whole series of meals from the vegetable patch after we should be done with it. Treasure hunters must have the same emotion when they find a small horde of greeny gold coins long after the main treasure is lifted.

One year when the black frost was brief and followed by days of mellow sun, I went a little mad. I decided to save everything there was to save. Racks of dill and sage and apple mint went in and out of the oven all day, celery tops hung in the woodshed, tarragon (that year we did have some) steeped in vinegar. Crocks of sauerkraut went down, relishes simmered on the old black range in the back kitchen. Green tomato pickles filled the shelves in the fruit cellar and catsup just went on endlessly.

In the end, Jill said, "I am not going to bring in a single thing more. Fun is fun, but we are never going to live long enough to use up all this stuff and if one more broccoli head comes or a single pepper more develops, well, let it." She said darkly, "remember you and the pepper year!"

I remembered. That was the year we were shopping in Waterbury and while Jill did some business, I happened to wander into one of those happy Italian grocery stores. By the time she got back to the car, the whole back seat was filled with baskets of scarlet and green peppers.

"A bargain," I said, waving at them.

"Yes?" she said coolly.

"The man said by the bushel he could give me such a re--duction—I forget how much but it was fabulous—and they are lovely peppers," I said breathlessly.

They were lovely peppers all right. And, as I pointed out, sweet pepper relish is a real treat. We seeded and chopped and chopped and seeded far into the night. The next morning we seeded and chopped again. We also ate stuffed peppers for four days, stuffed with rice, stuffed with tuna fish, stuffed with chili, stuffed with shrimp. We ate some sliced thin and broiled in butter—and this is a much underrated vegetable, by the way.

Our right arms were stiff as ham bones before we finished and the house was absolutely drowned in the odor of peppers.

It was three years, I think, before the last of that bout was done with, and we haven't made pepper relish since. A pity, too, as nothing is better with cold sliced meat than pepper relish. The red and the emerald make such a pretty accompaniment and the spicy peppery flavor is so good.

Jill's final comment was, "I sometimes forget how much you are like your father. Remember the bananas?"

This referred to the time Papa thought if a few bananas were good, why not buy a whole bunch and he did. I have never felt quite the same devotion to bananas since. For no family can keep up with a rising tide of ripening bananas even if they eat all day and all night and eat exclusively bananas.

Now is the time to go out to the woods for butternuts and hickory nuts and hazelnuts. The upper pastures are grey-green and tranquil, the deciduous trees flame against a sky as soft as the breasts of a dove. The old greystone ledges are warm, the light is golden on the fallen burrs. The butternuts are dark and sticky, the hickory nuts have a green plastic case, and underneath are smooth as ivory. The hazelnuts are fringed with cinnamon on the outer case and have an exquisite tri-cornered shape.

George's cows stand in pleasant aimlessness in the driftway as we go by. A big buck rabbit goes lippety lippety into the thicket. A wandering country cat pauses to eye us soberly, then sleeks away on her own serious business.

We carry old gunnysacks and we fill them, it is impossible to stop when the treasure is there for the gathering. Midway we sit on a big rock that is frosted over with lichen and eat our ham and cheese sandwiches and drink the hot coffee from the thermos. Even as we eat, nuts plop down, surely bigger and better than any we have yet gathered! The squirrels have been at work too, many of the nuts are only shells by now.

Staggering under the weight of the sacks, we finally come home, feeling we have done a very worthwhile thing. Never mind that we never do get all the nuts shelled. We crack some with a flatiron on the hearthstone, but we never really get to them all. I surmise it is more fun to adventure in the autumn woods than to dig out the tiny meats afterward with a pick.

Cracking and shelling butternuts takes real devotion. I get as far as one butternut cake—what could be more delicious—and then I decide to wait. The nuts can season. As for the hickory nuts, it would take a freight-car load to make a decent amount of meats. Hazelnuts shell easier, and are possibly more rewarding.

We used to have black walnuts too, but the black walnut tree was a victim of an early hurricane and is just a memory now.

After all, I think, as I sweep up the shells and nurse my bruised thumb and measure a half cupful of nutmeats, it is the joy of the gathering that is important, rather than the end product!

Last year a former resident of Stillmeadow came to call—her grandfather had farmed it here in the early days. She said she used to crack butternuts in the attic with the cousins every autumn. I liked the idea of the children up in the little attic with the sloping roof, cracking butternuts and having fun. Just as I like the idea that the minister who lived here seventy years ago had services in what is now my bedroom and the little reed organ stood where my bed now is. This should give me quiet nights, I think, with echoes of old hymn tunes floating in the air.

There is always one moment in a day when I think my heart will break. Such a moment I think all women have, and men too, when all the meaning of life seems distilled and caught up and you feel you can never, never bear to leave it. It may be when you turn and look down a blazing autumn road or it may be when you see your house under great ancient trees or it may be, in the city, when you look up at a towering apartment building and see one light and think "that is mine." It may be any one of a number of things, according to the circumstances of your life.

But there is the moment, and all the heartaches and sorrows of your life suddenly diminish and only the fine brave things stand out. You breathe sharp clean air, your eyes lift to the eternal wideness of the sky.

Anybody has moments like this to store up, but some people are too busy adding up their frustrations to appreciate them. And yet all we need is an awareness of the beauty in life to make us richly content. My definition of happiness is just the ability to garner the perfect moments.

Holly, like most Irish, has eternal charm. Never a morning but that George reports some special feat she has performed while he was in the kennel and she was helping him do the chores. "That Holly," he says, "she is smarter than a fox."

She goes in the kennel, flag waving, and eats a second breakfast. Then she comes back out with him as he fills the oil heater for the back kitchen stove. Then she inspects the bird feeders, for we always keep them full summer, winter, spring and autumn. If there is any stray suet or bread, she nips it up. George came in laughing this morning and said, "that Holly. She went quiet and still to the feeder and tuck out all the bread. She just slipped up."

"If you ever find that dog missing," says the plumber, "I got her. I never did see such a dog."

It is curious that a wayward and difficult Irish could so charm the world but so it is. If Jill takes her to the store, she stops traffic. When we drive around, people crane their necks and get fatuous smiles on their faces just looking at her.

And when she ate half the new soft fedora of the accountant who had come to balance the books, he only smiled and said, "oh well, I know—it doesn't matter, I can get a new hat!"

The universal appeal of a regal Irish is a strange thing to contemplate. When Holly collapses on the bed, she uses up over half of it, unlike the neat small curl-up of a cocker. When she strews oddments of paper and garbage all over, having stood on her elbows and nipped up the garbage container, we only sigh and sweep up after her. If we try to get her to do something she feels she doesn't care to do at that moment, she cannot even stand up.

When she was shut in briefly while we went to a party she was not invited to, she just chewed up the fence and got out. And instead of everybody being outraged, the general expression was, "well, isn't she the clever one—she didn't want to be shut in!"

I do not pretend to interpret this curious situation. We

have had three Irish. We had Maeve, the great Irish, we had Daphne whom we took to save from being put away because she had been abused and was incredibly wild and manic at first. And we have Hollyberry Red.

And even as she utters her high curious squeal if we leave her for five minutes, we get that *look*. "Isn't she a darling," we say.

The relation of man and dog is a longtime thing. From the first days when the dog moved into the circle of firelight as the cave man tossed him a bone, from the time the dog hunted with him, there has been a bond. Without dogs, man would have had a hard time.

In the beginning it was a working partnership. Dogs were better hunters and men had clubs or stone weapons. Men could build a fire and the heat felt good. From there it was a step to the dog lying at the mouth of the cave and guarding the man.

There must be some dim racial memory of those early times in most dogs, for they are happiest when working with their humans. Few dogs enjoy being idle, and most dogs like to use their intelligence. One has only to watch a trained tracking dog to see pure joy made tangible.

And in the Obedience rings, dog and handler are often overcome with their success. I have seen strong and reserved men break into tears after Roger has made a 200 score out of a possible 200. And Roger practically carries his handler out of the ring.

Putting the garden to bed is a satisfying chore. Burning old canes, carrying the cornstalks to be burned, pruning and tidying the border and raking leaves are all sound pursuits. Planting of bulbs goes on until the ground freezes, we always have some left over that do not get in, but that is partly because wherever Jill plants one bulb a whole clump comes out that needs to be separated and replanted.

"I wonder whether it's worth it," she says, "when I plant fifty and come back in with a hundred and fifty."

The mortality of bulbs is terrific too for the little ground mole is a murderer. One year we lost a whole stand of my favorite white daffodils, the King Alfred. And all the remedies are a nuisance. Poison I am afraid of, for who can be sure no cocker or Irish will not someday just once catch a mole? And who knows— Pouring old oil in the runs means all the dogs will come in the house looking like abandoned oilwells. Gassing the runs might be best, but it would be rather like the teacup and ocean business. And when we set mole traps, they never seem to be set in the place the mole is currently using.

All the dogs keep at it, however, which is why we never let anyone walk in the yard at night without a flashlight. Ed fills the tunnels weekly and reseeds all summer long and runs the roller over the humps. But as he says, the dogs are just trying to be helpful!

George brings in a load of wood for the fireplace now and stacks it in the barn. The smell of cut wood is delightful. This has been seasoning, so the ends of the logs have a soft greyish look. George cuts it on his land, or on ours according to where old trees have fallen or need clearing out.

His hired man, Jake drives the old truck, which should not run at all, but miraculously keeps on lumbering along. George stands on top of the load, and were I an artist, I should draw him so, broad-shouldered, slim-hipped, slightly stooped as most heavy-duty farmers are, his blue eyes are shining and he is smiling, as he usually is. I have never known such a disposition as George has. Overworked since twelve and with never a day off since we have known him, using old patched-up equipment, and running the big farm with one hired man, he is always cheerful.

This farmer's stoop, I think, is not entirely from too much heavy work, but somehow also has an overtone of the farmer's relation to the earth, he and the earth have a kinship, and he naturally bends a little toward it.

When the wood is stacked, George brings in an armful for the fire that night. This armful would almost fill a station wagon. I do not know how many pounds he could lift, I know his older brother once lifted 300, and George is just as strong.

When he splits kindling, it is an art. Not an unnecessary movement, just a swift rise and fall and the axe never a half inch from the mark. Now and then we have guests who split some and it is a revelation to see just how a typical city man splits wood. Usually he jumps on one end of the piece and smashes the axe down like a flail. This naturally sends the split part flying in the air, he ducks, if he is quick enough, if not he takes a neat wallop. He may then use both hands and whang the axe down in the middle of the wood. This gets nowhere at all, a few chips may rise, but that is all. Finally, in desperation, he will bang the axe on the end of the log, burying the blade in so deeply that when he tries to lift the axe, the wood comes right up in the air with it, the whole slab melded with the axe.

Sweating heavily, bruised and worn out, our city man comes in with a handful of chewed-up twisted bits which he deposits valiantly in the fireplace. We hand him a frosty drink and admire him no end.

One of the most difficult of country skills, it seems to me, is scything. When an expert scythes the long grass, the movement is poetry, beautiful is the sweep of the shining blade, lovely the angle of the body as the scyther swings easily.

The waves of pale green grass fall behind like green silvery combers.

And the scythe itself is such a traditional implement, it suggests far-off antique days.

Jill was determined to master this art when we moved to the country and she has become a fair scyther. Her first efforts were hampered by the fact that the grass, she said, did not cut, it just bent back, and after she swung on, there it was, strong as ever. I told her she better leave it for George —this seems to be my themesong always. But she said she purely admired scything and she saw no reason why since she had once been a champion golfer, she couldn't swing a blade on a stick.

Part of our early struggles were to achieve the respect of the countryfolk. From the day George told someone who asked about me "well, she works mostly with her head," we were determined to be accepted as equals in the end. And when the coal-and-feed man handed out a bag of fertilizer and drawled, "I suppose you don't know how to use this," Jill gave him a level look out of her grey-blue eyes and said, "if not, we'll learn."

Our first painting jobs were pretty sketchy, but when George said, "looks pretty good," we felt like professionals.

We also hung wallpaper and this, for my money, is the meanest task in the whole category. The minute you spread the paste on a length, it swings around and glues itself together all on its own. When you try to open it out, half of it slaps you in the face. And it may have seemed very tough while you were laboriously trimming off the trademarks for hours, but once it has been introduced to the paste, it tears in a jiffy.

After you climb up with a swatch of it draped over your arms and get the top part attached to the wall instead of (a) to itself (b) to you, you leap down and try to smooth out the lumps and bubbles and wrinkles. After which, you discover you made a slight error in your calculations and this piece doesn't fit there anyway. It was the piece that was supposed to go under the windows.

The paste itself is no mean adversary either. It is too thin, it is too thick. If you sit down to rest a moment, it turns into a gummy gob. It has, in so doing, sucked the wallpaper brush down in.

Further, every three minutes, you stop and wash up. If you don't the outside and inside of the paper will be equally covered with paste. I should never want to be gainfully employed as a paperhanger.

And it looks so easy when a professional does it.

One major lesson countrydwellers learn is to make do with what's at hand. It is just too far to drive to the nearest town, if one did that, one would be driving most of the time. If a screw is too long, we cut it off. If the curtain rod falls apart, we get out the adhesive. If a bed collapses, we wire it together pending the acquisition of angle irons.

In the food department, we keep extra supplies of butter and bread in the Deep Freeze, extra canned goods on an emergency shelf, and if we run out of something, we use something else.

In October we like to go to Cape Cod for a few days to walk the great shining beaches, drive along the dune roads, and watch the moon over the old unquiet ocean. I love the Cape any time, but especially out of season.

The natives have such a relaxed and happy air. They need the summer people for a living, and they know it, but oh what a relief to get their narrow land back again! Now the cranberry bogs are a garnet red, the scrub oaks along the roads are a deep purple-rosy color, and all the colors there are lie in the wet sands as the tide recedes.

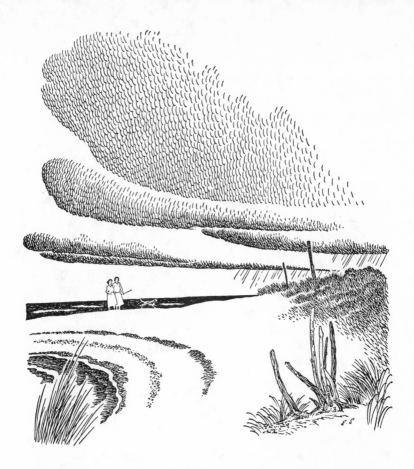

The gulls go over and drift on the bosom of the air and cry their piercing lovely cry. The little boats are asleep in the harbors, waiting for the tides of spring to come again. And the air smells so strongly of pine and salt that it is a wave of beauty in itself.

Colors are all intense on the Cape, possibly the sea is the cause, or the lack of high woodlands. The old weather-worn houses are silver, roses still bloom, the dark red ones against a split-rail fence have a jewel quality.

Alice and Margaret were with us this time, and Glenn and Burton flew in from Ohio. I always admire people who fly so casually. For Burton often phones from Akron at night and says, "how would you like to have me for lunch tomorrow? Or I'll make it by four in the afternoon anyway."

As for Glenn he would rather fly than do anything except sing or fish. He flew one of those early planes put together with bailing wire and loved it.

This time Burton said, "I am bringing your tenor." So I felt sure Glenn was out of voice with a cold or something. He is my tenor at such times, and Burton's tenor when he is singing just right.

Alice and Jill went clamming. I could see their bent busy figures as they raked around in the icy water. There is nothing more fascinating than bringing up those big greyish-purple quahogs, plump and cold and clean. Glenn had not been allowed to bring his tons of fishing tackle since he was supposed to sing his current concert for us, but he found an old bamboo pole in the cottage garage and began fixing it up at once.

Margaret and Burton talked music while keeping an eye on the ardent clammers. I skimmed through the *Cape Codder*, which I dearly love, and was pleased to read the news of this curiously separate little country. I was sorry to hear that Mr. So and so's career was cut short at age eighty-two when he ran into a telephone pole on a rainy night.

The Cape Codders, I believe, think nobody dies on the Cape except by some accident, because of the fish they eat. All the scallops and lobster and clams and striped bass and oysters must do something! But it may also be the relaxing quality in the air, so tensions are less. I notice people tend to move more slowly, to take things as they come. And not to bother about doing anything today which could just as well be undertaken next week. Or some other week, for that matter.

They are certainly not lazy, not at all. The fishermen work long hours in the wildest of weather, the tradespeople struggle with the roaring tide of summer folks. Nevertheless there never seems to be any pressure about anything.

The Cape is packed with history. One of my favorite spots is First Encounter Beach, where the Pilgrims first fought the Indians. What would I give for a look back in time to see just how they looked, those warriors. The beach is empty, the sea grass grown along the dunes, a wild and desolate shore, much as it must have looked then.

The Indians had been minding their own business a long time on this shore, and now these strange stocky men were invading their land. Did they know destiny had a hand on their throats? One wonders.

The clammers came in, with a pailful of clams. The chowder was under way in no time, salt pork diced and browned, onions sliced, potatoes cut up while the clams were ground medium fine in the grinder.

Then the simmering, then the hot cream. Plenty of true chowder crackers split and buttered and warmed. Plenty of coffee.

Later on Glenn sang his concert carrying us away on the magic wings of music to shores as distant as the shores of Spain, and yet as close as the heartbeat.

I like to hear his new songs very much, but I also want all the songs I ever heard him sing, and as Burton points out, that covers a lot of time. He just can't sing everything he has ever sung all at once!

After he finished, Margaret leaned forward and said sharply, "young man, is your voice insured?"

Glenn grinned. "No," he said, "but my outboard motor is!"

Which I felt was a very good summing up of this fisherman who happens to sing like an angel.

After the singing was over, Burton fixed a hot toddy and we were very merry talking the good talk of people at ease.

The tide was coming in, laying a line of dark silver on the sand, a high fall tide, very slow and strong and beautiful. The gulls were crying, and the light over the horizon was mother-of-pearl.

Nights are cold now, twilight is brief. We eat supper by the fire usually, and lean toward such rib-sticking dishes as barbecued spareribs or braised flank steak.

After supper we go out in the yard so the dogs can have a last race in the leaves. The wine-dark air, the luminous maples in the moonlight, and the lesser lantern of the fire shining through the windows of the little white house, these seem newly discovered, newly beautiful. The stars are very bright, they look like apple blossoms on the infinite tree of heaven. The sky, probably because of the cold, has a greater depth. It is like the ocean on a calm quiet night, so deep, so pure. So soft.

I think of Rupert Brooke's lines:

> I shall desire and I shall find
> The best of my desires;
> The autumn road, the mellow wind
> That soothes the darkening shires,
> And laughter, and inn-fires.

I can always substitute hearth fires and it fits so well. As we go in, Especially Me, the blond beautiful son of Jonquil, rushes to the refrigerator and makes hopeful hops by the door. He is a big cocker and is always in the mood for a snack. Jonquil goes directly to the fire and gets so close we fear she will burn up, she is a salamander. No dog we ever had in over twenty years of dog raising has so loved the heat.

"How can you tell the dogs apart?" someone is always and forever asking me.

"Can you tell people apart?" I always ask sweetly.

Now we all settle down, dogs on couches, in chairs, and on beds, each according to protocol. They establish this themselves. But Little Sister gets the other pillow on my bed and everybody accepts this.

Beautiful, dramatic October, I wish it could last for a year!

November

SOME OF THE DAYS IN NOVEMBER
carry the whole memory of summer as a fire opal carries the
color of moonrise. These are the days I especially love, when
the air lies soft and quiet over the dreaming earth; it is a reflective and thoughtful time.

"Season of mists and mellow fruitfulness," Keats called
autumn, "Close bosom-friend of the maturing sun," and so it
is.

Where are the songs of spring? Ay, where are they?
Think not of them, thou hast thy music too,
While barred clouds bloom the soft-dying day
And touch the stubble plains with rosy hue.

After the leaves come down, the countryside has an open
look. New vistas appear, hills unseen when summer's wealth
of green is spread, now stand, blue and hazy, in the distance.
In the cropped fields the browns and copper and smoky tan
make a sober symphony, not as dramatic as the blaze of October but lovely to look at.

We stay outdoors as much as possible for winter will soon
sweep in, and warm air is doubly precious. We like to eat
down by the pond, which mirrors such a pale still sky, and
just a few late-fallen leaves drift on it like upside-down stars.

Then the November rains come, so steady, so determined
and so fearfully grey. It can rain so hard in our valley that it
looks as if a wall of water advanced, you can not see a hand's
length ahead. The sky is pewter. The roads run with water
and the brooks make a thunder down the hill. George's barn-

yard gets flooded and he wades hip-deep with his boots flooded, his oilskins dripping.

This is hard weather for cockers and Irish, particularly for Irish. Holly keeps sloshing in and out, racing around the yard, racing in the house. She reminds me of a child "what can I do now, Mama?" And I wish I could get her interested in a crayon book or cutting out paper dolls.

Sister is very philosophical, she just goes to sleep. I suspect this is an ancient wisdom we would all do well to copy. Work on a fine day, Sister would advise, and when it is a terrible day, rest. Her small black and white cocker figure almost looks like a Staffordshire figurine as she lies so still.

I am reminded of the days when I lived in Virginia and had a very good cook. The day of the dinner party, she did not come. Did not phone. Just did not come. Frantically I basted chickens and made biscuits and went through a great flurry. It wasn't that I couldn't get dinner for ten people, it was just so unexpected!

My neighbor's cook was an interested observer of all this, and I finally said, "Essie, I just can't understand it—"

Her dark eyes were unfathomable as she eyed this odd No'-thener. "Why, Ma'am," she said, "it's rainin'!"

And of course it was raining. Why should I expect Lizzie to come to work if it was raining?

We have been sorting books for part of the fall cleaning. Hundreds of books have been dusted and piled in piles and packed in cartons to be given away to the little library. I find this a great emotional upheaval. Every book was somebody's dream once, the best as well as the worst. Every book represents, I think, dusting away, hours of struggle, anguish, some joy, much pain. For who of us can ever write the book which lies in the secret places of the mind?

I suppose Moses was satisfied with the Ten Commandments because he only copied them down. If he had made them up, he would have fretted over some of them afterward. But most authors know that what comes on the page is a small reflection of all that is in them. That clear dazzling vision never quite gets visible for all who run to read. If I ever met an author who was perfectly satisfied with his book, I would think something was wrong, the man must be quite mad!

Jill said she hoped we were accomplishing something but she did not notice the bookshelves were empty, even after we were through. We did move the books around some, she felt, and certainly all those cartons did have books to the top in every one—but why were all the bookshelves still bursting? This didn't surprise me at all, for every time I clean out a closet or a bureau drawer, it is always fuller when I finish.

There are many wonderful books which are fine to read, but there are very few that are better reread, and still fewer that should be reread every year. For one Thoreau there is a mort of best-selling books, ephemeral as mayflies.

For me, the test is, can I bear *not* to read this again? A fine book is like a mine. You get down strata after strata until the very deep lode is reached. This takes time and thought and isn't a business of skipping through once. On the other hand, a book may be pleasant as a shallow running stream and still well worth reading. But the ones to keep, to carry with one wherever one goes—these are precious cargo.

And taste is such a highly individual matter—even near and dearly beloveds can absolutely despise some book you are passionate about. It must, I think, take great courage to be a publisher.

For a publisher must measure—must weigh the book and at once juggle financial prospects with values to literature. An unread masterpiece butters nobody's bread. But imagine being the first to publish a romantic drama that seems moving and then turn out to have printed *Romeo and Juliet!*

Most writers I know are ambivalent. They would, on the one hand, like to write a masterpiece that nobody would ever buy, on the other hand such pleasing and understandable stuff that millions would rush to the bookstalls. This is a serious quandary.

If you are great enough a genius, this is not a problem. But you must be a Shakespeare to be at once loved by the masses and reverenced by the erudite. Only the really great reach all levels, which means to be universal.

Thanksgiving is gay with massed greens in the big copper bowl, with harvest vegetables piled in the old wooden dough tray, with red corn hanging against the mellow pine by the fireplace. Apples and raisins and nuts brim the bowls on the coffee table by the fire, the cheese board is decked forth with pale Swiss, bright Cheddar and creamy Port Salut.

Jill blisters her fingers on the chestnuts for the dressing for the plump turkey, but decides chestnut stuffing is worth it. When the turkey roasts, the savory smell of sage and chestnuts drifts from the kitchen and the onions glazing in honey and catsup add their fragrance.

The children are all at home for the week end, plus Jill's exquisite granddaughter, rosy and sweet as a young apple blossom. She is now over a year old, and busily absorbing every detail of this strange and wonderful world. We naturally see signs of very surprising genius in her every gesture, and I am reminded of that doting mamma who kept saying "look at my baby breathe!"

Well, it is pretty wonderful to breathe, at that.

The children sit quietly while I talk over with God what blessings we have, but I note they lift knife and fork the instant I raise my head. They are, I reflect comfortably, just as hungry now as they were when they were very little, and went out after dinner in bunny suits.

A family holiday, such as this, gives one a chance to estimate the changes in the children. As we pass the plates heaped with the crisply crackling turkey, mellow and delicate under the skin and golden brown on top—the conversation seems like a montage of their lives.

That serious young interne, surely only yesterday he was asking, "who is the leader of the stars?" The gay young mother, yes, she was the very one who fell off her bicycle and flew through the air a mile a minute. And Connie, as she relates some riotous happenings in her class at Columbia, must be the same little girl that came home from kindergarten and said, "Mama, T. J. kissed me. You know he's the one with the lavender up-top."

Sometimes one wishes they were little again, yet on the whole I think it is so rewarding to know them as equals that I would really wish the romper days back. Every mother must feel that occasional ache for her child's baby days and in retrospect even pushing spinach through a sieve seems fun. Nowadays, I think a baby would be no bother at all. Everything is puréed before you get it and what bliss! Disposable diapers or diaper services, nylon, dacron, orlon and what-not to wear that irons itself as you shake it out, whole meals from soup to nuts in little sterile jars—what a change.

As I was pondering this, however, it came to me that Jill's daughter spends all the time there is on the baby, and Papa's time is added to it when he is at home. This is a mystery. For all that timesaving seems to have gotten them exactly nowhere!

When the baby naps, they wash things, mix things, collect and wash toys, shake blankets. Get the medicine dropper ready for those miracle drops. And run up and down stairs every five minutes just to *be sure* she is not too warm or too cold.

So I finally decide things haven't really changed so much. A baby is a time-consuming affair even now.

I think on the whole I am glad I brought Connie up just as things went along. Now there are so many experts to consult, so many books to look things up in, it is dizzying. Parents watch like hawks to be sure the baby begins to crawl when he or she should, grasps things at the right moment, speaks in the right time, shows timidity at the correct age, shows stubbornness at the certain period he should. It keeps them on edge all the time, lest their own particular piece of heaven should fail Dr. Spock or some other great authority. I was spared this, for I never even knew at what age my child was supposed to be standing erect and saying Da Da. I wasn't alarmed that she first said "Abach," which translated into zweibach which she really adored. I just kept on taking things as they came, and confining all my worries to blankets and mittens and socks and bonnets, and at that, I worried enough.

After Thanksgiving dinner, the house simmers down to quiet. It seems cosy and natural to hear muted voices from all over, the baby upstairs waking up, Connie and Don talking, Don's wife tuning the guitar and humming. With all the food around, I reflect comfortably, we won't need to get another sit-down meal, they can raid.

Naturally in a very few hours, there is a kind of stir.

"When are we going to eat?"

"Is it almost supper time?"

"Mind if I eat a little more chestnut stuffing?"

It is very much as it was on Christmas when I said to Jill, "we can have the leftover turkey tomorrow," and she said, "what turkey?"

It turns out there is just enough to slice thin and have cold, plus extra dressing, and reinforced with a casserole of home-baked beans nobody perishes of starvation.

"And all of them as thin as pencils," I mourn afterward, "it just isn't fair! They can just eat alarmingly and never gain an ounce. Whereas I—no, no justice at all."

Thanksgiving is far more than the family dinner and national festival. I know all people have always had harvest celebrations of one kind or another, so there is nothing distinctive about a feast time after the crops are in. But our Thanksgiving seems very close to our relation with God. It has a deep religious significance not always spoken of, but I, think, felt.

I like to slip away for a brief time and sit by the pond on the one bench left out all winter. If it is a warm hazy day, the sun is slanting over the hill with a gentle glow. If it is cold, the wind walks in the woods. I think of everything I have to be thankful for, and it is a long list by the time it is added up. I am thankful for love, and friends, and the family gathering together. For starlight over the old apple orchard. For the chilly sweetness of peepers in April. For my winter birds, so brave, so hungry, particularly for my little chickadee with the bent wing that bangs away at the suet cake right while I type. He cocks a shining eye at me and seems to say, "life is really what you make of it, eh?"

I am thankful for music and books. And for the dogs bark-

ing at the gate. Well, there are so many things to be thankful
for that the list is infinitely long.

And it is good to take time to be thankful, for it is all too
easy to let the world's trouble sweep over one in a dark flood
and to fall into despair.

Reading Leon Whitney's *Complete Book of Cat Care* reminded me once more of the cats I have known and their
importance in my life.

I was very small when I brought home a brown paper sack
of kittens which someone had tossed in an alley. This was,
perhaps, my first introduction to cruelty and it was a bitter
one.

The tiny weak kittens were half-frozen, they were too
small to live, but Mama when she saw the anguish in my eyes,
allowed me to try to save them.

How I worked. I gave up playing with my friends, I kept warm soft cloths in an old shoe box, constantly re-heating them. I feverishly fed the kittens with a medicine dropper and warm milk. Drop by drop, I fed them.

In those days, nobody knew anything about formulas for unweaned animals. And in our little town the only veterinarian was a big bluff cow doctor.

I rather doubt if even Leon Whitney could have saved these particular tiny grey morsels, since they had been chilled as well as tossed away. But my sheer will kept them alive for several days, I am convinced of that.

Father was definitely not a cat man. His feeling for dogs was highly individual, too. On the big farm where he was raised there were dozens of cats and half-a-dozen English setters and a mongrel or too but everybody was pretty casual about them. They came and went as they pleased, the cats raised their families in the huge barn and aside from having pans of warm fresh milk set out for them, shifted for themselves. Father and the three other boys hunted with their favorite old pointer because this dog was always around, tagging along.

So although he was a highly sentimental man, he did not feel animals should be around inside a house. When we got Timmy, our first fine Irish, Father was a lost man, however. For although he built a dog house for Timmy large enough to house a horse, somehow Timmy never did spend a night in it, or even part of a day.

Timmy was Irish. So he just came on in the house and that settled it for everybody. By the time he died, at fifteen, Father conceded he was quite a dog. In fact, he would never have another, and felt I was highly disloyal to Timmy to think of having a single other dog ever. He buried Timmy under a hawthorne and planted flowers on the grave, and wandered around the house in a white fury for days.

A paper bag of alley kittens was his idea of a complete waste of time.

But when he saw how I grieved he brought home a pair of healthy grey kittens the right age to leave home and mother. I loved them dearly, but the ache in my heart persisted for a long time for the little abandoned babies. Mama couldn't explain to me just how people could be so cruel, either.

The cat is the only domestic animal that can support himself alone, in city or country. The alley cat in the city moves silently in the darkened areas, fishing out food from garbage cans, sometimes turning over a bottle of milk on a brownstone doorstep and batting the cover off with an agile paw. He is expert at keeping out of harm's way, and a mother alley cat will fight to the death to protect her kittens, housed in some old barrel or carton in a dingy back street.

In the country, alley cats are called strays. They can live in the woods indefinitely, catching mice and small rodents like rabbits, or fishing in the brooks. They sleep in old stone walls. This is a hard life, and one is amazed at the intelligence required to wrest a living in the cold winter and hot summer.

Cats are terribly clean animals. A cat may refuse to eat if the food is messy or the dish not clean. Even the alley cat fishing in the garbage can, picks out a bit and delicately cleans herself afterward, washing industriously. And most house cats will go into a fury if their boxes are not changed often enough.

The Egyptians called the cat Mau, and made him a god. Anybody who killed a cat in those days could be put to death. Cats could not be taken from Egypt but soldiers were asked to bring back cats from invaded countries. Later the Greeks sent spies to steal cats, for their granaries were being devoured by rats.

In Wales, in early days, cats were valued at a penny when kittens, twopence when their eyes were open, and fourpence when they became mousers. Since a penny then was as much as a dollar these days, cats were certainly worth their salt!

Mohammed was a cat-lover, I am glad to say. When his cat was sleeping on his robe, the story goes, Mohammed cut off the hem rather than disturb the cat!

But the most surprising cat tale is that when gold was discovered in California in 1849, rats and mice nearly ate up everything in the little shacks men lived in. A shipload of cats, a hundred cats, they say, landed in San Francisco, and the cats sold for ten to twenty dollars apiece.

When I see a country cat bounding along the roadside at twilight, I think of the long history of cats, and wonder if this wandering wayfarer has any idea of her regal ancestry. The proud carriage of tail and head would suggest it, and the thoughtful arrogant eye she turns on me as I slow down.

"Good hunting, Pussy," I say, and go slowly down the road.

Advice to women continues to be handed out largely by magazines and books. We seem to be in an orgy of confessions and case histories. Can my marriage be preserved?; what is wrong with my husband?; whom shall I marry?; I have a jealous husband; I have a stingy husband—my husband does not speak to me for weeks at a time, what shall I do?

I have a secret feeling we do too much of this kind of thing. I especially deplore grading one's mate. I can always imagine a reasonably happy little woman getting a list and grading her husband and finding he flunked the test flatly! What, I ask, is going to happen to *that* marriage?

Marriage is a pretty individual affair and I doubt whether it can be push-buttoned successfully. Possibly I am just old-fashioned, but, like John Crosby, I cannot care too much if Mrs. A and Mr. B are one way or another about each other. I would feel it their business, not mine.

I wonder whether this preoccupation with personal relationships has spread over into private lives from the Hollywood stars' on-again-off-again marriages? If so, it is a pity we do not let the Hollywood great have a little privacy in their lives off the screen. I am sure they would be grateful. They might even be more tranquil if people did not dodge after them every time they stepped from their front doors.

Barbara and Ed Shenton stopped by on their way to Maine to visit their son at Colby, and we sat late by the fire catching up on the events at Sugarbridge and Stillmeadow. There are friends one sees seldom between whom that delicate fine thread never breaks. With Barbara and Ed, they climb out of the car and come in, and it is as if we had all been together right along, and it may be months have passed with just letters and cards.

Much of the time, we talk at once, that is Barbara and I do, picking up the tag ends of each other's sentences as our minds race ahead. Ed sits relaxed and thoughtful, adding a bit of his dry wit here and there as needed. I wish I were a painter, as both of them are, to capture Barbara's shy slim elusive charm and Ed's darkly intelligent face. Ed is always modest, and considers himself a homely man, but he is the kind of man that can't walk down the streets without turning the head of everyone who passes. I often think he should pose for the Man of Distinction.

Barbara is a quick and sensitive person, observing every detail about her while not seeming to notice anything at all. This is an endearing quality, for long afterward, she will make some comment on a bouquet that was on her bedside table, describing every flower and the way she felt about it. She is a gourmet cook, but never makes one feel uncomfortable about any kind of meal tossed together in a hurry.

When we are all together, Jill sits quietly. She says with three verbal people in the room, she feels her place is to listen.

Jill can always take conversation or leave it. She can talk, if need be, as well as anybody I ever knew, but she never talks if anybody else takes over. Her ego never seems to need inflating by adding a bon mot to a flashing conversation.

Now and then I have been cross after a party and said, "you didn't say a thing!"

"Well," she will answer, "there was no need."

Once or twice when I have been knocked out for one reason or another and company was coming, I have said, "I just can't talk now."

And then I am amazed at how she takes over, stimulating people, keeping the conversation going, quite as if the social whirl was her favorite métier.

But unless it is necessary, she will just listen and give me her comments on the various guests after the day is over and we are having a last cracker-and-cheese snack before going to bed.

Most women, I think, need to feel a kind of security by shining in public, whether it be at a church supper or a literary cocktail party. But Jill never.

It may stem from her complete lack of the competitive spirit. When she was a champion golfer, she never could get worked up over beating other people. She wanted her game to be good, and that was all. In dog shows, she has always wanted the dogs to do a fine job, but whether anybody else goes over them is a small affair.

The one exception was when Maeve was to take her tracking test. At this point, Jill was as feverish as the next one, and bound her darling should get over that course better and faster than any dog ever had. I was glad Maeve did make a record for Maeve couldn't possibly realize how astounding it was that her handler had these unusual emotions!

My own competitive spirit is very jumpy. I rather like to fancy that I can catch a fish faster than anyone else in the boat, that I have fish "it." And I like to think I have a nice way with meats. I also like to think I can get along with people, and this may be my undoing, for nobody can always get along with everybody!

I get so easily crushed if anyone is rude to me. I have been so blessed, they seldom are. But I shall never forget the incident of the slip, when I lived in New York on almost nothing and had bought a slip at a little dress shop around the corner and it was definitely defective and I took it back. The salesgirl, slick and shiny, gave me the look of a haddock and said, "Madame, you never bought this here." I crept out and went sadly home. Tossed the slip in the trashbin.

My other great incident was at a dog show, when Sister and I were about to go to top Utility dog in the show. Sister just blew up, that is all I can say, and as I walked out of the ring, I gave her a small slap on her plump rear and said, "Oh, shame on you Sister."

I overheard a woman at the ringside say, "well, that is what I don't like about shows, the way they abuse poor innocent little dogs!"

Sister of course rode home in my lap, had her scrambled eggs when we got in, snuggled down on the other pillow on my bed, and thought nothing of it. But I remembered it. I made imaginary conversations with this spectator for hours. I told her of the hours and hours Sister and I had worked, of the hot suns and sifting snows, and of Sister's place as top person in the household. "Well, she could have for *five minutes* done that little exercise," I finished, "and that is it."

Sister just snuggled closer and indicated I better quiet down, I was making her *nervous*.

Around the first week in November, we realize that Christmas is imminent. We begin making lists, worrying over sizes. I am determined to get a small portable electric oven for Connie whose gas stove blows up every time she turns it on. I know she sits with one hand on the oven door as she roasts something, just to be sure. But how do I know the current in her old apartment house will support this gadget? I read the ads, they never give the wattage or whatever.

Jill goes around dreamily saying, "I wonder if they would really be able to use an electric frying pan?"

We have done better since we devised the Christmas chest. This is a pine blanket chest which we emptied of all the old linens and silver stored away. In it we put things which we suddenly find are *just* what we wish to give for Christmas.

The idea did not originate with us, it is Faith Baldwin's for she spends all year buying Christmas gifts. She will send a cryptic note in mid August saying "I found your Xmas gift—did it up."

This gives one a long time to wonder, but is a very sound way to operate.

Between Thanksgiving and Christmas a country family is busy. The house must be sparkling clean, this always involves repainting some woodwork, washing some curtains. Freezing some extra desserts.

And washing and grooming all the dogs, although just why this must go on between Thanksgiving and Christmas, I do not know. We feel it must.

Jill drove over to the Whitney Clinic yesterday to get some medicine for Linda. In the waiting-room, a big burly man was sitting with a bright pink bath towel over his arm. He looked up and spoke immediately, which most people do at the Whitneys'. The common bond of ailing animals keeps everyone friendly.

This man told Jill right away that he was a very tough guy. He had brought in his parakeet, but he wanted to say right then and there that if the bird couldn't be fixed up, well, put it to sleep, he said, scowling ferociously.

"What is wrong with him?" asked Jill sympathetically.

"Well, the cat took him outdoors," he said, shrugging his shoulders. "And it was five hours before we got him back.

And it was so cold. I guess one leg is broken anyhow." He went on glaring at the floor.

When Mrs. Whitney came in from the treatment room, she gave one look at this tough guy, and her beautiful eyes were gentle.

"No hope?" he said gruffly.

"Well," said Kate, "why don't you leave him with us and we'll just keep trying and do all we can—and then I'll give you a ring."

The tough guy mumbled something and went out with his bath towel.

Now this was, after all, a bird. But the Whitneys knew it was a very special bird to this man, they understood perfectly.

When Dr. Leon or his son George reaches out for a sick dog or cat, there is a sudden feeling on the part of the desperate owner that everything must be all right.

There is, I think, a special intangible quality a fine doctor has which is above and beyond his brains, or his training. It is something in the air when he walks up to a patient. A breath of hope and a renewal of faith seems to come.

Reading an article recently about hobbies, I wondered whether I am not just all hobbies! This was a disconcerting thought. And would I put cooking first? Collecting milk glass? Folk songs? Flower arranging? Just what is a hobby anyway? Well, I rushed to the dictionary and found out it is a small Old World falcon.

One can always depend on the dictionary for a surprise. It was formerly flown at such game as larks.

Reading further, I found it is a small or medium-sized horse. Hobbyhorse must come from that.

Finally I came down to a favorite occupation, topic, etc., pursued for amusement.

Well, my favorite occupation actually is writing, writing

almost anything. If I have no ideas for stories or books, I write letters like mad, or poems which I can toss afterward. Or just little notes to myself with observations such as "the chickadee's neckpiece is three-cornered, it is a cravat of jet silk." Or "the single birch in the swamp is like a pencil of moonlight."

But could one say I pursue it for amusement? Not at all. For writing is not an amusement, it is work. It takes just about all you have got all the time. No, not a hobby.

It is very often painful when the lovely images in the mind will not compose themselves into even reasonable facsimiles, in words. It can be so painful that I long to throw the typewriter out of the window and scrub floors all day. With a floor, I feel, you can see progress, you get somewhere.

Books and music cannot be hobbies. They are half my life and cannot be categorized as pursued for amusement.

Then how about dogs? Neither Little Sister nor Holly would thank me for suggesting that having dogs is a hobby. Over the years, reviewers and interviewers on radio and such have rather typed me as a woman with dogs and cooking and gardens as hobbies. But I never read such comments to the dogs. Raising puppies may be my favorite occupation but is a serious one, nothing slight about it.

Just possibly birds could be a hobby. But the relationship between me and the birds is a deep and profound thing. I do not feed and cherish them just so they amuse me, not at all. I heartily respect and admire them, and appreciate their beauty but they are much too wonderful and mysterious to be anybody's mere hobby.

A hobby, one feels, should be a light thing, a sometime affair. And viewed in that light, I decide I have only had one hobby in my life, for even cooking is far from a hobby, it is a life-time work.

My hobby, and this is obvious when analyzed, was doing jigsaw puzzles. There was a time when I had one set up all the time on a small table and every time I had a few minutes, I would go and try to fit in an odd piece of blue which should be sky and wasn't.

As for Jill, photography is not her hobby, but her vocation. Gardening is her job. Obedience training is a serious field in which she pursues her way, in snow, in rain, in hot sun.

Building furniture and re-doing antiques might qualify for her—not always amusement, however, often to get us some furniture.

So that leaves her with detective stories and me with my one-time jigsaws. I think we should really establish hobbies for ourselves, on thinking this problem over. Like making ceramics or painting on glass.

Scrabble is a good hobby, for playing with words is always fun. But I always wish it were arranged so that one could save up and make really fine elegant words instead of short plain ones. Mostly when we have played it we are reduced to cat and cow and save and lion and such. Once I made glebe and once I made quoin and I felt elated.

There is no doubt but that everyone needs a real hobby, something special and interesting, and pursued for amusement. It eases the stresses and strains of our competitive living, and also it increases the interest in something other than the daily grind. People are more fun to be with, if they have a lively hobby. It sparks their conversation.

China-painting was the main hobby when I was a child. Mama would sit up late at night in order to get the gold leaf on the last butterplate. She had a fine sense of color and design and her china pieces were not emblazoned with roses and pine cones and such. The only time she let herself go was on a salad bowl which had nasturtiums on the rim.

My aunts, I remember, went in for burned-wood glove boxes and cuff-link boxes and trays. The designs were burned onto the hapless soft wood with a long, pointed metal tool. Fearful were the results, but highly prized.

Almost every woman did needlepoint, chair seats and fire-screens and pillow covers. Embroidery was about to go out, but some of the Clio Club ladies did luncheon sets with such fine embroidery on them that you could hardly see the stitches without a magnifying glass.

And a drawn-work tablecloth was what Mama used for entertaining the college president. With the gold mono-grammed eggshell dinner set and the heavy antique goblets, the table was, I thought, elegant. Although I was always more interested in what went on the huge oval platter and into the covered vegetable dishes. I used to hope for the chicken with fluffy parsley dumplings, the asparagus with lemon butter and the Parker House rolls. With maple parfait in the tall parfait cups for dessert.

When Mama had a formal dinner, I had to wait on the table. Mrs. Novak would come and help with the dishes and mash potatoes and keep rolls piping and so on, but she would never, never enter the dining room to pass anything. It made her nervous. She was devoted to Mama, they were dear friends, but she drew the line at serving.

"Not that," she said fearfully, "just not that."

So I had a good deal of training as a waitress!

Since I never could bear to sit still very long, it worked out very well. I could always pop out to the kitchen for more currant jelly and have a chance to stretch myself.

As the season turns toward December, we are settling in. The woodpile high, the freezer filled, heaters ready to be lit in the kennels, snow tires on, we can face the world with a smile.

Now and then I get a yearning for a tropic isle with ivory or coral reefs and emerald seas foaming and a beach of beaten silver to walk on. With golden and green birds flying. And also with nothing at all to do but look at it. Every New England dweller knows the impending winter means work. Just keeping warm involves considerable activity in these parts.

But as I watch the still cold night sky deepening, and see

the quiet brilliance of the stars, I like the feeling of impending change. I think of Rupert Brooke's lines

> Then from the sad west turning wearily,
> I saw the pines against the white north sky,
> Very beautiful, and still, and bending over
> Their sharp black heads against a quiet sky.

The northern pine is a most beautiful tree, and hasn't been enough written about. I look out on seven, silvered with the rising moon and wonder if the tropics could be lovelier.

The air smells of frost. The house is making the soft breathing sounds very old houses make at night. Embers glow in the fireplace, and Jill is cutting a snow apple in quarters as she happily rereads *The Nine Tailors*. Jonquil is practically in the fire, a little salamander. Holly is in the coolest spot by the batten door.

A good night, I feel, to reread the recent cookbook, *With A Jug Of Wine*, and decide on a new receipt for tomorrow!

December

THE FIRST SNOWFALL IS WORTH HAV-
ing winter for. Comes the morning when Jill looks up from
her buttermilk pancakes and says, "look, this is it."

First a few tranquil flakes float down, then they come
faster, and with purpose. The old greystone walls silver over,
the swamp wears a mantle whiter than foam. The pine trees
on the slope begin to cast feathers of snow from their
branches. Inside the house there is a curious luminous look
to everything, and outside the sharp etchings of November
begin to blur.

Jill finishes her third cup of black steaming coffee and
climbs into her winter costume. She doesn't get sewed into
it, as they used to sew children into long underwear, but it
does seem a part of her from now on, the short fleece-lined
coat, the furry boots, the woolen tam and the lambswool
gloves. She flies to the kennel now to check on the heaters
and let everybody out for a run in the white mystery.

I struggle out laden with peanut butter, a spreader, a pail
of cracked chick feed, half a pan of sunflower seeds, three
slices of crumbled bread, two hunks of creamy suet, and a
portion of wildbird seed. Managing this load is no mean feat,
and I seldom have good luck because Holly tries to help me
and lunges at me, especially toward the fresh delectable suet.
I fend her off with the butter spreader and slide along on the
snow.

The air is so full of birds one could think them larger snow-
flakes. My chickadee with the bent wing waits impatiently
and says so. Nuthatches and woodpeckers and blue jays and

sparrows, including the solitary lark sparrow, a stray starling, and a flock of juncos are all there, hungry.

The pine trees flutter with wings. I feel as if I could fly myself if I just put my mind on it firmly enough.

We have all the kinds of bird feeders that we have room for, and the only one easy to fill is the one made out of an oil can which George Bennett designed and built and gave us. It is a ground feeder, you tilt up half the top and dump, and that is it.

The fancy green-roofed circular number is my despair and I often give up and wait for Jill. It has four parts and several screw things and the minute I begin they all fall apart. After I have successfully put it in shape and then attempt to insert the seed in the hole on top, the bottom falls off and all the seeds go down into the snow. Since I can't work the screws well with mittens, I am now quite stiff with cold. But if I put down a single piece of this wretched thing, Holly leaps away with it, it is a fine game.

Eventually I advance to the peanut butter stick. This has a squirrel baffle on top since we could not keep up with the large matronly squirrels who ate a quart a day. We discriminated, as they seemed stronger than the tiny neat little chickadees and brown creepers.

If I take the stick down, the baffle then baffles me. It knocks a circular path around the stick in a very human and sly way so that blobs of peanut butter fall in the snow. This stick is designed to take little dreadfully expensive cups of suet and seed, but we have given them up because the birds pull them out in a trice and not only Holly but five or six cockers play ping-pong with them. The peanut butter is fine, if you put it in just right so it doesn't go on out the other side.

The window feeder by my window has to be approached with caution when the dogs are away at the front gate hooting at George's dogs. Otherwise I can't get at it, as the level is exactly right for eager paws. It is also a roofed feeder so you have to spoon the feed in.

The two suet cages are almost higher than I can reach, but by jumping I can often make it and get part of the suet wedged in.

The small chick feeder on the sugar maple in back is always full of frozen hulls which have to be pried out.

After the birds are fed, I am ready to sit down and think about the joys of our feathered friends. If it continues to snow, the feeders will be empty by dusk, except for the suet cages. And the blue jays do their best by those by tearing out hunks as big as their heads and making off with them.

It all goes to prove, says Jill, that you only get out of anything what you put in. The birds, she adds, are about as much work as the dogs.

But we will drop anything to get the glasses and watch a new guest coming in for the winter. A solitary came in this year, all alone, looking like a sparrow but as if he had been half dipped in white paint. At first I thought he had been in some way. Dived into a jar or something. But Jill got the book and studied it feverishly and we identified him as the lark sparrow. "An accidental" said Jill happily.

At first the other sparrows were terribly rude to him. They elbowed him away, flew at him with harsh words, nipped at him with angry beaks. This went on for some time, yet every day he came back and came in around the edge of the flock.

A good lesson in perseverance, for in a week, he was eating in the middle of the gang, and as he is larger, obviously getting the best of everything. They had accepted him. We have no idea how he came to be here, all alone and in a territory he shouldn't be in anyway, but there he is, and making a very good living for himself.

The nuthatch likes to eat upside down, and I spent some time this week watching a very strong-minded nuthatch trying to arrange it so he could eat from the green feeder which has that roof. He finally made it by curling his toes around the edge of the top circle of the roof and swinging down and grabbing. Now I said any sensible bird would just stand on the floor and eat, but then there are a good many people who won't change their pattern either!

The chickadees may only seem more intelligent, but I think their little heads hold a good deal of wisdom. My little favorite comes to the feeder as I type and is no farther away than a pane of glass.

He sits down, bracing himself by his tail feathers, clings to the bars of the suet cage, and rocks his head back and forth. He is actually sitting on his tiny little rear end, and looks absurd and enchanting. When he arrives and when he leaves, he sings so merrily dee-dee-dee. It is a sunny note, unlike the harsh dramatic blue-jay voice or the club committee chatter of sparrows.

One day this week we had our three evening grosbeaks again and that made the day special. They were suddenly there, flashing with yellow color, looking like flowers in a spring garden. Occasionally we have a bluebird, once I saw a cardinal down the road, but never in our yard. Once we had a pileated woodpecker but he only came a few times.

But Ed, our yardman, friend, writer, called me to the door some time later and said, "there he is, can you hear him? He's in the swamp—the pileated makes just that sound, no other." We stood there listening to the sharp staccato ping and I felt it was fine to hear him going about his business in the swamp. He is a very shy bird, seldom seen around dwellings, and I suspect the barking of a bevy of dogs made him nervous.

But the dogs live here too, and we cannot discriminate.

The downy and hairy woodpeckers don't care how many dogs are whipping around, they go right on banging away at a square meal.

Without the birds, winter would be a very silent time in our home place. For snow muffles the sounds from George's barn, and from the Jeremy Swamp Road above where the cars go by at intervals. But the air is lively with birds, and they talk, they scold, they discuss, and they sing little songs. Now and then the chickadee will imitate a phoebe and the sweet little phoebe sounds like a lute string plucked in the grey day.

Before birds came into my life, a friend once advised me to write about birds. I wrote, said she, about dogs and cats and cows, but not about birds.

At that time, the only bird I knew was a solitary screech owl who found himself in the tree outside my bedroom window one night and screeched most of the night. After two nights, he took himself off and we parted in diplomatic neutrality.

Then we had whippoorwills who kept us from sleeping at all for as long as they whippoorwilled around. I had someway associated them when I was a child with *The Wept of Wish-ton-Wish*, one of my James Fenimore Cooper favorites, but nothing came of that.

And then somehow, birds began to infiltrate my life. I can't account for it, for although I loved to read about birds, I never expected to know any intimately. I doubted whether I could ever identify a single one.

And now, while I am a very amateurish amateur, I will run as fast as I can to get just one look at someone who is cracking a sunflower seed out on the back feeder.

It is as with much of life, I suspect, the richness is there, if one opens one's eyes to see it, and one's ears to hear it.

The Stephensons are as ardent bird fans as we are, and they too are recent converts, being still city week-enders. Steve will call up in great excitement to say they have spent two hours at the picture window watching indigo buntings. A cardinal calls for a celebration. We can talk endlessly of our respective birds and let anybody else just sit and be ignored. We exchange bird-food knowledge. And Steve in his first mad enthusiasm began putting up nesting houses in January just in case!

Steve and Olive are, by profession, interior decorators, but let us get on the subject of birds and we never mention a color scheme or a décor, we talk birds.

Sometimes people tell me they can't get interested in birds, never could. I never tell them what I have discovered, because I never tell people what they are not receptive to if I can help it. But I have found out, in my life, that to be interested in anything is only to observe it steadily and thoughtfully. I would think it unlikely I could develop a passion for, say, rattlesnakes, but it might well be if I got intimate with them, I might.

Any living creature has such infinite fascination, once you begin to learn about it.

Sometimes I have wondered whether we don't hate what

we do not understand. And, conversely, love what we know well.

This could translate to the field of human relationship too. Once we really see why anyone acts in a certain way, we are halfway to accepting it. I think Christ understood people and events with a divine sympathy and when He said, "Judge not, that ye be not judged," that was part of what He meant.

As Christmas comes around again, I find, as usual, I have mislaid some very choice Christmas presents bought last August. In a modern house, there would be no excuse for me, but in a house built in 1690, there is. For aside from a few shallow cupboards and a couple of closets under the steepest pitch of the roof and one chest, there is no place to put anything at Stillmeadow. Our very best closet can only be negotiated by crawling in, preferably backward, on hands and knees. Consequently we tuck things away in bureau drawers, in the attic, in the cellar, in the barn, and in the two pheasant houses which were built by a former owner for the pedigreed pheasant chicks.

The Christmas chest in the upstairs hall has definitely helped, but it is a smallish seaman's chest and won't hold everything. For the rest, we tuck away and then feverishly hunt.

Jill thinks a card index would help, and I point out we wouldn't be able to find the card index.

The children don't mind. They rather like to have a missing Christmas present turn up in March!

Christmas eve is my favorite time. Bayberry candles burning, fire glowing on the great hearth, the smell of turkey infusing the air with a promise of dinner, the drift of paper and the giggles and squeals as the children wrap last-minute gifts and rush down with them to the tree, the roars of laughter as they discover I am being given three recordings of my favorite Edith Piaf and Jill two duplicate Viennese waltzes. All this is heartwarming.

The trappings are fun, the holiday exciting, but more than that, I feel it has a significance not lost in the glitter, not really.

It is the birthday of Jesus. And it is good to remember that the carpenter's son was born, and taught, and died so long ago and yet is so alive, that we celebrate His birthday.

Once I wrote to this effect and a very angry woman wrote me and said Jesus was not a carpenter's son, He was the Son of God.

But to me it is not incompatible at all. I like to think of this very simple carpenter's son who was an artisan and worked with His hands, who dreamed, and suffered, and gave His life. I find as much divinity in Him as if He had come down on a golden cloud, robed in glory. In fact, more. I think without Jesus the man, we might not now be celebrating Christ the Son of God.

And what a miracle it is that down the centuries, in the midst of wars and destruction and famines and pestilence the spirit of this carpenter has proved more mighty than any other power for it grows and shines in our day as it did then.

And how wonderful that we can freely celebrate His birth in America, let our candles shine openly from every window, and decorate the live evergreen in every village square. Every door may wear its wreath, and the carols sound all over the country.

I am reminded of my friend Lois Holloway whose grandmother stopped every day in St. Mary's on her way home. Her son said, finally, "but mother, what do you find to pray about every day?"

"Oh, I don't pray," she said calmly, "I just sit there and look at God, and God looks at me."

Somehow I feel that at Christmas time, we may stop and

look at God and let God look at us. As we are lifted into a feeling of Christ being born again, we may think of all the things we have left undone that we should have done. And decide to try a little harder.

Everyone agrees Christmas has grown too commercial. It can be a tiring and exhausting chore to get ready, to send all the cards, to do all the cooking, make all the extra beds.

But I think there is a moment when it comes as clear as a wave rolling in from an infinite sea that faith in man is not misplaced. I think we tend to reach back and touch divinity, even if only for a quick perceptive instant.

And for people who do not believe in this little child born in an ox stall, they have their own quickening at some special time too.

The truth is, as I see it, we need to believe in a miracle, and for those of us who find it in the birth of Christ, Christmas is a kindling of new fires. I hear the Bible story again in our little hundred-year-old church, and I am amazed at how real it is, how vivid, and how contemporary.

I think most mothers get tired during the Christmas rush. I do. There is always a low moment when I fervently wish it were just over and I could SIT DOWN. I wish it were August. And nothing at all going on.

And yet, when the children say "Thank you for a wonderful Christmas, best we ever had," and one child whispers, "this was *just* all I wanted—how did you know?" and one child curls up to read the book you have chosen so carefully, and one says "we never had such a Christmas," suddenly then all the tiredness ebbs away, and a pure happiness floods in.

For in spite of the tinsel and wrappings and struggle over presents, we still have an idea, after all, that Christmas means giving some special joy, an unusual joy to someone. And that compensates for the commercialism which sometimes seems to threaten to engulf Christmas entirely.

I am sorry to see the dozens of Santa Clauses in the stores when I go to the city. Santa on street corners, too. I don't think it is good to exploit the little saint, and I am sure children must be confused and disillusioned when they have an interview with Santa in one store and walk two blocks and meet a different one.

As for the new type of Christmas music, if it can be called either Christmas or music, I cease to be a mild woman and feel all the emotions of a tiger. What a thing is this, to debase Christmas with mommy doing the mambo with Santa, mommy kissing Santa, and all the rest of them. I could well do without "Rudolf the Red-nosed Reindeer" as far as that goes.

With the beautiful and traditional carols and the decent modern pieces like "White Christmas," why must our children's ears and ours be assailed with cheap, tawdry stuff. With "Hark the Herald Angels Sing," and "O Little Town Of Bethlehem," and "Joy to the World," and the quaintly gay early carols such as "Good King Wencelas" and "We Three Kings of Orient Are," I should think the purveyors of Christmas music would be satisfied.

It would be fine to keep this one holiday dignified and filled with deep meaning.

Winter is the time to do odd jobs around the house. The pressure lets up outside as the weather takes things over. We made a project this week of re-doing the herb and spice shelves.

We were encouraged in this by the fact that the boys at the market have recently added herbs and spices to their stock. This little village store is rapidly becoming a gourmet's dream. They have everything from stuffed rock Cornish hens to frozen lobster pies, and now a whole wall of herbs.

"Hundreds," says George Tomey, helping me find the tarragon and oregano.

I hesitate to think how old some of our herbs were. Even our own mint and parsley flakes and sage and celery leaves came from two seasons back. Herbs lose their savor, and moreover, we keep on picking up herb mixes for fish, for salad, for meats, and they add to the collection until it overflows.

The herbs now come in lovely little clear bottles with good shaker tops, a great improvement over the little tight boxes we used to have. Jill piled the entire old collection in a basket for the dump, and I wondered whether a field mouse might investigate and get his little nose filled with curry powder!

Herbs, I feel, must be right at hand or the cook won't bother with them, at least not my kind of cook. I want to reach and tilt right by the simmering pot. So a narrow shelf runs along by the range the whole width of that wall.

This serves two purposes, it provides easy access to the seasonings, and makes my meal-getting romantic. For the whole world comes into the kitchen with saffron and sesame seed, chili powder, curry, basil and bay.

For instance, bay, which is laurel, or called sweet bay. I think of the golden days of Greece when I lift the jar, and victors' brows bound with laurel wreaths. It was then, I believe, a symbol of immortality. I think of Edna St. Vincent Millay who plucked two laurel leaves from the graves of Shelley and Keats and kept them always pressed in a book—and I wonder was it Aeschylus?

This leads me easily to reciting bits of Millay as I cook.

> For the sake of some things
> That be now no more
> I will strew rushes
> On my chamber-floor,
> I will plant bergamot
> At my kitchen door.

And then I go on to

> Oh beautiful at nightfall
> The soft spitting snow
> And beautiful the bare boughs
> Rubbing to and fro.

Miss Millay had such a deep perception of the beauty in every season, she was not a spring or summer poet as some have been. What a fascinating study it would be to take my favorite poets and find out just which season they liked best. It would take a year or so, but it would be fine. Someday, I resolve, I'll do it.

I could make a snap judgment on Keats, I think, as I stir up the meat loaf. "In a drear nighted December," comes to mind, and "The owl for all his feathers is a-cold." I fancy his being ill in the dark cold English winter made him long for warmth. He did love the open fire crackling among the coals, however.

The laurel leaves she loved were buried with Edna, and I feel it very fitting. But I think of her now as holding sweet converse with those others who loved and lived by beauty. The great Greeks, the incandescent Will Shakespeare, and Shelley and Keats would welcome this small slight woman with the moving voice and flashing mind.

Well, I think, as I carefully press two leaves of bay on the top of the meat loaf, who could ever say housework is dull? It is packed with excitement. I have been to Athens, to Rome, and to Steepletop in the mountains, all while stirring up a meat loaf.

Then I think that Jill almost always does the meat loaf for she has a Russian meat loaf, from a dear Russian friend. And it is better than best, so rich, so moist and so crusty. Grated raw potato is the magic, and that seems so Russian somehow!

But a meat loaf without those two bay leaves is a most pedestrian food.

If I am deviling our fresh country eggs with curry, I am carried away to India and I imagine all the mystery of India. I may never see it, but I can travel there as soon as I lift the little curry pot.

As to which herbs are basic, that is a problem I can consider while adding rosemary to green beans. It's fun to think of the old desert island—if I had only etc. etc. I get very agitated over whether I would settle on garlic and whole peppercorns and freshly ground salt, of course. "If the salt have lost his savour," I say to myself, "wherewith shall it be salted?"

Of course herbs take up such a small space—perhaps there would be room for, supposing I knew I was to be cast away—for let's see—

chili powder   oregano
rosemary   curry
thyme   basil
crushed red pepper   bay
dill seed (for salads especially)
whole cloves (what's a pot roast without these? Or ham?)
saffron (rice and saffron are like pork and applesauce)
sesame seed
pickling spice (for shrimp and crab and lobster a handful
    in the water)
salt (plain, onion, garlic)   celery seed
whole peppercorns   mustard

This leaves out mace and monosodium glutamate, a wretched name for a good friend to any dish, and turmeric and so on. But then one must draw the line.

Alfred Lunt, on the one memorable time I saw him, made Swedish bread for me, and that, of course, calls for crushed cardamom seeds. Delicious, but the cardamom seeds are very hard to deal with, I found. He is a more persistent cook than I.

When you go into condiments generally, there are so many mustards. I would hate to do without the violence of Bahamian, but the Bavarian with its musty mildness is so good with cheese sandwiches, grilled. Plain store mustard is needful for dressings and sauces too. And Jill is devoted to horseradish mustard. Then there are the steak sauces and I am just amazed at how they taste when they appear from the label to be made of oranges and tamarinds and water, salt and sugar. And chili sauce and catsup and soy sauce—which is a very excellent sauce for many things other than Chinese dishes. Spread on a roasting chicken for instance. Or a dollop in gravy.

Yes, cooking can really give food for thought as well as for the body. Even flour and corn meal have romance in them, if you stop to think of it. I wonder who first ground out a kind of flour and mixed it with water and made a little cake to put on a hot stone before some ancient fire? And who before the Indians ground the maize between two stones?

Salt is a story in itself. Men have died for salt in the past. Have evaporated sea water, have stolen salt, have fought over it. Countries blessed with salt have been rich, countries without it have struggled to get it.

Man must have salt, evidently, as he must have air and water.

As I casually lift the salt box, I think how fortunate we are, we get salt for a small sum, and all we want. We neither have to go to the salt mines and dig it, nor trap the sea and worry it for a small deposit in a wooden trough.

But I wonder who first tasted salt and how he managed to discover it? There are many mysteries in man's eating.

As for coffee and tea, there is a volume. The eighteenth century English coffeehouses gave much culture to the world as men sipped the bitter brew and talked. Tea, I think, got England through the war. These little dried fragrant leaves have comforted men and women in dire times, and as we lift our cup of Darjeeling in the afternoon, we are linked with all the past once more.

My Aunt Minnie, at well over seventy, always takes a thermos of tea with her when she goes after her annual deer.

I understand the first tea bags, by the way, were made of silk and designed to provide samples of tea for people to try out. I wish they had stayed that way. I do not like my tea flavored with string and paper or cheesecloth. It's perfectly simple to use the leaves and then you have true tea. The delicate leaves need free motion in the freshly boiled water to infuse their fragrance.

As we once again lug the Christmas tree ornaments to the attic and begin the battle of pine needles, which fill all the cracks in the old wide floors, I think of all the past Christmases with a little sadness tugging at my heart. We keep the same cherished old ornaments from year to year, but this year we did give up the candy canes and cookies hung on the tree. The children, now they are grown, prefer to cut a wedge of rich golden Cheddar for a snack to sucking on a striped candy cane. The excitement of picking cookies from the tree waned, too. So our trees are no longer bearing edibles.

They also in these years like popcorn with garlic butter or cheese butter rather than the big molasses balls.

Yes, things change, I reflect, as I unwind the tinsel and lay aside the Christmas cards to reread.

I have always so hated to see the last of the Christmas cards. I keep them around into January and look at them from time to time. The sweet old-fashioned ones with sleighs and silvery snow are pleasant and the ones with snapshots of the children are always lovely.

I don't care for the humorous ones any more than the new Christmas music. I like sentimental and romantic ones.

A good many Honeys were named for my golden Honey, as I wrote about her for fourteen years. And I always get pictures of the other Honeys who are still on this side of the door. Christmas was Honey's favorite time. She loved to sit and listen to the carols, she loved to help unwrap packages, and she adored the Christmas cuisine. I often feel her shadowy presence, but especially around Christmas time. Her dark amber eyes and golden velvet muzzle are visible beyond the edge of the firelight, and it is a very comfortable feeling to know she is there overseeing the end of Christmas as she always used to.

Connie and Dorothy this year went through the cards too, and chose an assortment for their youngest friends to make scrapbooks of, cutting and pasting. All the little angels and reindeer and bells and candles and houses with lighted windows and the fawns and bluebirds and cockers and kittens make a wonderful occupation for rainy days for the small ones.

Some of the especially lovely ones, I cut out myself and save to decorate next year's packages with. I like the feeling that they go on to another year instead of being burned up and forgotten.

One friend of mine did a whole tree with Christmas cards and I think that is a very good idea if one had the patience to string them all up.

I have wondered what would happen if one year everybody in the country sent two-cent postals with their greetings and put the money saved into the heart fund or the Save the Children Fund? This is, I realize, one of my impractical ideas, for what would the artists who design the elegant and charming cards do to pay the dentists' bills, and what would the companies do who make the cards? It is an overwhelming business these days, and all of those people involved would not thank me for wiping them out!

But what a lovely hunk of money for a cause would roll up! For that matter, all the Christmas trees we burn up on

Twelfth-night planted in groves would reforest most of the denuded areas in the country. I used to feel so sad when I lived in the city to see on all the streets the fallen dying trees waiting for the garbage trucks to haul them off. But of course city people need Christmas trees too, and who could plant an evergreen in a New York apartment? The whole street I lived on used to smell of pine for several days, I could close my eyes and forget the canyoned walls and walk in a far-off forest for a moment.

Sometimes, when I get in a fanciful mood, I can see great slopes of barren eroded land planted with one year's Christmas trees, with birds sheltered in the soft depths, with a soft carpet of needles underneath where visitors could walk softly and at peace.

We have done pretty well in our valley, through George Bennett's efforts. Most of us have planted anywhere up to five-hundred Christmas trees and I have yet to hear of a single soul cutting one after planting. So in due time, I daresay, our part of the state of Connecticut will be a great pine woods.

Alas, I do not cotton to the idea—as Mama would say—of artificial trees. Be they ever so beautiful they are still artificial. Silver or blue or pink, revolving to music or whatever, they do not spell the magic of Christmas.

So I suspect we shall go on, not cutting our own trees, but buying trees already cut, and burning them up afterward. In the early days, we did cut trees from our own land and made a great game of it, but then we got so devoted to anything growing that we lost heart.

Somehow the growing trees always fit the place they grow in, and the sense one gets that they are happy there persists. While we do not know how much a tree can feel, I for one, think it might be that a tree also likes life.

As we go on endlessly garnering pine needles throughout the house, I remember my childhood in northern Wisconsin when we would go out and pick balsam for pine pillows. That was the day when any well-furnished sofa had at least one pine pillow, usually embellished with a lurid green bough and a sentiment, "I Pine for You."

The woods there were deeply green and dark and awesomely still. No sound broke through the wall of green. We snipped the ends of branches and since there were millions, we had no sense of being too predatory. We carried sugar sacks and filled them and then went to sit on the veranda while we pulled off the needles. Such an aroma rose, so rich, so sharp. My hands got prickery and sticky, and I earnestly kept at it until I had enough balsam for a small pillowcase. I used to tuck it next to my real goosedown pillow, and breathe the breath of the great woods all night long.

Father always cut our own tree in those days, and this was a real job for he never liked the tree at hand, he always wanted to go farther and find one exactly perfect. One had too many branches at the bottom, another had a side that wasn't quite as full, one had the wrong tip. It was always around zero if not well below and we went out to the edge of town to the wild swampy Black Creek area. My mittened hands would be blue and numb as I struggled after Father who carried his axe like a banner and strode manfully ahead.

Mama never went, she knew better. "Just bring a nice small tree, Rufus," she would say.

We would come home with the biggest tree Papa could carry, and then he had to cut off the base to get it in the house at all, and cut off the top to get it in the living room.

But Father was a perfectionist, the biggest and best tree was none too good for me. And we had it, no matter how much trouble to both Mama and me!

I always think of Papa at Christmas time, he was an erratic giver and an emotional receiver. I always get one gift that is so supremely thoughtful, so very dear, that I burst into tears when I open it. It may be a lavender sachet or a bottle of white lilac toilet water from someone who has remembered my love for lilacs—or it may be an electric fryingpan, which I have yearned for for so long and never mentioned. But there is always something. Well, Papa would open something and his brilliant lake-blue eyes would just brim over. He would say cross as a woolly bear, "What's this? what's this?" and then, "it's too expensive, you shouldn't have done it."

Mama was perhaps the most completely unselfconscious woman I ever knew. She had been raised in a minister's family and her cultural background was excellent, but there was not enough money for college when she would have gone, so she did not go. She couldn't spell cat, but I don't think a Ph.D. degree would have improved her spelling a jot. She was a born non-speller.

Father would get furious with her for misspelling some ordinary word. Anybody could tell how it should be, he always said. But then he was a born speller, and fortunately passed it on to me. In fact, if anyone ever questions my spelling, I simply say that is the way the word is spelled and should the dictionary give an alternate spelling, I feel the dictionary is being too loose. But I feel spelling is an innate thing.

It is good to remember past Christmases. Memory may play tricks on us at times, but Christmas seems to pinpoint things, preserve them like a fly in amber.

From the first little squared-off silver locket from my beau to the Irish setter that was a graduation present, there are memories.

I take them out on Christmas always and think of them. And possibly this is one of the chief values of Christmas, that we remember the good things, the love, the friendship we have experienced.

My last words, on each and every Christmas for over twenty years have been spoken from the heart to all the world, and they are simple, but heartfelt.

> God rest you merry, Gentlemen,
> Let nothing you dismay.

9

January

SEEING THE NEW YEAR IN SEEMS TO involve much paper caps, night clubbing, and hangovers for some people. This is not my idea at all, never was. I wish to start my new year with a few people I dearly love, and in front of an applewood fire, with bowls of popcorn and apples, and hot buttered rum, and Port Salut cheese and crisp crackers.

And playing some good music, and reading aloud some choice bits. And feeling so secure in the fact that beginning a new year is a beginning with the same old friends.

This year was memorable because Burton and Glenn flew in from Akron for three days, Johannes came, and Connie was here. Jill's children had gone back to the city for various commitments, but the house was pleasantly full with six of us.

The ham was a special one ordered from one of those special places, baked in sherry and so on, and it was butter-tender. The glaze was exactly luminous and candied on the sweet potatoes and the Italian ripe olives tossed in Johannes' salad were *really* Italian, those little black-green nuggets. So dinner was, as Don would say, very O.K. Since all of us but Glenn and Connie have to watch those miserable gremlin calories, we had a fancy dessert for Glenn and Connie and the rest of us ate cheese and sliced rosy apples and more cheese.

Then we played the Schöne Müllerin recording, not by Glenn, the other one, which he said made him suffer but he did want to hear it. Then Burton read aloud, and it didn't upset my joy that he chose some passages from some early books of mine. I thought they sounded quite lovely, but it may have been the company and the fire and the residual spicy smell of that ham.

Later on Glenn took a lantern and padded out in his woolen slippers to look at the pond, just to see if it might thaw enough so he could fish through the ice in the morning. Burton and Connie talked semantics. Jill and Johannes discussed the use of the rest of the ham next day, with all kinds of ideas as to omelets and mousses and things.

I just sat and was happy.

I pulled myself out of the dream long enough to mix Smiley Burnette's buttermilk pancakes for New Year's day breakfast while Connie fixed more hot buttered rum, according to the Revolutionary Rogers' Rangers recipe. We have no loggerhead to immerse in it, we have to heat it on a modern electric stove but it still gets hot!

Around midnight, that hour of wonder and doubt and question as to the future of our world—and who would not, even in a night club, wonder about it—we played a last record and Glenn sang "Auld Lang Syne" in his crystal-clear tenor.

We thought it was the loveliest New Year's eve we ever had.

New Year's resolutions are a chancy thing. I make mine simple. I only pray that I may be a better person the coming year than in the past. More tolerant, kinder, gentler. Not impatient when things are difficult. I remember Bruce Gould telling me once that he had figured it out that nobody, but nobody, at best had more than a thousand months to live. Well, if that be so, one should not waste any of them in unworthy affairs or thoughts. A thousand isn't many.

This is the month we get viruses and such. If it is mild, we say it is unhealthy for New Englanders to be so warm in

mid-winter. If it be zero and snowy, we say it is the cold weather.

First I catch it from Connie, who has, presumably brought it from the teeming city. Then I pass it on to Jill, despite boiling of cups and silver and glasses and plates. You can't, after all, boil the air.

Dr. Ghiselin, who left New York to give his four children a country life, is so overworked that we all worry about it. Often he finishes a long day and gets to bed only to be called out on a long call. His charming wife acts as his office nurse, and has won the hearts of the whole valley people. She comforts, encourages and waits on the patients, works long hours in the office, but is never too busy to call up and ask if you are feeling better.

Alex comes over, and he comes in a lovely light suit, wearing no hat. He is a big rosy man (called Pinky when in medical school) very vigorous and athletic-looking. When he came yesterday, it was hovering around 20 and I crept to the door to admit him. He blew in like a breeze, and I said, "Oh Doctor Ghiselin—no coat and no hat—"

"Spring's just around the corner," said he briskly.

The odd thing was I felt better right away. I am sure he doesn't go about in summer garb just to cheer up his patients, but nevertheless his cheery assumption that it was nearly spring stopped my cough at once.

I cannot really understand how any man can bear to be a doctor, I am lost in admiration of the temperament that can endure it. Physically the life is unadulterated misery, for sleep and meals and leisure are no part of it.

If the G's take one day off and go to the theatre in New Haven, they are as happy as honeymooners. They get home around one, and he is called out on a case at three-thirty, another at five. After a quick breakfast he is off on the fifteen-mile drive to check on his hospital patients.

But aside from the physical discomfort, there is the thing of always being with people who are in trouble one way or another. Who suffer. Mrs. G's quick sympathy never seems exhausted, it is a bottomless well and Dr. G in his brusque casual way manages to convey a real sense of personal feeling for every person with a headache.

I have absolutely no patience with people who say doctors get too high fees. The doctors I know charge as little as they can.

True, I haven't had much experience in doctors' offices, as I was brought up to believe if you just tried you could "throw anything off." No matter what ailed me, I just tried to throw it off until the Ghiselins came to our village. Now I will pop down with a sinus or a virus and think nothing of it.

Such men are rare, I know, but I believe there are more good doctors than can be counted. And surely nothing could be a greater gift to suffering humanity than a man who gives his life for little pay in a rural community. I would place such a man almost above the minister in selfless service to mankind.

Socialized medicine I hear much of, pro and con. I am emotionally against it, for I feel the family doctor for you yourself, individually, is the nearest to heaven-sent aid one can get. For it isn't the pills or the surgery or the injections one half so much as the feeling of security, the faith because it is your very own doctor, it is a highly personal kind of security we all need.

Sometimes, as a matter of fact (and this is a phrase that should be permanently erased from our language, it is too much used), we may just call Mrs. G up and tell her we have such and such a pain and/or fever and so on. Even a chat over the phone restores us to a feeling we are fairly rugged individuals.

There must be a terrific sense of satisfaction in knowing your full working life is for the good of others. Most of us wish to help those in trouble, we can baby-sit or make broth or do errands or fix a roast, but it is the village doctor who drives through the night and brings hope and healing.

The family doctor was all there was when I was growing up, now we have seen specialists take over so much. One man does your sinus, another does your heart, a bevy check on X rays. But I think we are swinging back to the idea of one man as a family man, and this I believe in heartily.

One man, and only one, knows the whole picture, knows about all the sinus and virus and whatever you are subject to, knows what your children have had. He has an over-all picture, and a person is an over-all proposition.

When I was growing up, our family doctor had just abandoned his fast horse and sold his light buggy. He had an old Cartercar which he cranked. In the bleak winter nights in Wisconsin he would be chugging along, stopping to shovel when necessary, and many a baby he delivered by the light of a smoky oil lamp, many an operation he did on a kitchen table scrubbed clean.

And half the children in the county were named after him! I doubt whether any socialized medicine would provide this type of thing. Everyone needs a "Doc" in his or her life.

We refer to Dr. Ghiselin as "the boss" and he is just that. "The boss says." "Ask the boss."

And as he dashes around in mid-winter sans coat and hat and gloves, we all worry lest he himself *catch* something!

We do not have as many terrible blizzards as we had twenty years ago, this makes me believe in the men who say our climate is getting milder. But when we do get a Norther with stinging sleet and snow and a harsh wild wind, it is good to know our linesmen are ready. If the electric as we call it, goes off, they are there in no time at all. No night so bitter but that we can see their lights as they come to climb the poles and hook up fallen wires that carry the heat and light to the people of the valley. I think they seldom get thanked, but I always send a heartfelt thank you as I see their dark figures climbing in the night. With us, as with many country-folk nowadays, the furnace goes off, the water goes off, and the Deep Freeze stops all at once. The electric current keeps the lifeblood of our homes pulsing.

They do their best work when the weather is the worst. If the roads are impassable, they are on them. They often work all night to restore power. I have never personally been able to understand what electric current is or why it makes things go, but I revere it.

Now and then in January we get what I call a dividend day. The sun is clear and warm and the sky soft as lake water. The tree trunks seem to glow in the light, and a hundred misty colors appear in the swamp. The birds are very gay, they seem to fly with a lighter wing somehow, and the dogs sit by the well-house and dream quite as if it were spring.

Squirrels whip around in the maples, always so busy and so important. I think a squirrel would make a good bank president, he saves, he is thrifty, and he feels important, and he must have a very sound head on him.

The Quiet Garden on such a day is lucid with sun, and looks as if we might even eat there. I toy with the idea, but Jill says firmly, the benches will be cold as glaciers. And I realize they will.

So we settle on trays by the fire. But it is incredibly exciting to get such a day in January. It is not even the January thaw, it is just a small jewel of a day set in the silver band of winter.

"Let's take a ride," I say suddenly.

So we drive along the wintry country roads, looking at the snug farmhouses, the tidy barns. Light falls on the greystone fences, here and there glinting with a sheath of ice. As the sun goes lower, it intensifies the colors, the white church steeple is whiter, the red barns are set on fire. All the browns of the thickets and meadows are touched with a rosy tinge. The snow, where it lies in the hollows, has blue shadows on it.

Mittened and furred children go past carrying their ice skates slung over their shoulders, the steel catches the light and flashes like white fire. A hitchhiker waves a red thumb, but we dare not stop.

Time was we picked up everybody on the road. In those innocent days, I picked up a wayfaring tramp with a guitar, incredibly smelly and dirty, but very nice. He sang "Red River Valley" to me for some miles, and then a few others and I loved it, although I had to run the car window down to be able to breathe. We used to pick up soldiers and sailors and teen-agers en route to the nearest movie or bowling alley and it was all very neighborly and good. But the *Reader's Digest* cured us, may have saved our careless lives also. Listing the murders done, the cars stolen, the crimes committed by the pick-ups, the one sentence that floored me was to the effect that when you open the car door and invite someone in, it is like opening your living-room door and letting anybody march in there. Few of us would admit a grubby slant-eyed tramp into our houses, but on the road, our car is all the house we have.

One of the saddest things about the terrible increase of crime in the country to me is that the kindliness of the road must be forgone.

I still feel sorrowful when I drive by some tall boy with a lifted hand, but reason tells me I had better do just that. The college boys we used to take on their way were delightful—but now we know anybody can put stickers on a bag and get in. Such an easy way to steal a car or knock a driver cold! And some of the more violent crimes have been committed by teen-age girls, and who would ever think it a mistake to pick up a wistful teen-age girl? It's a sad commentary on this day and age that I feel there should be a Federal penalty for picking up strangers on any turnpike or highway.

It was such fun. I dare say no kind of bureau could be established with placards for the good hitchhikers, for they would be copied! I am glad, however, that all this had not come up when I picked up that guitar player, for I did enjoy him. Though he had been unwashed for a long time.

Well, much has been written about the country telephone. Ours rings apparently without reason, and with nobody on the other end. If we try to call anyone, we get five people in odd places who are justly annoyed at being summoned when we do not want to talk to them anyway. If I get called to the phone, I always hear another conversation going on, and I get so bemused listening to that that I never hear my own. Ofttimes in the stilly night, as the song goes, the phone rings wildly. And there is never anybody there after we stumble up to answer.

After being on a nine-party line for years, we graduated to

a two-party line. We felt elated, but it was a short-time elation. For now we only have a sort of dual conversation with the other party on at the same time. And if I get on, as I rarely do, I always hear this clear clipped voice saying, "is this the New York Medical Center?"

Phoning my daughter in New York is a lost cause too. Recently I tried, and tried and tried. And phoned Columbia University in the end to ask her to call me when she could.

"I just couldn't get you," I wailed.

"Now, Mama, you know you have to ask the operator to ring twice. Ring once, then ring again at once. If I am studying I never answer any other calls. Just tell her to ring twice. Right away."

Knowing our telephone service as I perforce must, I decided to communicate solely by wire with my daughter from then on. Let the telephone cope, said I.

My telephoning is hampered anyway by the fact that I can never understand anybody's name over it or what they want. I hear a dull glug glu and then I say brightly, "Oh yes?"

This can lead to real trouble if people phone they are coming in half an hour. Also since it is constitutionally impossible for me to utter a negative over the phone, we are in hot water again. I always accept all invitations thankfully and cheerily and it is left to Jill to point out we are due in three separate places at the same hour. She knows this, and is quite patient but sometimes gives me *a look*.

Mama didn't feel so charitable, she got quite angry. "Now Gladys, you can't be three places at once" she would say, "why did you say you'd be at *all?*"

"Well, it seems so rude to say no," I would answer.

We have now settled that only Jill answers the phone. She may be in the barn when it rings, and my natural instinct is to rush to answer and then I think, "Ah no, you will only get in trouble. Leave it be."

Hot and bothered, Jill lopes in and says bitterly, "It's the *Journal* calling you."

That is all right. I am sure I can't make a fatal error on that. All I do is say yes to whatever they want.

But for regular phoning, I can only get in terrible trouble.

If Jill is taking a shower and I answer the imperative peal, I may call up and say, "people coming for tea."

"Are you out of your senses," she calls back, "we have to be at a party at three thirty—"

Then we juggle. Often it takes some juggling, too.

Long-distance calls agitate me too. We know which they are as the phone acquires a curious sibilance.

If it isn't one of the children wondering how we are as we haven't written, it is likely to be Faith Baldwin.

In that case, I go and sit down. The phone is no hazard to her. She can chat over it. I am lost in admiration, in fact so lost that I often miss part of what she says.

She can do a whole novelette in five minutes and all I have to do is say OH. Or, in a great burst of inspiration, YES.

Most people who feel they must phone me start by saying apologetically, "now I know you can't talk over the telephone but—"

Usually I don't have to, at that. They do, only occasionally saying, "are you still there?"

I am definitely there, clinging to the receiver like a lifeline, but uttering nothing.

I cannot think just how my telephone phobia developed. But the ringing of the phone always seems ominous to me, a kind of trump of doom. In my business life it has often been, for I would just be ready to go on a small gay jaunt when the phone would ring and I would start off for Lake Isle in Jersey instead. But it goes far back of that.

Our particular country phone is maddening. For one thing the company changes the numbers every little while, and our former number invariably goes to some week-end shack by the river. Any misguided soul who tries to call us gets an empty shack. This goes on for a long time. Telegrams are undelivered, once a dear friend died and was buried before the news ever percolated to us. When we get restive about this, we are advised to just be sure to tell everyone the new number!

Laboriously we send cards to everybody—missing, of course, people we never think would call us, and unable to prepare for all probable business calls.

The phone rings a good deal, but of course it isn't our number but the number of someone else who has now another number!

When the dial phones went in, we were happy. Now it would be all set. We wrote tons of cards. We phoned people. But the honeymoon is over, for yesterday the man came to, yes, to CHANGE the number again. This time it is even more complicated, for it is changed on the phone, but the actual change doesn't go in until summer, says he airily.

I have known places where people had the same number all their lives, what's more they had it after they died, for their children inherited it. So I cannot understand this curious penchant of our company in the valley. Can it be they get bored?

The postman brought a letter from Faith Baldwin on a very cold snowy day this week. Even a siege of grippe doesn't dim her sense of humor. She wrote painfully:

> I think that I shall never see
> A sight less lovelier than me;
> A me whose driply flowing nose
> Blooms mid the Kleenex like a rose;
> A me who gruesomely must wear
> A wreath of curlers in her hair
> While daily living I deplore
> And virus smites me aft and fore.

To comfort her, I wrestled with the telephone and won. I got her! As one always does, I proffered the cheery news that others were sick too. Louella Shour, said I, had breakbone fever.

"Not at all," said Faith in a low croak. "Breakbone fever is *D E N G U E*, Dengue, and is tropical. You tell her she has something else!"

I instantly felt I must tell Louella it was something else, then I thought better of it. People have a certain kind of pride about their illnesses.

I can well remember how Father always diagnosed his own and told the doctor what it was and what kind of medicine he needed. That settled that. Then he would add some of his own medicines from the big black case he had carried in the Mexican mountains in the early days. He believed if one pill was good, five were bound to work quicker.

Also, he mixed the pills. First he would take what he had ordered the doctor to give him, then add some Rhinitis or aconite or a spoonful of some early remedy of mine. A glass of Bromo Seltzer helped out and a little later a raw onion sliced and placed between two slices of bread, well buttered, salted and peppered was a final sovereign remedy.

It may be, as well, that he was the healthiest man that ever lived, so he never got upset by any of his health measures. Mama on the other hand never took so much as an aspirin. She felt one should just keep a stiff upper lip and throw it off.

Consequently I alternated. One time, when a cold was rampaging, I had to raid the medicine cabinet. Just taking a sample of everything. The next time I would try to throw it off. One worked about as well as the other.

How fast times change can be measured by the medical ideas as well as change in fashions. Laudanum, paregoric, macrotin and sweet spirits of nitre—these seem as far gone as the snows of yesteryear in most medical advice. The leech has gone his way—one wonders how much more poetry Keats would have written had he not been bled so constantly.

In the nineteenth century a sure cure for consumptives was a draught composed of tamarack bark, spikenard, dandelion root, hops, three pints of best brandy and three pounds of honey. This was to be drunk freely three times a day—at least a gill or more. I hope the brandy and honey tasted good anyway.

When I lived in Virginia my very dear colored cook made a remedy for my cough out of scrapings of wild cherry bark and other mysterious substances. It was the best cough medicine I ever had.

And of course our friend Chief Grey Fox, the handsome, erect Indian who has the antique trading post down the road, has knowledge of many herbs and medications.

On the whole, we find many outdated treatments do prove to be valuable according to the modern science. Now we find curare is a fine thing—not to paralyze but to heal. Foxglove, used for generations, really is a heart medicine. Herb teas are beneficial and are coming back in fashion.

I hope we never revive leeches, however.

Our small neighbor skips past on her way to the school bus these snowy mornings. We have watched her grow. Just yesterday, it seems, she went in her bunny suit holding mama's hand. She looked like a small shy bird. Came the day she went to the bus corner all by herself, alone. And how proudly her head was lifted, and how she swung her small body arrogantly! And now she runs and skips for it is a casual affair, just going to school.

On Sundays when she sings in the Junior Choir, her little rosy face is very serious, dark eyes big as butter plates, cropped dark hair brushed and brushed. Above the white-collared blue robe, her pink mouth forms elaborate round O's. She takes this singing career not lightly.

Now I know the day will soon come when a freckled thin leggy boy comes down our road carrying her books, since she is obviously too frail to carry them! And before we know it, she will be coming home from college with a beau and they will walk down the hill hand in hand, rapt in their own dream.

Lois Holloway's young daughter had to write an autobiography for her composition class and came up with the following:

"My great-great grandfather was a very disreputable man, and in some ways my mother is a lot like him!" Poor Lois felt a bit agitated until she discovered Penny really meant unconventional!

The young can be so graphic! When Pen says "Mother, I haven't dislocated your purse once this week," it is a telling picture.

Hollyberry is going to school too, to Obedience Class. She has difficulty because she wants to play with every dog on the floor, it seems like a marvelous party to her. As she heels along, her tail waves like a flag in a hurricane, and she swivels her head constantly. She wants to see everything! Then when it comes to the Long Down, she is overcome with melancholy. The Irish almost never care about lying down. So she turns to jelly, rolls weakly on her back and holds sad paws up in the air. Down the long line of dogs lying so trim and even there comes this spot where Holly is, and everyone who sees her gives up and roars with laughter. She doesn't mind being laughed at. A cocker cannot bear it, but she thinks it is all good fun and lying in that silly upside-down fashion, legs in air, she begins to thump her tail again on the floor. If the down goes on longer than she feels is right, she yawns widely, accompanying the yawn with a long peculiar squeak.

With hunting dogs, we find it advisable to get their primary Obedience degrees in the indoor shows. Until they are quite far along in their education, their heredity can get the best of them. Our first experience with Daphne outdoors was unfortunately in a show ring abutted by a stretch of good deep woods. In the middle of the Sit Stay she lifted her head, wrinkled her nose, gave a bound and took off with lightning-like rapidity. She went through two other rings scattering dogs and handlers and judges at random, dove into the thicket. The pheasant had just time enough to get under way.

It was a beautiful sight, but not to us. The bronze and scarlet thickets, the wild bird rising and the Irish skimming along. I cannot describe, although I have tried many times, the look of an Irish running. I can say it is like poetry or like music. I can say the lovely shining head is lifted, the long lines of the body flow along and the great plume streams behind like the wake of a racing boat. But it is more than that, it is something about the way those long legs move, and the proportion of the whole.

However, that day we were not admiring our darling as she flashed away. All the Irish owners deployed and we went through a wild hour before we reclaimed her. She had quite literally stopped the show.

"My what a nose she has," said the Judge, "that pheasant was so far away—and hidden—you ought to train her for field work!"

We mopped our brows and looked at him, mute.

A thoroughbred cocker has a pretty fine gait, too. And they can cover the ground like the wind. A champion running brings a lump to the throat, the small compact body flying along, the deep ears swinging and the strong legs with the absurd big paws twinkling steadily in and out. But it is not, to me, as wild and free a flight as the Irish. It makes me long to gather him or her up and praise extravagantly the sturdy little traveler. When I see a cocker in a Field Trial getting through thickets the bigger dogs fail to negotiate and coming back with the bird held so carefully, I am lost with admiration, for the bird may seem almost as big as the brave-hearted cocker. But when I see an Irish run, I think—oh how free—could there be anything more free in this fettered world? And I feel the nostalgia all pedestrian beings feel for flight.

Of course, every dog has his own special gait, too. I can tell who is running in the back of the house if I am up front. Little Sister sounds as if she were on her way to an important meeting, busy and bustling. Especially Me ambles, moving his golden paws lightly, carelessly. Tiki just scours about in a state of high excitement over whatever he is excited about—and it is always something, he is the eagerest beaver we have. Hildegarde clicks thoughtfully along like a gentlewoman coming from her boudoir ready to pay genteel calls.

Jonquil has a dancing gait.

Linda skips like a butterfly, only touching the floor now and then. And so on.

Dark comes so early these days. We seem to have practically no afternoon. Around four-thirty the snow has a blue tinge, and the sky has a faint pale glow. The woods are dark charcoal, and most of the birds finish their feeding and begin to settle into the thick fluffy white pines by the swamp. The chickadees that have been singing all afternoon utter a few last Dee-Dee-Dees and snap up a few last sunflower seeds.

By dusk-dark, around five or five thirty, you would never know we had a bird on the place. And then, immediately it is night, faster than a third-act curtain. The whole world of day is at once shut away, the pale delicate winter colors, the amber sunlight, the wing-filled air, these are vanished.

And I am minded again of how light regulates our country living. The kennel heaters are filled at night. Firewood comes in at dusk. Bird feeders must be filled before dark for the birds who feed early get up long before we do in the morning.

With all the chores over, I feel it is time to make an onion pie, and begin turning the sliced onions in hot butter until they are gold and transparent. Holly begins banging her feeding pan on the floor to indicate it is supper time for her too.

The fire burns warm on the old stone hearth, and Jonquil gets right in the fireplace beside it. And Jill says, as she lights the candles, "you know, I don't mind winter at all. I find it rather a snug season."

And so it is!

February

THE SEED CATALOGUES BLOOM LIKE
the fabled Rose of Sharon. Now the difference in Jill and me
becomes apparent. I am for ordering a few packets from
everybody that sends us a catalogue, as a kind of thank-you
and to encourage them in their work. Jill is for consolidation,
getting all we can from just one place. She says it is better to
have one order that is a good one, than to spread around.

"What difference would it make to Mr. Burpee," says she,
"to send three packets of Crosby beets?"

So she makes out a firm order for everything from just one
seed company and despatches it.

Then it turns out that this is not the firm that handles Bibb
lettuce. So we order a packet of that.

Then we check our list and find edible-podded peas are not
on it so an order goes to somebody else for that.

It is true that every one of the top companies has some varieties others do not have, and a cross-section gives the ardent
gardener complete choice.

> Ah never blooms so red the rose
> As in the garden pages glows,
> Never crops so free from pest
> As on P.20 and the rest.
> And all the beauties we'll be growing
> Blossom in catalogues without our hoeing!

It is time now to bring in the branches to force into flowering. I am told that even pear branches will come to bloom,
but we have never tried them. Apple and quince and for-
sythia are favorites, the delicate sprays in an old glass battery

219

jar bring spring in ahead of schedule. We have never had much luck with bulbs in the house but I lay that partly to the restless life they lead. The wide window sills all over the house are perfect lookouts for cockers. And Hollyberry, by standing on tiptoe, spans the little loveseat entirely and leans a large half of herself against my study windowpane.

The sound of a crash usually means we forgot and put something on a window sill to get sun. And we find narcissi and hyacinths don't like to be tossed to the floor, even if they are gathered up and put back in the bowl.

I keep my beloved African violets in a quiet and secluded corner in an east window behind a fairly staunch couch and with a good stout Windsor antique armchair deployed in front. This works very well, as a rule, but one day this week there was an unusual commotion as two strange dogs, speaking a strange dialect came down the road and leaned against our fence and made communist statements.

And I found Jonquil sitting in my violet garden, right on top of one of the best Blue Heiresses. Snow Girl was flat on her side and Red King leaned dangerously. As I gathered little Jonquil up, she had a sort of wreath of African violet leaves in her hair.

But I reflected that Jonquil is irreplaceable and much as I love my violets, I can take a leaf and put it in vermiculite and start again on Blue Heiress. And I further reflected that living with dogs gives you a very sound sense of values. For you rather extend your belief in the importance of love and loyalty and a gay heart into the rest of the world. So if a friend does something that seems quite dreadful, you are already conditioned to think, ah, but what a heart he has!

We set our values very early in our life with dogs and cats. We never knew why Silver chewed the middle out of my one and only American Beauty down-and-silk puff, but she did. She was just a lonesome puppy, because we had gone away and left her briefly. And when she died, suddenly and terribly a short time later, that patched puff was incredibly dearer with the patch.

From then on, whenever a gay Irish tail has sculled across a coffee table, as Ed Shenton would say, and a bit of milk glass goes down, I only say, "better move the milk glass."

With children, too, I feel one should keep the most important things in mind. Nobody wants to skate across a cascade of blocks and bring up flat in an electric train, but I had an aunt who was an immaculate housekeeper. (She was not a blood aunt, a marriage one.) And when my cousins and I would get all set up to play an elaborate game of store, with shiny navy beans in piles here and there and a Teddy bear or two and five rag dolls sitting around, and a pony, in case they wanted to ride away, and so on, my aunt would then appear in the door and order us to put everything back in the closet, on the proper shelves. It was time for lunch and we couldn't leave a solitary bean around.

On Papa's side of the family, everyone did more or less as he pleased. With eight lively children, Grandma would sit and play the piano and sing while the house rocked with thunder. She did object mildly when the four boys got to doing target practice in the bedroom, because it made holes in the ceiling and walls. But mostly she played and sang and looked beautiful and let them go their way.

I loved to visit there, when I was little, because I thought apple pie for breakfast was a very sound idea.

One enchanted season Mama and I stayed on Grandfather's farm while Father was off gold-mining or something in the wilds of Mexico. The little one-room red schoolhouse was wonderful to me. At recess it was only a step to the brook which purled along between cool cress and forget-me-nots and had plenty of shiny good frogs along the edge. We ate our lunches under great trees overlooking a sweet meadow. And since I was a city-school product, the work was a vacation too.

The school was full of cousins. In the migratory life of a mining engineer, ties have little time to form, and I had none. Before I would get to know a few children, we would move. Here were a ready-made group, mine by relationship. The extremely wealthy cousins in the pink stone mansion had a store complete with little wires that carried the money boxes back and forth. The poor cousins had a henhouse which we could make into a palace of our own.

In the mansion, I could have tea and biscuits. In the raggedy house I could help collect eggs, warm and polished and beautiful in the little woven basket.

Years later when I drove back down what had become a superhighway, and passed the little red schoolhouse, such a pang shot through me as one must feel shut out of paradise and seeing it in a dream.

Some of the houses in the valley are closed now, while their people are in Florida. They have a lonely look, shuttered and still, and wearing the State Police signs on their doors. Icicles hang from the eaves in long silver needles, and around the unshoveled walks, the small prints of stay-at-home rabbits make fascinating patterns.

It is a fine thing to follow the warmth to the South, I always think, but I am always sorry for the house left lonely.

Those of us who stay in the valley make out very well. We build up the fires, light the candles, and the soup kettle over the hearth makes a pleasant simmering sound. No hearts of palm here, but on the other hand, corned beef and cabbage and flaky potatoes cooked in the rich liquid make a handsome meal for anybody. The corned beef (good done at home, too) slices in tender rosy slices, the cabbage is in delicate ivory wedges, the carrots from our own garden are honey-sweet. Open a well-done potato and spoon over some of the long-simmered juices, and there you have a dish fit for any-

body. Not Bahamian mustard on the corned beef as it is too
rich, but a mild musty Bavarian mustard.

In lieu of roaming a moonlit tropical beach, we play Scrabble by the fire, later on pop big fluffy popcorn and get out the
red apples. And then, perhaps, play a few records. César
Franck's symphony or some old Caruso, thrilling and rich
over the thin reedy sound of the early accompaniments.

Or folk songs. From "Borrachito" to the "Eddystone
Light," I love them all. The Latin American folk music has
a nostalgic quality, the English a robust melancholy as a rule.
Andrew Somers to Frank Luther—we can really run the
gamut.

Or if we do not feel like changing records, we read. And
stretched out by the fire with a really good book to read and
popcorn at hand is not a very dire fate to wish on anyone.

Making a hilarious discovery like *No Time For Sergeants*
is better than a trip any day. Or I can pop right back to the
Middle Ages reading *The Cornerstone* and feel just ready
for a Crusade.

Country living in these days may be rather effete, with
music at the turn of the knob, news over the air waves every
few minutes, books coming in by mail—and then you can see
and hear a whole opera if so minded, on television.

We live in an age, it seems, when the whole world is at
our doorstep, no matter where we may be.

I often think how it was here in the early days when the
mail came delivered by a man on a horse. Often he drove a
pig or two to deliver somewhere along the line. It wasn't
exactly air mail!

For music, there was no knob to turn. There were even
times when it was sinful to make music. Although I dare say
mothers then hummed secret lullabies as they rocked the little
wooden cradles, for it is in a mother's heart to sing to her
baby.

News came by riders, or travelers who came post chaise

from Boston might bring it. Books and magazines were found rarely in ordinary homes, except the Bible and possibly *Pilgrim's Progress*.

A home was a pretty private place then, with no John Cameron Swayze or John K. M. McCaffery or Ed Murrow large as life and delivering news so hot it smokes every evening.

Letter writing has fallen out of common practice of late, but one fine feature of cold winter evenings is time to write to dear friends far away. A leisurely chat via paper is rewarding. One has only to read some of the letters of the past to realize how well people portray themselves when writing to friends. Much of the best of Katherine Mansfield, for instance, is in her letters. Keats and Shelley wrote letters which reveal their genius as much as their poetry does. If only we had one or two letters of Shakespeare—

I wonder at times why so many people have been so fevered to prove Shakespeare was not Shakespeare. He was Bacon, he was, as of now, Kit Marlowe, he was the Dark Lady, and so on. I suppose genius is so astounding that one can hardly believe it, and it is easier to take if it comes from a high place. I personally do not see how anyone could read Bacon and Marlowe and not feel how different their whole beings were, but that is my opinion. I find no trouble at all in believing in Will. Any more than I do in believing in Abraham Lincoln, the most unlikely to succeed, one would have said. What could be more incredible than that this log-cabin boy with his shambling gait and attacks of melancholy and lack of polish should dominate the life of our country through a terrible war?

Documents and pictures will keep future questioners from trying to prove Lincoln was somebody else, thank goodness.

Valentine the saint was a Christian martyr who died about 270 A.D. in Rome. I wonder whether he leans over "the gold bars of heaven" like Rossetti's "Blessed Damozel" and watches while on his day heavily ribboned boxes of candy and bouquets of roses in green waxen armor go merrily from one to another!

Perfume seems so appropriate to Valentine's Day as a token to "the object of one's affection" as the dictionary says with such reserve. Possibly perfume is more romantic than most things, for a whiff can transport us to the sandalwood groves or the land of far Araby.

Flowers certainly, for flowers breathe of young love. Roses especially. But when I was turning sixteen, my beau brought violets, a rare luxury. The cool dark purple was beautiful as a dream, the glossy pointed leaves framed the flowers, and the stems were wound with silver foil. The air on Olympus could not smell sweeter than those violets. I laid them on my pillow at night. It did not matter that in our little town by the time the violets had been carted in on the old sweating Northwestern train, they were half dead, nor that by the next day the leaves rusted, the flowers crimped with death. Those violets were immortal, for I can smell them yet.

I sprinkled them with cool water. I laid them in the icebox—too near the cake of river ice Mr. Lutz had just tonged in as it turned out—but never mind, I had my violets. The whole world was a blossoming garden to me!

Years later, after my little Mother died, I found a small box tied with pink ribbon in her big walnut dresser. In it were all the valentines I ever had made for her from the first wavering I love yu Mama to the erudite Sugar is sweet and so are You. From blue and pink crayon on oatmeal paper to a fancy deckle-edged pale blue paper with an original poem by the rising young writer aged fifteen.

So Mama was sentimental too! Who would have guessed it? As Papa and I emoted around like rockets, she was so quiet and serene and so sensible. And all the time she was saving those valentines!

This was a holiday for her to give parties, and oh the table frilly with rose-colored ribbons and shining with newly polished silver. Oh the little heart-shaped cakes, a bite apiece and cloud-pink with icing. The maple nut parfaits and the candied roseleaves. I remember these better than the main part of the dinner, naturally being young and dessert-minded. I can recall thin slices of rosy sugar-cured country ham, glazed with brown sugar and deep with clove. The vegetables I cannot remember at all. Sweet-potato soufflé was there. And thimble-sized light rolls.

This would be a faculty party when History and Latin and Geology and Mathematics would forget their differences and have a merry time. Followed by charades with a sedate Professor stamping around in an old bear rug being, naturally a BEAR.

The valentine tea would be more quiet, ladies only, and the clink of silver tongs on fair china cups as I passed and passed wee rolled and open sandwiches, eating several every time I turned around.

Followed a party for my gang. We just swarmed all over everything and ate like mastodons. Rolled up the Orientals and danced. Finished off with hot chocolate beaten with Mama's Mexican beater and with cinnamon spicing it, and dollops of heavy sweet whipped cream—plus the rest of the tiny heart cakes.

And finally, when Valentine's Day was really over, a whole half week of it, a moonlight walk with my beau along the snow-deep streets of the little town.

Dreams spinning silver pathways over the snow. We always began with a million dollars, that was all accounted for and settled. But the yacht was a problem. I held out for a rose-covered cottage. I said quite frankly that life on a yacht was not for me because I got seasick even in a canoe.

There are still people who ask us if we aren't lonely in winter, way off in the country. Jill says that it would be a real trick to be lonely with dogs and cats swarming around, birds whipping in and out of the feeders, neighbors popping in for a snack, and the woodwork to repaint in the Maple room.

People scatter so in summer, but in winter we are closely knit as a community. We can have eighteen people for a buffet supper without even adding them up. And even if a sudden blizzard whirls in as a last gesture from winter, most will arrive, snowy and triumphant. Only those who live at the top of some place like George's hill can't make it.

My theory of entertaining is simple, have a lot to eat and let everybody help themselves. We used to cook up fabulous and difficult dishes when we entertained trying to emulate some mental Waldorf-Astoria. Now we have a couple of hot casseroles, something with burgundy savoring it, and a roast of beef, perhaps, with juices following the knife down as it cuts. A salad in the big wooden bowl with everything in it, and a cheese board furnished well with various cheeses.

Last year we decided on an innovation. We had a winter picnic. We used a checked cloth, paper plates, cups, napkins. We had fires in both fireplaces burned down to good coals. And we had hamburgers and frankfurters and coleslaw with pineapple chunks and celery seed and toasted buns and all the mustards and relishes in the category of such.

We had picnic ice buckets with cold drinks and big jugs of hot coffee and ice-cream sticks in an iced thermos pail.

We had more fun than ever in our lives and Jill says it is just as well, for we shall never have the energy to do it again. Jill said "a five course dinner with turkey would have been easier."

For one thing, I spent half a day on the mustards and relishes and pickles and such, and putting up picnic tables. Jill spent hours on the fires, getting them right for grilling. What is so simple outdoors in summer, proved to be a lot of work inside in winter. All the little heated units we set up under the casseroles were a bother too.

Then there were the dogs, who are not accustomed to platters of meat being set on the floor without its meaning something to them.

We were madly splitting buns when the guests came, so we turned over the cooking of the hamburgers and franks to Phil and Steve. They hardly had anything to eat because they cooked so much.

Afterward we played the word-guessing game until around one, and everyone said a winter picnic was a fine idea. But as we cleared up the next day Jill said, "after this, in winter, we eat a regular meal."

It was fun, though. I even thought so as I screwed the caps back on fifteen different mustard jars.

Jill has been reading the current mysteries. I read two and

got so cross. My quarrel with mystery writers is that their heroes and heroines behave so stupidly that I lose patience with them right off the bat. The heroines always go sneaking about dark houses at midnight after a murder, just looking for a good book to read. The heroes rush into black alleys looking for a guy who knows all—and find him all right.

Nobody on the right side ever carries a gun. If he is a cop, he leaves it at home, if a newspaper man, he doesn't care for guns.

Hero and heroine always *tell all* to anybody around, who is, naturally, the murderer or his best pal. They get into strange autos, they go into dives just for the fun of it apparently.

And when they really know who murdered Mr. Bascom, they go right up to his hide-out like a Fuller Brush salesman and take him to task in a very moral but impractical way. At this point, I feel they deserve to be killed. If they haven't what the old lady called "the sense God gave a goose," they aren't going to contribute much to the world anyway.

The author always saves them, but are they worth it, I ask.

I realize the exigencies of the plot make it necessary that they get kidnapped, shut up, half killed, or tossed from a racing car and all that, but I think the authors are a bit lazy about the way they get them into the various fixes. I just find it hard to believe people can be quite as dumb as the heroes and heroines of most mysteries.

Another thing I wonder about is how they get along without eating and sleeping. Possibly the beautiful blue-eyed maidens take a snack while the private eye or newsman is rushing along into another blind alley, but it isn't cricket for the man to eat. He drinks black coffee, or whiskey—and how much whiskey! He takes dozens of cold showers, and believe thee me—as George Gobel would say—those showers are wondrous. He can be knocked flat, jumped on, banged on the head with a pistol, kicked, tossed across a room. But let him just get back to his cold shower and he is fine and dandy, all set to go out and begin again.

If I ever chance on a mystery where the people sit down and eat so much as some scrambled eggs and bacon, I decide it is a good book. This may be why I like the Nero Wolfe stories for Nero Wolfe not only watches his orchids and drinks tubs of beer but he eats good meals. Even Archie, his overworked assistant, gets a sandwich now and then.

The main time food enters into the lives of any character is when it is poisoned, and then it is generally something in a carafe which they just toss off, or in a martini pitcher.

I will except the Lockridges from these complaints for Pam and Jerry North are so unutterably charming, as is Inspector Weigand, that I wouldn't care how little sense they had nor whether they consumed anything beyond their favorite just-perfect martinis. Besides, they have the Siamese cats who would hold up any book by themselves. Gin and Martini are so much like my own Esmé and so Siamese!

We used to see deer often, lately they are rare as the side roads began to be built up. But we never go down the Jeremy Swamp Road without seeing again in our mind's eye the four deer we once had to slow up for. Father led the way so proudly, mama came behind and two little twin fawns tipped after. It was a moment to hold in memory always.

It is a comforting thought that beautiful moments never die. One can collect them, store them away, and they are always at hand to bring forth again and appreciate. There are many of them, and all one needs is an awareness to have them.

The little Victorian love seat is doomed. Holly has used it as a taking-off jump for some time, and a sixty-five-pound Irish bouncing on it has done the springs little good, or the frame either. We now sit on it with trepidation, hoping it will hold up just a little longer. It is a valiant little piece, it has gone all over the country with me, been re-done innumerable times, survived the children's games for years, and I suppose might be rebuilt once more provided it could then go into genteel retirement. But something more rugged ought to go in that place, for the view on that side of the room is such an important view for the dogs—the road lies down the hill and you can see trucks and cars and cows and all kinds of fine things. In winter you can even see Jeremy Swamp Road which is beyond the swamp and marks our boundary. Farm wagons roll along there in season, children ride bicycles, and the postman comes by. Of course if Holly would just tiptoe up on the love seat it would help. But she prefers to take off from the top of the couch in the next room and sail through the air, bounding once lightly on the floor and landing like a jet plane.

She carries her current bone with her. The boys at the store are so good about saving her good marrow bones. The cockers can take a bone or leave it, chew awhile and go on to higher things. But Holly has to have her bone right with her. When she goes out, she grasps it firmly in her mouth and leaps out with it. When she scratches at the door to come in, there is the bone in her mouth. She takes it to bed with her, resting a happy paw on it as she sleeps. When she goes riding, the bone goes riding too. She would no more leave it behind than a lady would abandon her purse.

When Louis put the groceries in the car yesterday, she rose up on the back seat and looked out at him, bone in mouth, and he was so overcome that he rushed back to fix her a fresh bag of them.

I tell her we could support the family on her bones, for they are elegant fresh bones, full of marrow and with much meat on them. The ones that have doubtful value for a dog I make soup of and what soup it is. Holly gets only non crushable, non splinterable, firmly rounded knuckles or leg bones. The rest, scrubbed and simmered with herbs and onion and vegetables and spaghetti or rice, or done with lentils or dried lima beans, makes a soup that one could live on. I never make it without thinking of all the hungry people in the world and wishing I could share it with them. Why, why, why, I ask again, must children go hungry in so many far parts of the world when just a few plain bones could furnish forth a feast?

Here in our green valley or snow-deep valley or blazing autumnal valley, we have so much. It seems dreadfully much if I stop to think of it. I tell myself there is no reason for me to feel guilty eating a soup made from Holly's extra bones, but there it is. I often do. Surely someone soon will come up with a way to send food and clothing for everybody where it is needed.

The many fine organizations such as Save the Children fund and Foster Parents Plan and above all CARE are at least a small finger in the dike of human need. They do a superb job in a wilderness of suffering.

But food is the world's problem, and far from being solved.

Economics is a strange and mysterious world to me. I wish I could learn more about it. It would be fine if one could go back to school for a year every now and then and pick up all the knowledge missed before. Any adult education is a valuable thing, I think. It is good to learn, nothing takes the place of opening vistas in one's mind. But there are all kinds of things practical to know about that would be good to investigate. Aside from economics, I would like to know more about music, to be able to understand Bach as well as enjoy him. It is all very well to sink blissfully in the beauty of Bach, but it would be even better to have some idea of what was happening.

Then it would be excellent to have a course in modern

poetry because the modern poetry I had in school is no longer modern.

And everyone could do well with a knowledge of design and decorating. For the impact of color and shape on our lives is always vital.

Comparative religion would benefit most of us, for with understanding of other religions would come greater tolerance and sympathy.

On the whole, I thought, while ironing pillowcases today, we all ought to stop everything and go right back to school!

Going out to the kennels this morning, I was surprised to find George standing in the doorway to the barn, staring up at the roof. He had the dog pans in his hand and was just standing, staring.

"Sh," he whispered, "look—a nest!"

And there it was, on the beam over the door, a new nest. Made chiefly of straw, but with a few feathers, some of which had fallen to the floor.

"I saw her, too," said George, "she's a sharp-looking little bird—a long bill and tail. What a time to build a nest—February!"

"It can't be," I said, staring too.

George got the wheelbarrow and stood up and felt, and yes, there was one egg in the nest, he said solemnly.

Then we were in a quandary, for the barn door is supposed to be shut to keep the heat in the kennels. And on a day with the temperature at twenty, I hated to leave it open. But how could we shut the little bird away from her nest?

We settled on leaving the door open all day, but closing it at night when she ought to be snugged down on her nest anyway and not roving around. So far I have not identified the sharp little bird but I hope to see her before long—and I wonder whatever made her try to raise a family in New England in the coldest of winter?

I often think it would be fun to travel as far as the migratory birds do. To set sail in a ship laden with "ivory, peacocks, apes, sandalwood, cedarwood and sweet white wine." To put in at coral isles where sapphire seas foam in. However, I come back from these journeys when I realize how far it would be from the children and that it would not be easy to take nine dogs around the world.

So on the whole it is a good idea to pile another log on the fire and travel instead to the Middle Ages while finishing *The Cornerstone*.

Or we can pop corn and talk about trips we have taken in the past, and live them over again.

One of the best, we decide, was the trip to Montreal when Jill judged the dog show there. It was early spring and the mountains on the way up incredibly lovely with their misting of emerald. The rivers tumbled with mountain snows, and all along the way farmers were out doing their spring chores.

We came to Montreal about sunset, the sky a pale fire above this strange city with its Mount Royal rising so abruptly in the midst. The mountain is an extinct volcano, and now clinging to its sides are parks and steeply slanting streets of houses.

We stopped to ask directions when we got in but we could not find anybody who spoke English and our French had long since evaporated. By the time our willing and affable man had found out what street we meant by our writing it down, since we couldn't pronounce it so he understood it, we listened with awe to a long voluble description of where we should turn, and thence where, with arm waving and gay smiles. Of this was understood not a word.

It was getting late, and we were tired and hungry, and I was nervous. We made various sallies around the city, getting farther and farther from our objective. And then, in the end, when we had come full circle like lost hunters, we stopped at a tiny filling station and a handsome Frenchman in a blue beret and a dark suit came out.

His dark eyes shone, he clapped his hands and laughed.

"Ah——ah—— Con—neck—ticoot," he said. "You from it, yes?"

We said yes, we were.

He spoke English, he thought, and it was enough so we were made to understand he had a daughter who lived in Naugatuck, which is only a few miles from us. He had been there to visit. So we were old friends, neighbors.

And he put us on the right street and we parted with mutual expressions of joy at having met.

Further trouble developed because I could not read the French signs well enough or fast enough. Jill would whirl past something and I would cry, "oh that's Cote de Neige—we should have turned there."

Then I just figured out it is forbidden to enter here when we had already entered.

When I wasn't madly trying to decipher signs and watch, I was praying for Jill, for the drivers who whipped past were rather difficult. Everybody in Montreal seemed to drive in the same place at once.

Then I began to worry about the money. I had made the horrifying discovery when we stopped inside Canada to buy some oranges, that our money was not worth as much as Canadian money.

"But it can't be!" I cried, "you mean American—United States money isn't worth as much?"

"No, it isn't," said Jill firmly, "and don't get your feelings hurt about it, it is just the way it happens to be."

But I brooded over this. It developed I couldn't even depend on the stamps I had in my purse. So then I began to wonder whether we would run out of money and then what would we do?

Jill got really out of patience with me as she made turns,

dodged little taxis, and tried to avoid those streets forbidden.

"I wish you'd relax," she said crossly.

"Relax!" I retorted, "with us way off here and our money hardly worth anything!" And I added, "and nobody can understand a word we say, either."

Finally we came to our destination, and this was funny too. We had reservations in the Town and Country Motel at the edge of Montreal on the theory that we would stay outside the main city overnight and brave it in the light of day. The only trouble was that the Town and Country Motel was on the *other* side of Montreal, which, added to all our devious driving around and about, meant that we had covered all of Montreal anyway before we got there.

As we fell out of the car, a Doberman pinscher came to meet us, followed by a French—or French Canadian manager, who blessedly spoke English. With a dog and this man, I felt at home right away, and when we were ushered into a delightful big room with a good bath and easy chairs and a coffee table, I felt still better. After cleaning up, we had a French dinner which was enough to restore anyone from the brink of the grave. We even negotiated the French menu, since we have, from time to time eaten in French restaurants in New York.

The next day we met two perfectly charming men at the hotel for breakfast, the president and trainer of the Montreal Obedience Club and they were as English as anything out of Cambridge.

The show was a real experience. Jill judged for six hours, I should say, and in all that time there was hardly a sound. The gallery sat so still that one had to whisper if one wanted a glass of water. There never was anything like this in the United States. At our dog shows you yell to be heard. The concentrated attention was terrific, Jill said it took her an hour to get used to her voice being the sole one booming out as she gave commands.

There was no argument between handlers, nobody protested any score, everyone thanked the judge, thanked the stewards. It was a lesson we shall never forget. Such sportsmanship is a rare and wonderful thing to behold. It was a big show, and yet smoothly run to the last detail.

Afterward we went to dinner at a member's house on the mountain, where all of Montreal was spread below us, dazzling with lights, mysterious and beautiful. The only thing I have ever seen to compare with it at all is the view of Los Angeles from the top of the mountain there.

The buffet dinner was suitable for an article in *Gourmet* and we picked our way among boxers as we served ourselves at the long table, which fascinated me as it hung from the ceiling by what looked like silver chains. The dog talk was good and comfortable and we felt we had known these people for years.

We did the sights in the morning, creeping around in chalky crypts and admiring McGill which is higher up than the stars, and seeing cathedrals. The best of that was watching a bevy of pretty pink-cheeked nuns taking pictures on the steps of St. Joseph's. They skipped about holding up their heavy black skirts, they laughed, and they were delightful. This was obviously a special pilgrimage and a very special treat.

When we packed to leave, we wondered whether we could ever retrace our way back through Montreal, but as we moved out to the car, a laundryman jumped from a truck by the main gate and ran over with a slip of paper. "Here are the directions," he said, "I know you want them in English. I speak it."

We couldn't get over the courtesy of everyone we saw, even the policemen who waved us by forbidden streets were polite about it, and the time we got hopelessly embroiled with two buses and four cars going the wrong way, nobody shouted at all.

"This is one place we are coming to again," said Jill, as we

crossed the St. Lawrence. At least we thought we were crossing the St. Lawrence.

It left us in a very thoughtful mood about our own country, however. I would rather hate to have a Canadian estimate
us on the basis of a few days in New York, shoved and
shouted at. And as they come down more and more to our
dog shows, I hope they don't copy some of our manners.

"You Americans seem to take it so hard," said one Canadian
handler to me.

Perhaps that is the answer. The American rules have been,
up to now, stricter and less flexible. And after Mrs. B goes
to thirteen shows with Reginald and he still fails to pass, she
gets "nerved up" as we say here.

Possibly Americans take everything hard, I wonder. Do
we have a national drive to be the best, get the farthest, outdo
everyone else? This competitive spirit can backfire. After
all, the dog world is a reflection of the other worlds we live in.

Most of these Canadians were interested in one aim, to have
their dogs educated, to do a better job themselves. If they
failed, they accepted it quietly. Whereas often in our country, a judge can be mobbed by disappointed handlers.

I gathered that there are stresses and strains plenty in Montreal, as there must be with two nationalities living together.
Even our taxi driver pointed out a small cemetery with the
words, "there is a pro-test'unt cemeterie," as if it were a freak.

I noticed that our hosts made a point of being bilingual.
But as far as the dog show was concerned, French and Eng-
lish sat side by side, and the dogs worked equally well to
French or English commands.

Coming back from Montreal we made the drive in a day,
eleven hours. We could have stopped and done some sight-
seeing, and taken a leisurely trip. We had provided with
George for it. But somehow when we got as far as Burling-
ton, Vermont, we thought we might go on to Massachusetts.
We began to wonder how the dogs were. There they were,

all alone, said we. Would George let the Irish out or would
he keep her in the run? Would Jerry and Tiki get mixed up
over a rubber rabbit they love—and had we put away that
rabbit before we left?

Would George remember to go over at night and feed
Holly that extra meal. Would Sister eat at all with me gone?
So we drove just a little farther.

"We can stay in Williamstown," said Jill, "and get in
earlier in the morning."

I love to eat when I travel and I had in mind a festive dinner but we decided that would take quite a time. Lobster
can't be hurried. So we stopped at a Howard Johnson's and
had a good hot jumbo frankfurter and a glass of milk and
drove on just a little farther.

So then it was silly to stop just eighty miles from home
when we could go on and get in by just keeping at it. And
around eleven at night we came around the corner of Jeremy
Swamp Road and heard the sweetest music this side of
heaven, the welcome barking of all the dogs. All fine, all
warm and well-fed but wishing to state they were the lone-
liest creatures on this earth. So Jill put the yard lights on
and let half a dozen in the house before we even took our
coats off.

Sister cried bitterly for twenty minutes, and then forgot all
about the whole thing, being a forgiving person. Everybody
clustered around as we fixed a hot cheese sandwich and we
told them there wasn't a dog in Canada to compare with them.

And so to bed!

Since Jill is a pretty popular judge, being always so fair, so
steady, and being herself a handler, which gives her a good
knowledge of the obedience problems, we pop off from time
to time for a show, and have to spend the night. The Montreal
trip was a longer haul; one night is easy, for we think the dogs
just get around to missing us by the time we get back.

But it has given me a chance to see the complete change in

travel in America since I was growing up. Papa was a terrific wanderer and we were always going somewhere. In summer we camped, because he adored being a woodsman, and we carried everything from tents with porch awnings to a homemade refrigerator. Nothing could have been more uncomfortable or more ghastly than a camping trip with Father, except a winter trip when we had to stay in hotels. The times I have slept on the outside of a bed, or propped up in a chair because I did not *trust* the bed at all, are too numerous to list. We were always driving beyond any city, because he felt we couldn't get started early enough in the morning from a city and he was a dawn-chaser. So we ended in little villages in dreadful little hotels.

How Father would have adored motels. If motels had been in existence, poor Mama could never have stayed home a single week end all her married life.

I think, therefore, that I am peculiarly fitted to appreciate motels. They dazzle me. Jill says I would like to just take a trip from motel to motel never mind where we went.

But you drive up, you have a reservation, you go into a room as big as an auditorium, practically everything is wrapped in cellophane and I have fun breaking the seals. A pitcher of cracked ice appears at once, a local newspaper, postcards. Double Hollywood-size beds with foam mattresses and pillows, easy chairs, reading lights, coffee tables, television, phones. And as a final gesture, wall-to-wall carpeting!

Then if you want another book that is in the car, you pop out and get it. If you decide on a drive in the moonlight, out you go.

Once you are in a hotel, and the porter has lugged all your things in that you *think* you might need, and the car has gone to the garage, you are trapped. It takes an hour to get it back.

I like the people who stay in the next apartment too. They are always, it seems to me, families taking all the children on a grand tour, or sons taking mama for a trip after papa has died.

The sons are so gentle and sweet, the mama's so appreciative that son would leave wife and children just to take her somewhere, it is touching.

We stayed once in a new kind, a super, super-colossal motel. It cost twelve dollars a night, and was worth it. It had everything. One could spend a month there. French cuisine, with the best sauce for the shrimp I ever ate, gift shops, soft desert colors in the décor. And the beds were amazing. A troop of cavalry could be accommodated in each bed.

We had stayed in a hotel just before. In the hotel none of the old-fashioned standing lamps worked. The bathroom was dingy. There was one chair. The curtains were that greyed Victorian color of lace. Jukeboxes blared in our ears all night, and there wasn't a scrap of air.

The carpet was worn, the wallpaper crawling with livid flowers.

"Well," said Jill, "at least we can have breakfast in bed."

Not at all. The dining room was closed all day the next day, it being Sunday, and we had to stagger out and walk three blocks to a very greasy tin-spoon place.

I don't quite know what is to become of the hotels, except of course in New York and Boston and such cities. For on top of everything else, you can get up in the morning, start the car and be right on the highway where you want to be.

Possibly hotels can manage with train and plane travelers but for the ones who take to the road in cars, I wonder.

Jill says it isn't my problem. I have no stock in any hotel, and I couldn't conceivably run a motel. She says I would invite all the nice people to just stay on for the summer.

Naturally, with our American talent for excesses, we shall soon have too many motels. More motels than people. Even though we are nomads and constantly on the move, the rate at which we see motels going up is appalling. The entire road to Hartford is paved with them already.

On the American scene, also relatively new, are the Howard

Johnsons and the Glass Houses and so on. These are a great boon to the traveling family, for they insure clean, safe, economical, quick food. When Connie was a baby, we traveled a lot, and I can still remember the horrible moment when a waitress in a restaurant in Lima, Ohio said to me, "I wouldn't give the baby that. I have a child of my own."

I had ordered beef for her. And as I looked at her round little face framed in misty curls, by heart gave such a lurch. A waitress less kind would have let my darling eat that beef and maybe die of poisoning. Those were pioneer days for travel.

A really fine hotel is lovely to be in, I would be the last to say not. To stay at the Williamsburg Inn is worth living for, for quite a time. There one has yellow roses in a silver vase, sent with the compliments of the manager, a bowl of fruit with a silver knife and a folded snowy napkin when one gets in from doing the Governor's Palace. When they bring your car, they do not walk, they run. And the rooms—and this is a compliment—are even more elegant than a quality motel room. Engraved stationery is a delicate gesture and push-button service is ready at any minute.

But this is rather rare.

Many of the New York hotels are fabulous. Because New York is a city of apartments and hotels. Naturally my favorite is the Roosevelt because the spaniel show is there, in the ballroom and it seems so cosy to be in a hotel with several hundred dogs barking madly.

But I wonder, thinking of the American scene, whether the ordinary little hotel is not doomed. It will be interesting to see in the next few years.

Meanwhile, here in the country, passing visitors can stay in the 1750 House. There isn't a motel until you get almost into Danbury. I don't know what our zoning committee would say if anyone wanted to build one, I suspect they would not like the idea. And if people get hungry as they come through our village, they can get a hamburger at the little stand by the crossroads and just drive on.

As I came in from burning the trash I thought of Millay.

White sky, over the hemlocks bowed with snow,
Saw you not at the beginning of evening the ant-
lered buck and his doe
Standing in the apple orchard?

The thermometer was dropping like a skier on a good slope. Snow forecast for the week end and cold. The old house settles in the crackling cold. I pulled off my mittens and listened to the voice of the house. All this talk of motels, it seemed to say, stuff and nonsense. Everybody should stay at home and keep their fires going.

Can anything, asked the old house, take the place of home?

Jill was doing something delicious with onions and tomatoes and crab meat. Holly was lugging her bone around the kitchen. Sister was on the couch and the others were severally happily arranged, Jonquil, of course, right in the fire.

"Well," I said, "here's a good cliché. East, West, home's best."

"My goodness," said Jill, slicing an onion, "you mean you don't want to start for New Orleans tomorrow?"

"No," I said.

"I thought you'd give that idea up by suppertime," she said. "You would travel anywhere, if you could get home for supper."

The light falls slanting across the swamp. Color is deeper now in February, the stems of shrubs that I never shall know begin to glow with deeper tones of garnet and yellow and green. It is still winter, we shall have a heavy snow this week end. There will be bitter weather, dark days, for March has winter in it too in New England.

But the sky has a different look as the sun drops down. More apricot, perhaps. Less lemon color. I decide I must constantly observe the shape of the branches on every tree while they are still bare and sharply etched in the white light.

The first star comes out, so pure, so cold. And I think Miss Millay's lines must have been mine

> But the roaring of the fire
> And the warmth of fur
> And the boiling of the kettle
> Were beautiful to her!

Any day now the imperative footsteps of spring will fall on the snow-cold ground. And winter will be laid aside!

March

NOW GREAT WINDS ROAR DOWN THE canyons of the sky. Branches crash, brooks race, snow scuds along greystone walls. The world is incredibly clean as the strong vibrant music of March pounds in the pulses and invades the chilled lungs of winter.

As for the wind, despite the scientists I feel nobody knows whence it comes or whither it goes. The dark of north woods is in it, the white breath of polar ice, and underlaying this just a whisper of melting warmth as it passes some sun-warmed hollows where the secret little flowers of spring woods are already stirring, oh so gently, so strongly under the sheath of moist earth.

How it blows away the settled feelings of snug hearth and flickering candlelight! Now I think suddenly, with Millay

> It's little I care what path I take
> And where it leads it's little I care;
> But out of this house, lest my heart break,
> I must go, and off somewhere.

I can fancy taking sixpence in my pocket, a loaf of crusty long bread and a wedge of sweet fine Cheddar and setting off for the world's end to see where the wind comes from. I suddenly know just why my forefathers in 1672 left the secure little English village and went on the wild seas to the new land. Of course they were brave, as I am not. That first Richard Mather, a man of God, prayed when the storm nearly foundered the ship and wrote complacently that his prayers saved her.

I have always loved those English stories about men who took to the road, eating under leafy hedges, sharing their bread and wine with fellow wayfarers. It is all mixed up with hawthorne blossoming and nightingales singing and the silvery rattle of a tinker's pans as a cart jolts down the road.

I think in spite of poverty and political troubles along the way, the strolling play companies of Shakespeare's day must have had a merry time. The pennons flying over the cobbled inn yards, the small boys scrambling about, the ladies of the villages and town peering demurely from leaded casements as they dismounted, the music sounding in the blue of evening and then the play. Torches flaring, lutes being tuned, the smell of damp leather jerkins, of ale, of stables, and the voice of a young player sounding bravely—

> Was this the face that launched a thousand ships
> And burned the topless towers of Ilium?

Possibly, Kit Marlowe was there himself and thought he had excellently turned a line. And indeed that description of the fatal beauty of Helen of Troy would have been enough to make him memorable if he had never written anything else.

Well, I am not wandering the byways of merrie old England, I remind myself. I am hanging blankets on the line in Connecticut. I have been standing with a clothespin in my mouth for some time, bending against the wind and wandering far away.

But as I hang up one blanket I begin to think of Will Shakespeare himself. It is just not possible that this man's plays, written three hundred and fifty years ago, and count that time, three hundred and fifty, have never, but never, stopped being played. And read, and studied. He survives all fashion. Extremely English, he is claimed by all nationalities. He is played in modern dress without scenery and with the most elaborate fanfare and elegance the atomic age can devise. He is analyzed according to Freud. He is studied in high school English, which sinks many a minor poet.

Giggling girls and gawky boys labor through *Midsummer-Night's Dream* for graduation plays. Dramatic students memorize the old familiar "To be or not to be," "If music be the food of love, play on," and so forth. Most great actors and actresses are unfulfilled unless, at least once, they DO Shakespeare for they and they alone really know how to do him. And the miracle is, he cannot be dulled or diminished. The more he is exploited, the more gold turns up. Who else has been the common man's property for three hundred and fifty years as well as the scholar's?

I was a very fortunate child when I was growing up, for nobody ever laughed at me when I was serious. When I was being an Indian in the back yard, attired in Papa's heavy Navajo blankets, nobody whistled as I played the Bridge of the Gods and declaimed, "The Bridge of the Gods has FALLEN!"

And when Shakespeare came into my life and I began staying home from church to memorize *Romeo and Juliet,* I was allowed to do so. It was the only time in the week I was alone in the house, and the house just reverberated with "No, 'tis not so deep as a well, nor so wide as a church door; but 'tis enough, 'twill serve: ask for me tomorrow, and you shall find me a grave man," as brave gallant Mercutio dies.

I always thought Shakespeare had to kill off Mercutio or he would have stolen the show from Romeo in the next act. He was what the children now call a doll.

In any case, the excitement of saying the play aloud always uplifted me so that when Mama and Papa came home, I could only eat a few helpings of fricasseed chicken with dumplings and a couple of pieces of deep-dish apple pie.

Came the time when I felt I ought to impart the beauty of this to the town. I had discovered Shakespeare, and I was fevered with it. Somehow all my family's friends were persuaded to come to a neighbor's house while I did *Romeo and Juliet,* all alone, by myself. The neighbor was chosen because of having a stairway with a sort of balcony effect. By hanging an Oriental rug over the banister, it gave a really fine, I thought, imitation of Juliet's balcony.

The only remarkable thing about this is that I was a very timid child, a mouselike person. I never talked in gatherings, I just passed the sandwiches. But borne on the wings of Mr. Shakespeare, I did the whole play for a quietly respectful audience of adults who may have been puzzled but were indubitably polite.

In my later years, I have made a good many public appearances, but nothing could ever compare in any way with leaning over that Oriental rug and saying with passion "Farewell, farewell, one kiss and I'll descend."

Naturally descending would have meant landing on the grand piano in the parlor below, but that was nothing.

I can only think that Mr. Will Shakespeare had given me a kind of madness at that time, I just had to let everybody know how wonderful every word was. And after this remarkable exhibition, I went right back to school in my navy-blue middy suit, my hair in neat braids with a barrette on each end, and did not dare recite unless called upon. It all goes to show, I thought, hanging the last blanket on the line, just what Shakespeare can do!

This week end Connie came home and on Sunday morning went to church with me. In the middle of the sermon, a terrible crash sounded, a crackling, bashing sound. "Mama, what was that?" she whispered.

"Church falling in," I whispered back.

I looked for cracks in the ceiling, and found none.

The minister was talking about Paul, and he only paused a minute and went on about Paul and the shipwreck. Paul

said the ship would not be wrecked, in Acts something or other. I admired Paul's courage. Another crack came.

Then the sweet-faced little organist stepped over and murmured something to the minister and moved to the back of the church.

It turned out the organ pipes had sort of blown up as it was a very cold day. It sometimes happens, announced the minister.

"I thought the church might explode on us," said a young choir singer to us afterwards as we gave her a lift home. "It was right by me."

Then an eight-year-old girl, alone in the front pew began to make a glider of her program. She had already combed her long hair with her fingers, straddled the pew, half-climbed into the next pew, and turned to inspect the congregation vacantly person by person.

The minister stopped in the midst of the Cypress voyage and asked her to sit quietly.

"I think we *all* better find out about what happened to Paul on this voyage," he said.

I decided that being a minister in a village is quite an occupation. A big city has problems but not like these.

Faith is a strange thing. In our little church one feels it strong and firm among the farm people and the retired people and the city week-enders who have been able to stagger out for service. To lose faith in the ultimate good in life is to lose life, I thought, as I came down the steep ancient steps of the little white building. The world news may be especially grim, disaster strikes in a home, any one of the ills flesh is heir to may strike us, and it becomes easy to give up. And yet the gathering together of people to pray and worship God, according to their choice of church, whatever it be, is a strong bulwark against defeat and despair.

The very act of saying, "I believe," is a renewal of faith. As for the world, it has been in a parlous state so long that there is no sense in worrying about the future. It is better, I think, to go on believing in goodness and beauty and truth and in God, no matter how we define these terms each of us for ourselves.

And better to live a day at a time. This is a hard task, often, for we tend to keep going to the past and trying to live it over again or looking ahead and uselessly trying to forecast tomorrow and next week and next year. But somebody has said all the time we really have is the NOW. We have today.

To use this day well, that is about the sum of it.

As De la Mare says it:

Look thy last on all things lovely,
Every hour. Let no night
Seal thy sense in deathly slumber
Till to delight
Thou have paid thy utmost blessing.

In grief, one can endure the day, just the day. But when one also tries to bear the grief ahead, one cannot compass it. As for happiness, it can only be the ability to experience the moment. It is not next year that life will be so flawless and if we keep trying to wait for next year's happiness, the river of time will wind past and we shall not have lived at all.

But when I begin thinking about time, I remember Gibran, that strange mystic and his saying "Yesterday is today's memory and tomorrow is today's dream." And of course, one can't live without memory and dream!

Most of my thinking, I notice, has a circular pattern. And I also find it is hard to express exactly my very best thoughts. They are invariably winging by like purple and golden butterflies, and I see them, but cannot catch them.

Gibran spoke truly when he said, "the wave of words is forever upon us, yet our depth is forever silent."

Jill called me early this morning in hushed excitement. Right outside the kitchen window were a pair of eastern mourning doves. She saw them as she was grinding the coffee, and they walked right across the yard and toward the house, pausing now and then to select some morsel of food from the frozen lawn.

They walked right on past the ground feeder, ignoring its buffet. By the time I got to the window, some noise had startled them. They had made puffballs of themselves, a soft brown-grey suffused with pink tones. Presently they pulled themselves into shape again, and moved gracefully on, one a little ahead, probably the male. With their long tails and beautiful slender bodies and pointed bills, they made a most striking pair.

We were enchanted for we had never seen a mourning dove near the house before, and the sight of the two of them tiptoeing along in the soft early-morning light was something to remember always.

Louella Shour gave the glamorous Especially Me a blue terrycloth bathrobe, complete with zipper and ties for his golden neck. We gave him a bath yesterday and zipped him up in it and he was docile and polite about it. As soon as he was dry and I had hung it up on a rack, he went right outdoors and made a mud pie of himself again.

"Well," says Jill, "you just can't have everything; nice clean dogs have to be kept shut in. Nice clean houses have to be practically empty. Take your choice."

"I take the dogs," I say firmly, "but he could at least have stayed clean half an hour."

"He's had a change of mud anyway," says Jill.

When I opened the door and he came flying in with Holly hard on his heels, they looked happy as could be. I was suddenly reminded of the time when Mama had scrubbed me and dressed me up in a blue silk smocked frock for a party and she turned around twice and I had fallen flat on my face onto a large sheet of fresh flypaper. So I told Especially Me I understood how hard it is to stay clean.

I went out to burn the trash and found the yard as sticky as molasses. At every step I took, a strange sucking sound came from the thawing earth. Nobody could dream that this would become more or less of a lawn in another month.

There was still an edge of ice in the air, it smelled incredibly pure and fresh and the brave March wind tumbled my hair and the battle with mud seemed inconsequential. Tomorrow, I thought, we can do all the floors again and lay newspapers down in the traffic lanes.

As I was stirring the lentil soup today, I reflected that every woman must have a favorite utensil. I am deeply devoted to a certain wooden spoon. It has worn down at the edges and has a faintly pinky glow from having stirred so many ruby jellies and jams. But I always reach for it, it fits so comfortably in my hand and stirs so well, and it feels like a companion. We have been through a lot together, crises of sticking chili sauce or carrots in a precarious state. I am very fond of the old black iron spider too.

I love the new gadgets, the shining utensils, the smooth modern efficiency, but I still like to have the old friends right there within reach.

Small things can be important anyway. A spoon, a pan, a special dish, they make one's kitchen peculiarly one's own.

Small jobs can be important too. Washing the milk glass would never go down in history as an achievement, but how good I feel after I have done it! I sit down and look at the old corner cupboard and think about the days when the milk glass was made—and all the people who cherished it, and they did cherish it or it would have been broken long ago. The swan compote has the swans forever swimming on their white stream, the lacy edge plates are lacier than ever. And the little log cabin looks as if tiny folk must be inside, snug and happy. The hens look out at the world with a fierce eye as they sit on the woven basket dishes. The little sleighs look as if they were ready to take on passengers and skim over imaginary snows. I can imagine the tiny figures, waving muffs as they glide away.

We used to set the table with milk glass on a dark-green linen cloth to bring out the translucence, but now we are growing lazy. For the milk glass has to be washed by hand, the torrid heat of the dishwasher cracks the lacy edges. After all this is old, and needs gentle warm suds.

So we use the Leeds which is tough in fibre. Steve and Olive have a complete ironstone collection, and this is lovely as well as practical, for the dishwasher cannot crack it. Their dinner table, set by the big window overlooking the trout stream, is beautiful to see for one seldom does see every single thing in a collection. They even use the tall handleless cups for the coffee, and when I hold one in my hand and feel the good warmth coming through, I wonder why anybody ever put handles on cups at all. Olive uses the big tureens with the acorn tops on the covers for her hot dishes, and she even has an ironstone ladle in perfect condition.

Good wine may need no bush, I always think, but good food is enhanced by being served on such lovely dishes.

Connie collects mugs, and this has been a fine idea. She serves hot soups in them, as well as hot chocolate and tea, uses them for chips or bread sticks. Small ones make cigarette holders, a big pinky one holds an African violet. I like best the small ones that say "Remember Me." Or "I love you." We have a footed milk glass mug which should, by rights, go with hers. It has four little paws for feet, and I cannot imagine how anyone dreamed them up.

We use milk-glass cups to hold pencils, milk glass on the bureaus and the bathroom dressing table, and milk-glass lamps on the mantel. And so even though we don't eat from our collection, we do use it. I feel strongly that a collection should be used. We keep the milk-glass candlesticks in constant use and the H-and-L bowl for fruit, and in season, I do bouquets in everything from saltcellars to spoonholders.

Of course, as I say rather often, a collection is only really the memories that go in it. You cannot go in and write a check and own a collection. A collection means to collect. It means piece by piece. It means remember the day we found this in the junk pile at the auction? Remember the dear old ladies that found the matching tiny tureens with one wee ladle? Remember that darling woman who said this piece was her grandmother's but she had only one and it should go with ours?

At its best, it also means you figure the pennies. You give up something to get that swan compote. You save and pinch and squeeze and then proudly buy the eight Gothic plates all at once, all eight.

And oh, the excitement of having one square, blue, wheat-design vase and years later finding a mate in Maine or Vermont.

One piece we have not, and may never have. A friend of ours has it, a long, narrow, covered dish, with a lady's hand elegantly laid on top. On one finger is a ring *with* a green stone in it, and the stone is still there, after all the years of living that hand must have done. I do not covet things, but I wish I could once find one like this.

This friend is a very wise woman. She is the one who started us on the milk glass in the beginning. We had a great deal of illness and sorrow in our families and life had a grey visage for us.

"Collect something," said she, "there is nothing like collecting to revive your interest in life. Try milk glass."

And she helped us find our first small piece. From then on we were so busy scouring around that we got a lot of exercise and had less time to brood over our troubles.

I do not think the monetary value of a collection is very important. Connie's mugs and our milk glass happen to have increased astronomically in value because they got to be the fashion, but we had nothing to do with it. I know a woman who collects and presses ferns, which only cost her time and energy, and her fern collection is now a museum piece. We have a friend who collects African violets, and often she only has a single leaf from some rare variety which she is given. And her violets are like a tropical garden, incredibly rich and beautiful and a rainbow of colors.

Another friend has simply collected dog cartoons from magazines and pasted them in scrapbooks. From Clancy the Irish tied up in a million streamers or stepping on a box of tacks to Ted Key's doggy dogs getting in trouble tracking paint all over the house, she has a complete record of American humor at its warmest and best.

I love special dog-eared books, and an old pewter plate battered from much puppy-lugging and Mama's old red basket which Holly ate up the other day, and many other things. Jill is not a clutterer and she is very patient with my addiction to little bottles with flowers on them stuck around on sills, and carved boxes on tables, and old decanters and such. Her heart is with the milk glass alone. Her idea of a perfect house would be one with great sweeps of open spaces, furnished with only books, the milk glass and the dogs. Nothing else. Possibly she would concede the electric frying pan to cook on and the coffeemaker. But she says, she knows I like things around.

While we began to spring clean this week, I resolved to CLEAR the decks in capital letters. I did retire one magazine rack and one Bohemian ruby glass bottle, but that I only retired to the back kitchen and any minute it will creep back to its little home on the hall window sill. It is a pleasant bottle.

I know if Steve did this house over, it would be a dream of perfection. But I would have to visit with a good many items in the storage house.

Pictures are another problem. As we were dusting and polishing, Jill said thoughtfully, "do you have to have all the pictures of all the people you love on the walls? I mean, three or four of each?"

"Only three of any," I said meekly.

But I did a fine sorting job and did retire a few, and then began figuring on some new ones I could put up.

While I was doing this, Holly ate two of our four chops which were to be our entire dinner.

Jill says Holly should be trained not to help herself but I feel it is reasonable for her to suppose that what is ours is hers since we obviously adore her. Why discriminate against her? It isn't stealing, she is just taking some of her own, she feels. She never takes anything from the table while we are eating, she is an angel about it, no matter how sad her eyes. But what is left inadvertently on a counter, is left at anybody's risk.

I never can understand people who punish animals for helping themselves to the family food. We make companions of them, we educate them in all sorts of Obedience, but they are part of the family group, and who would deny that food is communal property.

In any case, no matter how one reasons, our chops are gone.

Of course, Holly is so beautiful that as Jill says, she gets away with murder. We were glad to see that her father, International Champion Red Star of Hollywood Hills, won the award for siring the most champions of any dog of his breed of this year. But we felt he had sired Holly and needed no more honor.

We feel a little guilty sometimes when we look at her, knowing she ought to be a champion too. We also know that any person who can smell a yellow rubber rabbit inside a high closet cupboard ought to be field trained.

On the other hand, it is all very well for the dogs who never know anything else to live in cages and travel all year and run in a show ring and go back in a box. But how would Holly feel? She would feel just awful. No free wild running in the acre yard, no tidbits, no chops, no helping open the mail and cleaning up the kitchen. And positively no foam rubber pillow for her at night. No television either and she particularly loves "The Halls of Ivy."

Also no Especially Me to drag around by the ears and romp with. No, it is not her dish, she would say.

As for Especially Me, our other prospect, he is so gentle and mild that I could not wish a show circuit on him. His little heart would be brave, but he would suffer every hour.

My conclusion is that you can't mix members of the family with the competitive haul of making a champion. Obedience is a different affair, for there you go with your dog, you come home with him or her, you wait around until you can both get out. You ride together, you work together. You have a team. No handler enters into it except you yourself. And the net result is a fine companion dog and a fine educated owner.

In the breed circuit, your dog may be in Abilene, Kansas, and you don't even know it. In the Obedience ring, you have to be there too, so you only go to shows you can get to. It works out very well. In the vast number of shows, there are always enough within a day or a day-and-night haul, and you go to those. You don't care whether they are three point or five point shows as you are not in breed anyway.

As we add some hamburger to our supper to replace the missing chops, I reflect on the days when I had no dog at all, not even one small one. My idea of heaven then was to have one dog. Now I open the door and six sweep in, and suddenly I am overcome at my good fortune. Nine dogs, I decide, isn't many. Three in the kennel, six out. I think with nostalgia of that summer when we counted and found we had thirty-six. It wasn't practical and we gradually came down to nine. But a bevy of dogs running around the yard is a fine and happy sight to see.

If they were all alike, one could settle for a couple, but with every dog so different, so individual—it is hard to limit the number.

However, we are both eminently unsuited to having a commercial kennel. We never liked to sell puppies. I could always think of more reasons not to sell them.

Which is one reason we found ourselves with thirty-six.

This is definitely the month to clean up after winter. For soon we shall want to be outdoors all day long. Jill has been painting woodwork, waxing furniture. I sort things. Old winter clothes can go out now. Blankets get a wash and a blowing on the line, to fill with wind and sun. Rugs go out on a fine blowy day to be filled with fresh spring air.

In my childhood spring cleaning was a serious proposition, all down College Avenue as soon as the deep snow melted, carpets were laid on the grass and beaten with wire whisks. In the elegant houses, carpets were wall-to-wall Brussels, and pulling out the tacks that kept them anchored the rest of the year was a terrible job. In modest homes, carpets were called druggets and could be lifted and swung in the air. They did not reach to the walls.

In those days also, furniture was moved to the yard during spring cleaning. Husbands wandered homelessly about, getting cross and adding greatly to the problems of the housewife. Men do not like to be upset. But spring cleaning was a moral responsibility and it went on, husbands or no. Curtains blew on the line, were stretched on stretchers with tiny pins holding them taut. Windows were washed with vinegar and water.

Even cellars were scrubbed and scoured and a fine damp smell came from them for days afterward. The fruit jars were washed, ranged in serried ranks on shelves freshly papered.

And finally it was all done. The house smelled of wax and oil and naptha soap. Everything glistened. The carpets were tacked back down with clean shiny carpet tacks.

Mama and our cleaning woman, dear Mrs. Novak, would

sit down and have a cup of hot black tea together in the moment of triumph. They laughed and visited and Mama's flyaway brown hair would make a cloud in her little neck. Mrs. Novak, who was Polish, would flush pink, her shiny narrow black eyes filled with success. Her thin mouth smiled.

And just at that point, Father would lope in from college, bearing a whole load of cobwebby mouldering specimens of one sort or another, a dried blowfish, some bits of meteorite and a few skins of long departed animals.

"Grace!" he would call, in his boyish light voice, "I have some wonderful things!"

And the cleaning honeymoon was over as Papa strewed sand and dirt and webs all down the hall and into the living room.

Nowadays most women, I find, clean all the time. The modern theory is to do a room a week, room by room thoroughly and then you never do a turn-out. It works very well, except that the whole house is never immaculate at once. You miss the fine frenzy of everything being polished and scoured at once. There is no great triumph, only a series of little jobs going on endlessly.

The vacuum cleaner is no friend of mine. I eye it with distrust. I know if I vacuum every other day, cleaning is not a problem. So the books say. We have, in our twenty-odd years of country living, tried all types of cleaners, and I can heartily say none is easy.

Our current cleaner is as simple to manage as an octopus or giant squid. In fact I try to imagine myself at the bottom of the sea battling a squid as I snake it around, thinking it might be easier if I could fancy myself a deep-sea diver. The cord hooks on every piece of furniture in the room, and at once jerks out the plug so the whole thing sits inanimate. Then the main part skids along awkwardly, catches on the sill and balks like an old grey mule. Meanwhile the long snaky tube slides along, winds about a chair, and I fall on my face trying to guide it. The nozzle snorts in a great manner as of one overworked. But it turns out it is not DRAWING ANYTHING. So we take it all apart and reverse everything and hold the nozzle to the great outdoors and blow out a ton of mixed dog hairs and lint. Then we begin again.

By now, I am tired. I approach the contraption firmly but wearily and manage a good grip. I plug in. Just as I am nicely started, the thing darts away and sucks up a half box of Kleenex which Holly has left on one of her gay excursions about. By the time I sort out the Kleenex, it is time to empty the dust bag.

Now this should be simple. It just never is. The lugs do not wish to unlug, for one thing. The filled bag does not wish to come out. When it does, one end is open and a whole ton of dirt falls back on the floor. Then the new bag turns out to not quite fit. It is (a) too small or (b) too large. We screw it around and insert as directions say. Then we take it out and begin again.

Finally we start the whole cleaning over again only to find we are using the wrong nozzle anyway.

Putting the vacuum away is the last straw. Since in a 1690 house, storage space is not at a premium, it just isn't, we try to sort out the cleaner according to its various parts and stow. I lug the main body of the squid along. The cord trails after, catching on everything in the house except the window sills, and it would catch on them if it could only reach up that far. The hose slides under the sofa, then under a radiator. The nozzle falls off and turns out to be under my bed. Making about five trips, I finally get most of the thing in the back kitchen, at which I give up and just call for Jill.

Getting it in the tiny closet is more than I can do.

Jill gives it an ominous look as she untangles cord and hose and nozzles and so on.

"I think we ought to just use a broom," she says.

I love to look at pictures of slim gay girls vacuuming their houses from a single stance, like a putter on the golf green. But in my life it doesn't seem to be so simple. I just feel that with all the push-button ease of our modern living, it is too bad I still have to fight my vacuum cleaner.

It may all be due to a lack of dexterity on my part, I freely admit I have no dexterity. But I cannot be alone. I feel other women must be battling their cleaners all over the country even as I do. Somebody should dream up a really portable high-powered thing that would eat up floor dirt.

The question of help in the country is a serious, a grave one. When we first came, we could get a very nice cleaning woman by the day for twenty-five cents an hour. This just about fitted our then budget, and we had her. With her help we painted and papered the entire house.

After she moved away, we went on to various and sundry. That was it, various and sundry. From the girl who kept her horse by the kennel and spent most of the day attending to him, to the soldier's wife who brought the children, we had a good deal of experience.

We even had a Finnish couple with cats, a lot of cats. And a girl work-camper named Phoebe that we wished to adopt except her parents didn't feel that way about it.

We had, for a halcyon period, Belle, who had been my cook in Virginia and came North for a time. Belle was one of the finest women I have ever known, a tall, spare colored woman with a fine high aquiline nose and high cheekbones, suggesting Indian ancestry somewhere along the line. With almost no schooling, she was as wise and intelligent a woman as one could find, and she was gentle and charitable and with a fine wit.

While we had Belle, she ran us all with a firm hand, we were superbly taken care of.

The only trouble was that we worried about her for she had no friends around, and her own church was down in Virginia. We used to sit up nights figuring on ways to entertain Belle so she wouldn't be lonesome. I may say we never saw so many movies in our life as while Belle was with us. Almost every night, we would dash through dinner to get to the next town in time for the movies. We were a fixture, Jill striding ahead to get the tickets, the three children and I coming along midway, and Belle, in her neat dark dress and kerchief bringing up the rear like a general.

We took her for drives when there was no movie, and on picnics. And when she went back to Virginia because of illness in her family, we felt as if a special guest had departed.

Belle would sing in the kitchen as she fried chicken and made spoon bread or her fabulous shrimp creole. She said she had learned to cook on the hearth in a log cabin when she was very young. "I always used a turkey wing to sterilize the hearth," she said, making sweeping movements.

She could take cleaning or leave it, preferably leave it, but her cooking was gourmet. And she always doused the dishcloth in bleach once a day, which was a nice gesture toward cleanliness.

She dearly loved our black Manx. "That my man," she would say, "he my man."

And he justified her admiration by fetching her a young rabbit one day. We stayed in the other part of the house while Belle had a fine rabbit stew with herbs.

Nowadays, there is little help to be had in our valley since factory jobs in nearby Waterbury or the institution for the feeble-minded a few miles away attract most people. The whole countenance of living is changing. The big elegant mansions, formerly staffed by three or four servants are now run by their owners with maybe a high-school boy to mow the lawn.

And the thing that impresses me so much is how easily the women in America adjust. One goes to tea in a great house, and finds out accidentally that the lady pouring the tea has no help at all any more. She manages, and she manages very well. She will scrub the paint from her hands in time to set up the silver service and slice the bread paper thin. And never feel sorry for herself at all.

When our last cleaning woman moved away, we felt a momentary panic and then Jill said briskly, "now all we do is plan so much a day. We let it get dusty part of the time. We do so much, we shall make a list."

I often think Jill will arrive at the gate of heaven with a list which she will submit to St. Peter. And I am sure he will read it and check things off.

In any case, we made a list.

"And until we get someone else to help us," said Jill, "why don't we pay ourselves the money?"

This lifted my forehead a lot, as Belle would have said. Every day we had no help, we put the money in the milk-glass apothecary jar labeled Mastix. And it got to be such a game and it mounted so fast that I began to draw up plans for an addition to the house, a sort of studio library room where a grand piano could live.

There is not an inch of space for a piano in the house. All our musician friends come up with ideas of knocking out walls and adding bay windows and nothing comes of it. But a whole new room could accommodate a piano.

Of course neither of us can play a piano, but I just feel every house should have one!

I have finally made up my mind about television. It was because Alice and Margaret left us their set to care for while they went to their Florida island to gather shells and bask in tropic air all winter.

At first we gingerly turned it on for news, then we advanced to a single program. I had a feeling that we had gone far enough with radio and that was enough. But what really changed my mind was a lecture on the poetry of George Herbert, that mystic who followed John Donne, a very scholarly, college kind of lecture. The professor who read the poems and discussed Herbert's life was sound and expert. He announced that he would go on with the series, and I gathered I had already missed the Elizabethans.

Lawk a mercy me, I thought—as the old lady said—I had NO idea this could be television! I then saw two *Hamlet* productions—first as it was probably done in Shakespeare's day, and second as it is now done. Why, I thought, if they kept this up, we would all be educated no end!

I had thought television meant dancing girls and skits, and I was amazed.

And then I sat in on an interview between Ed Murrow and Oppenheimer, that sadly controversial scientist.

I decided that the time may come when there will be a university of the air, and one can graduate from XRCA as a B.A. as well as from an ordinary college. One can always turn the button off for the cheap hours, and wait for the few worthwhile ones.

And by the time Jill said hesitantly, "isn't this the night for 'The Halls of Ivy'?" I knew we should buy a set ourselves.

It is a dangerous medium, I think. Children should not replace reading with television skits. Howdy Doody may be all very well, but books offer something invaluable and there is danger the next generation may not read at all, just look. But if we can control it, it is immensely important.

Jill does not worry about the implications of this new dazzling medium at all. She simply says, " 'The Halls of Ivy' has the best Alma Mater next to Cornell." Turns it on, watches the gentle college people, turns it off and goes back to her letters of Freud or whatever.

She says I can do the worrying about the future of television for both of us.

But the vast power of this new thing does worry me. It comes into any home. It comes into hospitals, to the bedside, it can teach and inspire and illuminate. The bedridden can enjoy it as much as the casual passer-by. And it is a terrible responsibility for the men who choose and shape the programs.

If they realized their power, they might sleep badly of nights. Presumably they are worrying mainly about staying on the air.

My feeling is that it is a wise person who knows when to turn television off. It is quite possible to select such programs as a fine analysis of Beethoven's *Fifth Symphony*, or Ed Murrow. Or for pure relaxation to watch George Gobel turn a shy sober face toward the camera. Pure humor is a rare and wonderful thing, and Mr. Gobel has it in every inch of his stocky lonesome little figure.

I suspect it is partly because he is an extension of our own confusion with such things as the electronic brain, and as he flounders his way through life, he is a pretty basic interpretation of mankind.

Now and then we have snow in March, but it has a theatrical look, not quite real. Big feathery flakes fall with an idle grace. The road up the hill to the mail box turns silver again, but a light, lacy silver. And when George goes out with the milk, the truck leaves dark ebony marks. The sky is pale, but not as low-hanging as a February sky. The swamp is veiled, it looks mysterious and lovely in the falling snow.

When it clears, the world has a brisk look, sky a startling dynamic blue. All the wet branches glow with color, the osiers, the alders, the young willows, and the wild berry canes. The brooks rush down the hills with splendid thunder.

By August, they will be modest little trickles, but now they have their day as they sweep down the watershed.

We watch for the skunk cabbage to poke up her pointed cone down by the pond. Such a dramatic plant to have such an unfortunate name. The leaves, when open, are a most brilliant green, and look so tropical that I feel they cannot be indigenous to this northern land and must have gotten mislaid somewhere in the course of history.

Then there are the snowdrops, so pure and silken on their fragile stems. The delicate bells look as if they might be rung in faeryland. I have spent a long time over the years trying to describe the white of the petals, and have given up in despair. It is snow, to be sure, but it has a glowing tone. Possibly it most resembles a freshwater pearl such as Father and I used to get from the clammers along the Winneconnie.

Often the clump of snowdrops is footed in actual snow. When I gather them, the little stems are cold as glass. In the house, they go in a milk-glass saltcellar and the advent of spring could not be more delicately announced!

Crocus and scilla and grape hyacinths all set me to thinking that it is strange the most fragile flowers come first when wind and rain and melting snow and mud are rampant. One thinks of alpine flowers, that are small and gentle too.

The sturdy violets begin to come up now too. Small pointed leaves poke up as a suggestion that April and violet time is not far off.

Jill has been raking the yard and burning up the debris of winter. This is a fine satisfying job, the left-over soggy leaves come away from the border and leave a neat clean look, room for the bulbs to come freely into the upper air. In the yard itself, old bones, bits of rubber rabbits, and a few dog-food cans turn up, for Holly makes it a point not to go outdoors without carrying something. Three of my missing socks appear too.

On the first warm day, I begin suggesting the storm windows come off. I do not like looking through two panes of glass, Jill says I would have no windows at all, if we could support life that way.

If we lived in California, or Florida, we would probably have complete outdoor living. I love to look at pictures of patios and living rooms that have a whole wall that slides away. But I think ranch houses look very alien in our New England landscape. They are not functional here. The steep roofs of our old houses were designed to sheer off the great snows, to make the house warmer and tighter. The little windows kept out more biting blasts, exposed little surface to the icy cold. The small rooms, not so elegant as the huge Western ones kept folk snug. And a typical New England house is cool in the hottest summer day. The thick walls, the little windows see to that.

Our own, since 1690, has withstood hurricanes and near-floods, and although it has nary a picture window, every little window looks out on beauty.

If we ever toyed with the idea of adding a wing with a glass wall or something like that, Steve would probably never speak to us again, so it's as well we are content to be traditional. Having a top-decorator friend does make one mind the period and no mistake. I once tentatively suggested a bay window for my violets but Steve said he did all the research possible and no bay window was ever in a house of this period. He was polite, but firm. If we had edged into the eighteenth century, he felt we might manage the bay.

Never mind, said Jill, it would be a lot more window washing.

Putting up an aerial for the radio was a hazard too. We really needed the aerial but I felt it would ruin the house. I went away for a drive while it was being put up. But so adjustable are human creatures that now we never even see the aerial, although I predicted it would make the house look as if it were about to take off for Mars.

While making a cheese soufflé last night, I thought what a noble thing cheese is. I couldn't begin to count the varieties that even we use. According to the experts, the Egyptians had cheese, so it is an old friend of man. And from the big curds of pot cheese, so creamy and mild, to the sophisticated flavor of a Port Salut, it is all good.

The hard, the semi-soft and the soft cheeses each have their charm. Parmesan belongs beside the herbs on the herb shelf, for adding just the right touch to so many dishes. A wheel of Cheddar on hand gives the housewife complete confidence, she can always make a meal for unexpected guests if she has good fresh Cheddar. Soufflé or a rabbit or rinkum tiddy, that happy blend of tomatoes, onion and cheese.

Pot cheese blended with freshly boiled noodles and a dab of sour cream stirred in would feast a Lord.

Swiss fondue is a very elegant way to dunk. Wedges of crusty French bread dipped in, and the whole hot and smoothly simmering. And then for salad dressings, crumbled bleu—for hot canapes any number of things with cheese added and all run under the broiler.

Then pizza would be impossible without two kinds of cheese, the Mozzarella and a sprinkle of Parmesan too.

I admit I like my cheese to be a cheese. I do not want it mixed with other things and turned into a cheese spread, pasteurized. I would go so far as to admire a cheese blended with port or white wine, on occasion, for snacks, but there is a good deal of fine pure cheese being made in this country, and I prefer it unadulterated.

We get most of ours from the Swiss people in Monroe,

Wisconsin, and feel it is about perfection. The Camembert is notable, as is the Glarus and the Rexoli—I never know which is best, except that which I am eating is the very best.

I can remember going to Monroe for cheese with Father when I was very young. The shop windows were full of wooden shoes, and I longed to live in a village that sold wooden shoes! We bought great wedges then, and carried them home wrapped in brown paper.

We also used to get cheese from a Bavarian family outside our own town and this was a ceremony. We would go down in the cellar and see the cheeses, so pure and cool, aging according to their habit. After Father had decided on just the right age—he liked them, as I do, green, we would sit in the tight little parlor and visit with the rosy-cheeked family. They had been cheesemakers for royalty abroad and were fully conscious of it and when they poured us tiny glasses of homemade wine, it was a real celebration. I always had a wonderful sense of sin, too, as we never had strong drink in our house. A thimbleful of rosy wine and a wedge of fresh cheese with a slice of homemade bread was heavenly.

Father would always explain afterward that we couldn't offend them by refusing the wine, but I noticed he always had three glasses and smacked his lips.

Mama made her own pot cheese. The big grey enamel pan was set on the very back of the old range and I could hardly wait until the cheesecloth was laid over and the whey poured off and I could have a bowl of fresh pot cheese with a warm slice of bread just out of that old gas oven.

Thus fortified, I would be able to go out and play several sets of tennis with my beau. Or go to a neighbor's barn and try to shoot rats.

March is for buttoned jackets, woolen gloves, for wild wind and a trumpet sun, for sharp exciting nights with scudding clouds and a white moon sailing. March is for considerable sneezing, for muddy paws, and for scouring and scrubbing.

March, says Little Sister, nibbling my elbow, is for being alive, and thankful to God for breathing the first breath of spring! And any minute now, April will walk in her daffodil skirts along our New England valleys.

Let the winds blow!

Full Circle

A YEAR MAY BE MEASURED ON A CAL-
endar, with holidays as mileposts, and the rhythm of the seasons is a repeating rhythm, but actually, to a countrydweller,
there is never a beginning, and never an end.

The river of time flows as gently as an August brook with
water cress marking its banks, and now and then we lift our
eyes with amazement and say, "the trees have grown so!"

Those small pines we set out—surely it was only yesterday
—their tips are tangled with stars at night now. And the purple lilac outside my bedroom window touches the sill of an
upstairs window!

And yet the passage of time seems of little consequence.
As I go out in the morning to pick the white daffodils, I think
of the bulbs secure under the snow in the past winter, of the
first green spears that lance the early spring light, and I think
of next year's garden, too. And I have no feeling of finality
when I cut the faded tips of the lilacs that have again budded,
blossomed, died. For by now the homespun sweetness of the
Dorothy Perkins is covering the picket fence, and Silver Moon
opens pale ivory buds by the gate.

It is, of course, quite possible that man will destroy this
world a week from tomorrow. He has finally learned how
to blast all of humanity, and all living creatures into oblivion
in one final blaze. It may well be the race of man is doomed.
But I do not believe so.

The constructive urge is strong, and may yet prevail. Love
against hate is not bound to be a lost cause. It may be that
because we live in our quiet green valley in the little house

which has survived so many storms down the years, we have such a sense of permanence that we have too much faith. But better too much than too little!

And there is a kind of immortality in every garden.

As I close the garden gate and follow the crooked flagstone walk to the house on an amethyst evening, the dogs run before me, the Irish skimming as if she were airborne, the cockers scurrying, ears flying, bits of tails ecstatic.

Jill is bending over in the garden, planting young lettuce, pressing the earth gently around the pale roots.

And the ancient splendor of the evening star shines above Stillmeadow.